# Lotos Leaves
by William Fearing Gill

# LOTOS LEAVES.

ORIGINAL

# STORIES, ESSAYS AND POEMS,

BY

WHITELAW REID, WILKIE COLLINS, MARK TWAIN, JOHN HAY, JOHN BROUGHAM, NOAH BROOKS, P. V. NASBY, I. H. BROMLEY, JOHN ELDERKIN, THOMAS W. KNOX, W. J. FLORENCE, CHANDOS FULTON, J. HENRY HAGAR, CHAMPION BISSELL, J. B. BOUTON, W. S. ANDREWS, GILBERT BURLING, CHARLES I. PARDEE, M. D., C. McK. LEOSER, HON. R. B. ROOSEVELT, WILLIAM F. GILL, C. FLORIO, C. E. L. HOLMES, CHARLES GAYLER, JAMES PECH, MUS. DOC., H. S. OLCOTT, EDWARD GREEY, J. BRANDER MATTHEWS AND ALFRED TENNYSON.

EDITED BY

## WILLIAM FEARING GILL.

## Illustrated.

CHICAGO AND NEW YORK:
BELFORD, CLARKE & CO.
1887.

R. B. L.

COPYRIGHTED:

W. F. GILL,

1875.

DONOHUE & HENNEBERRY PRINTERS AND BINDERS. CHICAGO

TO

# ALFRED TENNYSON,

*THE POET OF OUR TIME,*

𝔗𝔥𝔦𝔰 𝔅𝔬𝔬𝔨

ⁱꜱ,

(WITH HIS SPECIAL PERMISSION)

AFFECTIONATELY INSCRIBED

BY

## THE LOTOS CLUB

OF NEW YORK.

Farringford,
    Freshwater,
        Isle of Wight.

March 13

honoured by
&c &c — leaves
propose. I have
    & this same
    — town to
it certain
by your
Tennyson

Lotos Leaves

1 8 7 5

# PREFACE.

*TO THE SOVEREIGN PEOPLE OF THE UNITED STATES.*

MAY IT PLEASE YOUR ROYAL MULTIPLICITY : —

E, the subscribers hereto, appreciating the absorbing interest taken at the present period in the occult and the non-understandable, beg to call the attention of pansophic inquirers to the singular MANIFESTATIONS which will develop themselves in the pages following, emanating, as they do, from a group of edacious and bibitory media, who materialize daily at the refectory of the LOTOS CLUB.

YOUR AUGUST POTENTIALITY will not fail to observe that those spiritual adumbrations are not evanescent or fugaceous, a latrocinous cheat, repugnant to common-sense and an insult to the most parvanimous of human intelligences, but tangible entities, altogether stationary, and as visible to every eye as the readablest of printed work.

The embodied essences which will in due time appear, — psychologic offspring evolved from the mysterious union of the brain and pen, — being polygenous, will of necessity be variform and dissimilar ; but, however unlike in shape and feature they may be when compared with each other, yet individually they will be found to exhibit sufficient family resemblance to indicate their paternity.

In *Books*, as in *Babies*, one can readily discover — excepting in the cases of unequal collaboration, or of entirely pilfered matter, foreign or domestic — some characteristic trait hereditary, some trick of style or peculiarity of expression, through which to designate the author of their being.

The cerebral progeny of the Lotos will, in like manner, display upon their lineaments the shadowy sign-manual of their respective producers.

With this brief but perspicuous prolegomenon, we send our multigenerous youngsters out into the world, to be judged by their merits ; parental solicitude alone urging us to entreat for them a liberal indulgence, if it be only for their juvenility.

It only remains to say that the pecuniary profits, if any, resulting from the promulgation of these Leaves will be presented to the American Dramatic Fund.

J. B.
J. E.

# CONTENTS.

# CONTENTS.

# LIST OF ILLUSTRATIONS.

Engraved under the supervision of JOHN ANDREW AND SON.

## HALF-TITLE ILLUSTRATIONS.

The ornamental initials at the opening of each article were expressly designed for this volume by
JOHN ANDREW AND SON.

# SOME SOUTHERN REMINISCENCES.

# SOME SOUTHERN REMINISCENCES.

By WHITELAW REID.

HE Publishers' despatch demands, rather suddenly, a contribution to the Lotos Leaves. Thus energetically summoned, I can, on the instant, think of nothing better than to go back to my real lotos-eating days. They were passed in that pleasant land where once, to cotton-planters as well as poets, it seemed always afternoon, but where now, alas! it too often looks as if the blackness of midnight had settled. I spent a year or two, after the close of the war in the Southern States, mostly on Louisiana and Alabama cotton-plantations; and if I must "write something and at once," I shall merely try to revive some recollections of that experience.

It was one of those perfect days which Louisianians get in February, instead of waiting, like poor Massachusetts Yankees, till June for them, when I crossed from Natchez to take possession of two of the three river plantations on which I dreamed of making my fortune in a year. The road led directly down the levee. On the right rolled the Mississippi, still far below its banks, and giving no sign of the flood that a few months later was to drown our hopes. To the left stretched westward for a mile the unbroken expanse of cotton land, bounded by the dark fringe of cypress and the swamp. Through a drove of scrawny cattle and broken-down mules, pasturing on the rich Bermuda grass along the levee, under the lazy care of the one-armed " stock-minder," I made my way at last down a grassy lane to the broad-porched, many-windowed cottage, propped up four or five feet from the damp soil by pillars of cypress, which the agent had called the " mansion." It looked out pleasantly from the foliage of a grove of China and pecan trees, and was flanked, on the one hand by a beautifully culti- vated vegetable garden, several acres in extent, and on the other by the " quarters," — a double row of cabins, each with two rooms and a projecting roof, covering an earthen-floored porch. A street, overgrown with grass and weeds, ran from the " mansion " down between the rows of cabins, and stopped at the plantation blacksmith and carpenter shop. Behind each cabin was a little garden, jealously fenced off from all the rest with the roughest of cypress pickets, and its gate guarded by an enormous padlock. " Niggers never trust one another about their gardens or hen-houses," explained the overseer, who was making me acquainted with my new home.

To the westward the plantations sloped gently back from the house to the cypress-swamp, which shut in the view. Not a tree or fence broke the monotony of the surface, but half a dozen wide open ditches led down to the swamp, and were crossed, at no less than seven places, by long lines of embank- ments, each, as one looked toward the swamp, seeming higher than those beyond it. The lands were entirely safe from any overflow from the Mississippi in front ; but crevasses, miles above, almost every year poured floods back into the swamp ; thence the enemy gradually crept up on the rear, and about

June the fight with the water began.  An effort would be made to
stop it at the first line of embankment ; this failing, the leading
ditches would be closed, and the next embankment, a hundred
and fifty yards farther up from the swamp, would be strengthened and guarded.  Failing there, the negroes would retreat to
the next.  The sluggish, muddy sheet of water would scarcely
seem to move ;  but each day it would advance a few inches.
The year before, the negroes had only been able to arrest it
at the embankment nearest the river.  Some months later I
soberly realized that I had done little better ; out of twelve
hundred acres of cotton land, my predecessors had only been
able to save three hundred, and I barely rescued two hundred
more.  Then, as the waters receded, we planted in the ooze,
just in time to have the cotton beautifully fresh and tender for
the worms in August.

But as I rode out first, that perfect day, among the gang of a
hundred and fifty negroes, who, on these plantations, were for
the year to compromise between their respect and their new-
born spirit of independence by calling me Mistah instead of
Massa, there were no forebodings.  Two " plough-gangs " and
two " hoe-gangs " were slowly measuring their length along the
two-mile front.  Among each rode its own negro driver, sometimes lounging in his saddle with one leg lodged on the pommel,
sometimes  shouting sharp, abrupt  orders to the delinquents.
In each plough-gang were fifteen pairs of scrawny mules, with
corn-husk collars, gunny-bag back-bands, and bedcord plough-
lines.  The Calhoun ploughs (the favorite implement through all
that region, then, and doubtless still, retaining the name given
it long before war was dreamed of) were rather lazily managed
by the picked hands of the plantation.  Among them were

several women, who proved among the best laborers in the gang. A quarter of a mile ahead a picturesque sight presented itself. A great crowd of women and children, with a few aged or weakly men among them, were scattered along the old cotton-rows, chopping down weeds, gathering together the trash that covered the land, and firing little heaps of it, while through the clouds of smoke came an incessant chatter of the girls, and an occasional snatch of a camp-meeting hymn from the elders. "Gib me some backey, please," was the first salutation I received. They were dressed in a stout blue cottonade, the skirts drawn up to the knees, and reefed in a loose bunch about the waists; brogans of incredible sizes covered their feet, and there was little waste of money on the useless decency of stockings, but gay bandannas were wound in profuse splendor around their heads.

The moment the sun disappeared every hoe was shouldered. Some took up army-blouses or stout men's overcoats, and drew them on; others gathered fragments of bark to kindle their evening fires, and balanced them nicely on their heads. In a moment the whole noisy crowd was filing across the plantation toward the quarters, joining the plough-gang, pleading for rides on the mules, or flirting with the drivers, and looking as much like a troop flocking to a circus or rustic fair as a party of weary farm-laborers. At the house the drivers soon reported their grievances. "Dem women done been squabblin' 'mong dei'selves dis a'ternoon, so I's hardly git any wuck at all out of 'em." "Fanny and Milly done got sick to-day; an' Sally's heerd dat her husban''s mustered out ob de army, an' she gone up to Natchez to fine him." "Dem sucklers ain't jus' wuf nuffin at all. 'Bout eight o'clock dey goes off to de quarters to deir babies, an' I don' nebber see nuffin mo' ob 'em till 'bout elebben. Den de same way in de a'ternoon, till I 's sick ob de hull lot." " De Moody [Bermuda grass] mighty tough 'long heah, an' I could n't make dem women put in deir hoes to suit me nohow." Presently men and women trooped up for the tickets representing their day's work. The women were soon busy preparing their supper of mess pork and early vegetables ; while the plough-gang gathered about the overseer. " He 'd done promise dem a drink o' whiskey, if dey 'd finish dat cut, and dey 'd done it." The whiskey was soon forthcoming, well watered, with a trifle of cayenne pepper to conceal the lack of spirit, and a little tobacco soaked in it to preserve the color. The most drank it down at a gulp from the glass into which, for one after another, the overseer poured " de 'lowance." A few, as their turns came, passed up tin cups, and went off with the treasure, chuckling about "de splennid toddy we 's hab to-night." Then came a little trade with the overseer at " the store." Some wanted a pound or two of sugar ; others, a paper of needles or a bar of soap ; many of the young men, " two bits' wuf" of candy, or a brass ring. In an hour trade was over, and the quarters were as silent as a churchyard. But, next morning, at four o'clock, I was aroused by the shrill " driber's horn." Two hours later it was blown again, and, looking from my window just as the first red rays of light came level across the field, I saw the women filing out, with their hoes, and the plough-men leisurely sauntering down to the stables, each with corn-husk collars and bedcord plough-lines in his hands.

Somewhat different was my first sight of our third plantation. It was fifteen miles farther down the river, from which it was hidden by a mile of swampy forest. It had been freshly cleared a little before the war, had been neglected since, was overgrown with briers, and covered with fallen logs. Remote, wild, gloomy, it almost recalled that weird picture of the Red River plantation on which Mrs. Stowe abandoned Uncle Tom to the mercies of Legree. Nor was this impression lessened when I found that the overseer had for twenty years followed his calling during the existence of slavery. But the most cordial feeling seemed to subsist between him and the negroes. "Him allus good man, befo' dis time come in," they said. "He allus did us niggers jussice." Here he had them divided into three gangs, "the hoes, log-rollers, and ploughs." Riding through the quarters, one seemed to come out at once upon an immense Western clearing. Everywhere still stood the deadened cypresses : it was through a forest of their decaying bodies that the eye reached in the distance the living forest and the swamp. Half-way back was a scene of unusual animation. The overseer kept his three gangs near each other, the hoes ahead, pushing hard behind them the log-rollers, and, shouting constantly to the log-rollers to keep out of their way, the plough-men. The air was filled with a dense smoke from the burning briers and logs. Moving about among the fires, raking together the trash, chopping the briers, now seizing a brand from a burning heap and dexterously using it to fire half a dozen others, then hurrying forward to catch up with the gang, singing, laughing, teasing the log-rollers to "cotch us if you kin," were the short-skirted, black-faced damsels, twenty or twenty-five in number, who composed the trash-gang. Before the little heaps were half burnt, the log-rollers were among them. A stout black fellow, whiskey-bottle in hand, gave directions. At least half of this gang also were women, each armed, like the men, with a formidable hand-spike. They were very

proud of their distinction, and wanted it understood that "dey was n't none of you' triflin' hoe-han's ; dey was log-rollers, dey was." Selecting the log hardest to be moved as the centre for a heap, the driver shouted, " Now, heah, hurry up dat log dere, and put it on dis side, heah." A dozen hand-spikes were thrust under it, and every woman's voice shouted in shrill chorus, "Come up wid de log, come up wid de log." "Man agin man dere," the driver would cry, "gal agin gal ; all togedder wid you, if you spec any wate' out o' dis bottle." Sometimes before these heaps were fired the ploughs were upon them, every ploughman urging his mules almost into a trot, and the driver occasionally shouting, "Git out o' de way dere, you lazy log-rollers, or we plough right ober ye." The land was a loose loam, turning up like an ash-heap, and both negroes and mules seemed to thrive on the hard work.

The overseer rarely left the field. With one leg lazily thrown across the pommel of his saddle, he lounged in his seat, occasionally addressing a mild suggestion to one of the men, or saying to the driver that the other gangs were pressing him pretty close. Then, riding over to the next, he would hint that the trash-gang was getting ahead of them, or that the ploughs would catch them soon if they were n't careful. All treated him with the utmost respect. I am satisfied that no Northern laborers of the same degree of intelligence ever worked more faithfully, more cheerfully, or with better results.

Very novel, and sometimes very droll, seem to me now the experiences of the year on these plantations. One of the first was my effort to reform a " bad nigger." His old owner, so the gossip ran, had once or twice wanted him killed ; last year the overseer had snapped a pistol at him; altogether, there was no managing him. A genial old-time planter, my nearest neighbor, warned me that the boy was desperate, and ought to be driven off the place. In my Northern wisdom I laughed at the warning. "Of course your system drove any negro of spirit into revolt," I argued; "and so you had what you call a dangerous nigger. Now he sees that he gets the reward of his own labor, and so freedom makes a first-class hand of him." But the old slaveholder shook his head. It was not long till I saw he had reason. My model reformed negro was caught stealing pork and selling it, getting drunk, drawing a loaded musket on his brother-in-law, and the like. "I 'll never give in to your new-fangled notions agin," growled the overseer. "A nigger 's a nigger, and I 've only made a fool of myself in trying to make anything else out of him." And so a warrant was procured for his arrest. Hearing of the warrant, the boy ran away. In about three weeks he returned, very defiant, and boasting that no white man could arrest him. He had been to the Bureau, and knew the law; he was armed, and meant to go where he pleased. But he was promptly taken, without resistance, before a justice of the peace. Three negro witnesses established his guilt, and he was committed to jail to await a trial by court, with every prospect of being sent to the penitentiary for a year or two. Among the witnesses against him was the brother-in-law he had threatened to shoot. When Philos was being locked up he called to this man and said, —

"Arthur, you know I 's allus hated you, and talked 'bout you; but you was right, when you tole me not to git into no sich troubles as dis."

"Philos," ejaculated Arthur, precipitating his words out in shotted volleys, "I allus tole you so.    You said, when you come back, dat you 'd been to de Bureau, — knowd de law, — dat no white man could 'rest you.    I tole you den you did n't know nuffin 'bout law, — dat no law 'lowed you to carry on mean."

"Well, I t'ought I did know sumfin 'bout law den, but I shore, now, I don't."

"Dat 's so, Philos ; but I tell ye, you 'm got in a mighty safe place now, whar you 'm got *nuffin in de wo'ld to do but to study law !*    I reckon, Philos, by de time you git out ob heah, you 'll be a mighty larned nigger in de law !    Good by, Philos."

"The worst thing about these niggers," explained the justice, "is, that they seem to have no conception of their responsibility. That boy, Philos, can't see why a word from his employer is n't enough now to release him, as it would have done while he was a slave.    He does n't comprehend the fact that he has committed an offence against the State, as well as against his employer."

Most of the negroes seemed very anxious to learn to read, but now and then one sturdily adhered to his old belief that learning was only good for white men.    "Wat 's de use ob niggers pretendin' to learnin' ? " exclaimed one of my drivers. "Dere 's dat new boy Reub.    Missah Powell sent me to weigh out his 'lowance.    He brag so much about readin' an' edication dat I try him.    I put on tree poun' po'k, an' I say, ' Reub, kin you read ? '    He say, ' Lor' bress you, did n't you know I 's edicated nigger ? '    I say, ' Well, den, read dat figger, an' tell me how much po'k you 'm got dar.'    He scratch he head, an' look at de figger all roun', an' den he say, ' Jus' seben poun', zacly.'

Den I say to de po' fool, ' Take you' seben poun' an' go 'iong.'
Much good *his* larnin' did him. He los' a poun' o' po'k by it,
for I was gwine to gib him fo' poun'."

Early after my arrival, I had one of the overseers take me
to the negro church. On secular days it was the blacksmith's
shop. Now it looked fresh, and almost attractive, half filled
with the people of the plantation. All seemed pleased to see us
enter, and I soon found that we were not to pass unnoticed.
The old preacher, who was none other than the plantation gardener, was not one of those who fail to magnify their office.
He was delighted at his Sunday official superiority to his employer, and at the chance to level his broadsides at two white
men ; and he certainly showed us no mercy. " White men might
t'ink dey could git 'long, because dey was rich ; but dey 'd find
demselves mistaken when damnation and hell-fire was a'ter dem.
No, my breddering an' sistering, black an' white, we must all
be 'umble. 'Umbleness 'll tote us a great many places whar
money won't do us no good. De Lo'd, who knows all our
gwines in an' comin's out, he 'll 'ceive us all at de las', if we behave ou'selves heah. Now, my breddering an' sistering, white
an' black, I stand heah for de Lo'd, to say to ebery one ob you
heah, be 'umble an' behave you'selves on de yearth, an' you shall
hab a crown ob light. Ebery one ob you mus' tote his cross on
de yearth, eben as our bressed Master toted hisn."

This was about the average style of the sermon. Part of it
was delivered in a quiet, conversational tone ; at other times the
preacher's voice rose into a prolonged and not unmusical ca-
dence. He was really a good man, and whenever any meaning
lurked in his numberless repetitions of cant phrases, picked up
from the whites to whom he had listened, it was always a good

one. The small audience sat silent and perfectly undemon-
strative. The preacher once or twice remarked that there were
so few present that he did n't feel much like exhorting ; it was
hardly worth while to go to much trouble for so few ; and finally, with a repetition of this opinion, he told them " dey might
sing some if dey wanted to," and took his seat.

" D——n the old fellow," whispered the overseer ; " he don't
do no retail business. He wants to save souls by hullsale, or
else not at all ! "

The passion for whiskey seemed universal. I never saw man,
woman, or child, reckless young scapegrace or sanctimonious
old preacher, among them, who would refuse it ; and the most
had no hesitancy in begging it whenever they could. Many of
them spent half their earnings buying whiskey. That sold on
any of the plantations I ever visited or heard of was always
watered down at least one fourth. Perhaps it was owing to
this fact, though it seemed rather an evidence of unexpected
powers of self-restraint, that so few were to be seen intoxicated.

During the two or three years in which I spent most of my
time among them, seeing scores and sometimes hundreds in a
day, I do not now remember seeing more than one man absolutely drunk. He had bought a quart of whiskey, one Saturday
night, at a low liquor-shop in Natchez. Next morning early
he attacked it, and in about an hour the whiskey and he were
used up together. Hearing an unusual noise in the quarters, I
walked down that way and found the plough-driver and the overseer both trying to quiet Horace. He was unable to stand
alone, but he contrived to do a vast deal of shouting. As I approached, the driver said, " Horace, don't make so much noise ;

don't you see Mr. R. ? " He looked round, as if surprised at learning it.

" Boss, is dat you ? "

" Yes."

" Boss, I 's drunk ; boss, I 's 'shamed o' myself! but I 's drunk ! I 'sarve good w'ipping. Boss,— boss, s-s-slap me in de face, boss."

I was not much disposed to administer the " slapping " ; but Horace kept repeating, with a drunken man's persistency, " Slap me in de face, boss ; please, boss." Finally I did give him a ringing cuff on the ear. Horace jerked off his cap, and ducked down his head with great respect, saying, " T'ank you, boss." Then, grinning his maudlin smile, he threw open his arms as if to embrace me, and exclaimed, " *Now kiss me, boss !*"

Next morning Horace was at work with the rest, and though he bought many quarts of whiskey afterwards, I never saw him drunk again.

But the revival of these old recollections of Southern experience has already outrun reasonable limits. Let me close with some brief account of a visit — since made by many Northerners — to the now well-known cemetery of Buonaventura, near Savannah. It was in the spring of 1865. Aside from the army officials, we were almost the first visitors from the North since the war. " Doesticks " (Mortimer Thompson), indeed, had preceded us, and to our amazement was found in Savannah editing a daily newspaper ; and, true to the traditions of the craft, was breathing out threatenings and slaughter against the common enemy of most newspapers in war times,

—the commanding general. The sandy roads leading into Savannah were still crowded with the rickety wagons of refugees,— the whites fleeing from starvation, the negroes hurrying from the plantations they had never before been able to leave of their own free will, to get their first taste of liberty and city life. Out of this scene of squalor we suddenly turned into what seemed a great and stately forest. The finest live-oak trees I had seen in the South stretched away in long avenues on either hand, intersected by cross avenues, and arched with interlacing branches till the roof over our heads looked, in living green, a groining after the pattern of Gothic arches, in some magnificent old cathedral. One of the Tatnalls, probably an ancestor of the Commodore of our navy, of Chinese and Confederate note, long ago selected this site for his residence, builded his house, and laid out the grounds in these noble avenues. The house was burned during some holiday rejoicings. An idea that the place was unhealthy possessed the owners, and, with a curious taste, the soil that was too dangerous for men to live upon was straightway selected for dead men to be buried in. We would hardly choose a malarious bottom or a Northern tamarack-swamp for a burying-ground, beautiful as either might be. But what matters it? After life's fitful fever, the few interred here sleep doubtless as sweetly beneath the gigantic oaks in the solemn avenues as if on breeziest upland of mountain heather.

Even into this secluded gloom had come the traces of our civil wars. The only large monument in the cemetery bore the simple inscription of "Clinch," and within it lay, I was told, the father-in-law of "Sumter Anderson," as in all our history he is henceforth to be known. Some vandal had broken down the marble slab that closed the tomb, and had exposed the coffins within.

This very barbarism, and the absence of the rows of carefully tended graves, and the headstones with affectionate inscriptions that mark all other cemeteries, increased the impressive gloom of the lonely place. The sun strove in vain to penetrate the arches overhead. Here and again a stray beam struggled through, only to light up with a ghostly silver radiance the long, downward-pointing spear of the *Tillandsia*, or Spanish moss. The coolness was marvellous ; the silence profound, deepened indeed by the gentle ripplings of the little stream, by which the farther side of the cemetery was bounded. Everywhere the arches were hung with the deathly festoons of the Spanish moss, slowly stealing sap and vigor — fit funeral work — from these giant oaks, and fattening on their decay. Drive where you would, the moss still fluttered in your face and waved over your head, and, lit with the accidental ray from above, pointed its warning silvery light toward the graves beneath your feet ; while it clung, in the embrace of death, to the sturdy oaks on which it had fastened, and preached and practised destruction together. Noble and lusty oaks are these ; glorious in spreading boughs and lofty arches and fluttering foliage, but dying in the soft embrace of the parasite that clings and droops, and makes yet more picturesque and beautiful in decay, — dying, even as Georgia was dying in the embrace of another parasite, having a phase not less picturesque, and a poisonous progress not less subtly gentle.

Some day, when Georgia has fully recovered, this spot, too, will feel the returning tide of her generous, healthy blood. The rank undergrowth will be cleared away ; broad walks will be laid out among the tombs where now are only tangled and serpent-infested paths ; shafts will rise up to the green arches to commemorate the names of those, of whatever race, most deserving in the State ; the heroes of past struggles will here find fit resting-place, whichever side they fought for, if only they did it on their consciences and like true men ; and the *Tillandsia*, still waving its witchery of silver, will then seem only like myriad drooping plumes of white, forever tremulously pendent over graves at which the State is weeping.

# THE HYMN OF PRINCES.

# THE HYMN OF PRINCES.

## By JOHN BROUGHAM.

"By the blessing of Heaven, twenty thousand of the enemy are left upon the field. Order a TE DEUM!" — *Telegram from the King of Prussia to the Queen*

ORD! we have given, in thy name,
The peaceful villages to flame.
Of all, the dwellers we've bereft ;
No trace of hearth, no roof-tree left.
Beneath our war-steeds' iron tread
The germ of future life is dead ;
We have swept o'er it like a blight :
*To thee the praise*, O GOD OF RIGHT !


Some hours ago, on yonder plain
There stood six hundred thousand men,
Made in thine image, strong, and rife
With hope and energy and life ;
And none but had some prized one dear,
Grief-stricken, wild with anxious fear :
A third of them we have made ghosts :
*To thee the praise*, O LORD OF HOSTS !

We have let loose the demon chained
In bestial hearts, that, unrestrained,
Infernal revel it may hold,
And feast on villanies untold ;
With ravening drunkenness possessed,
And mercy banished from each breast,
All war's atrocities above :
*To thee the praise*, O GOD OF LOVE !

Secure behind a wall of steel,
To watch the yielding columns reel,
While round them sulphurous clouds arise, —
Foul incense wafting to the skies
From our Home-manufactured Hell ! —
Is royal pastime we like well,
As momently Death's ranks increase :
*To thee the praise*, O GOD OF PEACE !

Thy sacred temples we 've not spared,
For they the broad destruction shared ;
The annals of time-honored lore,
Lost to the world, are now no more.
What reck we if the holy fane
Or learning's dome is mourned in vain ?
Our work those landmarks to efface :
*To thee the praise*, O LORD OF GRACE !

Thus shall it be, while humankind,
Madly perverse or wholly blind,

Will so complacently be led,
At our command, their blood to shed,
For lust of conquest, or the sly,
Deceptive diplomatic lie :
To us the gain, to them the ruth ;
*To thee the praise,* O GOD OF TRUTH !

# AN ENCOUNTER WITH AN INTERVIEWER.

By, Mark Twain

# AN ENCOUNTER WITH AN IN-TERVIEWER.

## By MARK TWAIN.

THE nervous, dapper, "peart" young man took the chair I offered him, and said he was connected with the *Daily Thunderstorm*, and added, —

"Hoping it's no harm, I've come to interview you."

"Come to what?"

"*Interview* you."

"Ah! I see. Yes, — yes. Um! Yes, — yes."

I was not feeling bright that morning. Indeed, my powers seemed a bit under a cloud. However, I went to the bookcase, and when I had been looking six or seven minutes, I found I was obliged to refer to the young man. I said, —

"How do you spell it?"

"Spell what?"

"Interview."

"O my goodness! What do you want to spell it for?"

"I don't want to spell it; I want to see what it means."

"Well, this is astonishing, I must say. *I* can tell you what it means, if you — if you —"

"O, all right! That will answer, and much obliged to you, too."

"I n, *in*, t e r, *ter*, *in*ter — "

"Then you spell it with an *I* ?"

"Why, certainly ! "

"O, that is what took me so long."

"Why, my *dear* sir, what did *you* propose to spell it with ? "

"Well, I — I — I hardly know.   I had the Unabridged, and I was ciphering around in the back end, hoping I might tree her among the pictures.   But it 's a very old edition."

"Why, my friend, they would n't have a *picture* of it in even the latest e—   My dear sir, I beg your pardon, I mean no harm in the world, but you do not look as — as — intelligent as I had expected you would.   No hârm, — I mean no harm at all."

"O, don't mention it !   It has often been said, and by people who would not flatter and who could have no inducement to flatter, that I am quite remarkable in that way.   Yes, — yes ; they always speak of it with rapture."

"I can easily imagine it.   But about this interview.   You know it is the custom, now, to interview any man who has become notorious."

"Indeed !   I ha l not heard of it before.   It must be very interesting.   What do you do it with ? "

"Ah, well, — well, — well, — this is disheartening.   It *ought* to be done with a club in some cases ; but customarily it consists in the interviewer asking questions and the interviewed answering them.   It is all the rage now.   Will you let me ask you certain questions calculated to bring out the salient points of your public and private history ? "

"O, with pleasure, — with pleasure.   I have a very bad memory, but I hope you will not mind that.   That is to say, it is an irregular memory, — singularly irregular.    Sometimes it goes in a gallop, and then again it will be as much as a fortnight passing a given point.    This is a great grief to me."

"O, it is no matter, so you will try to do the best you can."

"I will.    I will put my whole mind on it."

"Thanks.    Are you ready to begin?"

"Ready."

Q.  How old are you?

A.  Nineteen, in June.

Q.  Indeed!    I would have taken you to be thirty-five or six. Where were you born?

A.  In Missouri.

Q.  When did you begin to write?

A.  In 1836.

Q.  Why, how could that be, if you are only nineteen now?

A.  I don't know.    It does seem curious, somehow.

Q.  It does, indeed.    Who do you consider the most remarkable man you ever met?

A.  Aaron Burr.

Q.  But you never could have met Aaron Burr, if you are only nineteen years —

A.  Now, if you know more about me than I do, what do you ask me for?

Q.  Well, it was only a suggestion ; nothing more.    How did you happen to meet Burr?

A.  Well, I happened to be at his funeral one day, and he asked me to make less noise, and —

Q.  But, good heavens! if you were at his funeral, he must

have been dead ; and if he was dead, how could he care whether you made a noise or not ?

*A.* I don't know. He was always a particular kind of a man that way.

*Q.* Still, I don't understand it at all. You say he spoke to you and that he was dead.

*A.* I did n't say he was dead.

*Q.* But was n't he dead ?

*A.* Well, some said he was, some said he was n't.

*Q.* What did you think ?

*A.* O, it was none of my business ! It was n't any of my funeral.

*Q.* Did you — However, we can never get this matter straight. Let me ask about something else. What was the date of your birth ?

*A.* Monday, October 31, 1693.

*Q.* What ! Impossible ! That would make you a hundred and eighty years old. How do you account for that ?

*A.* I don't account for it at all.

*Q.* But you said at first you were only nineteen, and now you make yourself out to be one hundred and eighty. It is an awful discrepancy.

*A.* Why, have you noticed that ? (*Shaking hands.*) Many a time it has seemed to me like a discrepancy, but somehow I could n't make up my mind. How quick you notice a thing !

*Q.* Thank you for the compliment, as far as it goes. Had you, or have you, any brothers or sisters ?

*A.* Eh ! I — I — I think so, — yes, — but I don't remember.

*Q.* Well, that is the most extraordinary statement I ever heard !

*A.* Why, what makes you think that?

*Q.* How could I think otherwise? Why, look here! who is this a picture of on the wall? Is n't that a brother of yours?

*A.* Oh! yes, yes, yes! Now you remind me of it, that *was* a brother of mine. That 's William, — *Bill* we called him. Poor old Bill!

*Q.* Why? Is he dead, then?

*A.* Ah, well, I suppose so. We never could tell. There was a great mystery about it.

*Q.* That is sad, very sad. He disappeared, then?

*A.* Well, yes, in a sort of general way. We buried him.

*Q.* *Buried* him! *Buried* him without knowing whether he was dead or not?

*A.* O no! Not that. He was dead enough.

*Q.* Well, I confess that I can't understand this. If you buried him and you knew he was dead —

*A.* No! no! we only thought he was.

*Q.* O, I see! He came to life again?

*A.* I bet he did n't.

*Q.* Well, I never heard anything like this. *Somebody* was dead. *Somebody* was buried. Now, where was the mystery?

*A.* Ah, that 's just it! That 's it exactly. You see we were twins, — defunct and I, — and we got mixed in the bath-tub when we were only two weeks old, and one of us was drowned. But we did n't know which. Some think it was Bill, some think it was me.

*Q.* Well, that *is* remarkable. What do *you* think?

*A.* Goodness knows! I would give whole worlds to know. This solemn, this awful mystery has cast a gloom over my whole life. But I will tell you a secret now, which I never have revealed to any creature before. One of us had a peculiar mark, a large mole on the back of his left hand, — that was *me*. *That child was the one that was drowned.*

*Q.* Very well, then, I don't see that there is any mystery about it, after all.

*A.* You don't ? Well, *I* do. Anyway I don't see how they could ever have been such a blundering lot as to go and bury the wrong child. But, 'sh ! — don't mention it where the family can hear of it. Heaven knows they have heart-breaking troubles enough without adding this.

*Q.* Well, I believe I have got material enough for the present. and I am very much obliged to you for the pains you have taken. But I was a good deal interested in that account of Aaron Burr's funeral. Would you mind telling me what particular circumstance it was that made you think Burr was such a remarkable man ?

*A.* O, it was a mere trifle ! Not one man in fifty would have noticed it at all. When the sermon was over, and the procession all ready to start for the cemetery, and the body all arranged nice in the hearse, he said he wanted to take a last look at the scenery, and so he *got up and rode with the driver.*

Then the young man reverently withdrew. He was very pleasant company, and I was sorry to see him go.

# My Hermit.

# MY HERMIT.

BY J. B. BOUTON.

### PART THE FIRST.

N the early summer it pleases me to take late afternoon walks in the upper part of Central Park. Its
natural scenery is varied and romantic, and judicious
Art has heightened its picturesqueness. Best of all,
it is not invaded by pedestrian mobs, whose feeble
legs and unambitious souls restrict them to the con-
ventional haunts below the Ramble. There, in a region
sometimes all my own, not even a policeman pacing its
foot-ways, I can stride along, swinging my cane freely, and
whistling, chanting, or reciting favorite bits of poetry, no
more noticed or obstructed than I would be in the wilds of
Minnesota. I imagine myself in the real country, minus
its dusty roads and frequent incident of dogs shooting out
from wayside huts and snapping at my heels. It is good
enough rurality for me.

Last year (1872), about the close of June, I became
aware — unpleasantly aware, to be candid — that the north
end of the Park had another *genius loci*. I came across
him in curving by-paths and odd nooks that I had claimed
by right of sole tenantry. He particularly affected that
snuggest and shadiest of retreats, the Grotto Bridge I call

it, beneath which one may sit on a ribbed and knobby bench, and be soothed by the drowsy monotone of the little waterfall in the Loch above, and rejoice what time the hot air is cooled by ribbon jets that spurt forever from the rough face of the grotto upon him. From the top wall of this concavity hang miniature stalactites two or three inches long, formed by deposits from water slowly trickling through limestone. These have been ten years in making ; and one idly speculates about them that, in a hundred centuries or less (or more), they will each be as thick as a man's thigh, and fill up the grotto till it looks like a bunch of organ-pipes. There is no place like it to sit and cool off, smoking a cigar and surrendering to a delicious stupor.

This new man — this rash invader of my domain — was not very remarkable in appearance. He was strongly built, a perfect bull through neck and shoulders, and had a commonplace face, which would not have caught my attention twice but for the furtive look that he cast at me when I first saw him. It was an oblique, suspicious glance, quick as lightning. Ever after, when I dropped upon him suddenly, as I wheeled a corner or dived into a hollow, he shot that searching eye at me. Then I began to study him. His face was one of which you may find a thousand duplicates at a mass meeting. Photographs show them pretty much alike, and verbal descriptions cannot do better. Nature's every-day pottery, — a low flat forehead, pug nose, high cheekbones, wide mouth, and thin lips. His cheeks were deeply bronzed, as if by frontage of wind and weather ; but I noticed once, when his hat was off, that his brow was white. He wore the brim well down over his eyes. His dress from

head to foot looked second-hand and seedy; it did not fit him anywhere. His eyes were clear, his face unbloated; he was evidently not a drunkard, though his miserable clothes and dirty shirt looked like the last unpawned possession of the sot. A grizzled beard, perhaps of a month's growth, gave him the concluding touch of ugliness.

Occasionally I surprised him in the act of eating crackers and cheese, bits of chicken, morsels of red herring, pickles, and other trifles as inharmonious. These odds and ends he carried loose in his coat-pockets, and when he saw that I observed him he hastily put away the fragments with a slight cough. I never caught him reading a book or a paper; so, plainly, he was not a poor scholar. Though when seated he was looking intently at nothing, I did not imagine him to be a thinker, grubbing at some deep social problem, or an inventor distressing himself over some mechanical puzzle. If this able-bodied man was poor, why was he lounging in the Park, when he could get work down town on his own terms at eight hours a day? If he was vicious and criminal, why was he not among his pals in the back slums and alleys? The more I saw of him, the more my curiosity became excited to know something of his history; and one afternoon it fell out that my desire for knowledge was gratified.

One hot day in the last week of June, I was out for exercise. My appetite being languid, I walked a little faster than my regulation gait to stir it up. Reaching the Grotto Bridge, I was somewhat heated and tired, and at first right vexed to find the rustic sofa occupied. The incumbent was MY MYSTERY. From the débris about him it was apparent he had been eating, of all things, soda-biscuit and pickles, and the very moment I saw him he threw what looked like an empty jam-pot behind the seat. Never did the poor fellow look so much confused, and I felt the impulse to pass on and leave him to his eccentric meal. But I was flushed and wearied, and needed coolness and rest. And then — that was a time as good as any to drop into his acquaintance.

I sat down and heaved a deep sigh of weariness. The man looked at me askew, and put out his hand to take up a walking-stick, made of the branch of a tree. I saw that I must act promptly.

" Warmish," said I, mopping my face.

" Ye-yes." And he moved as if to rise and be off.

Something more decisive must be done. " Take a cigar," said I, offering him one. " Nice place this for a smoke."

This touched his heart, and opened his mouth, as I knew it would. His eyes sparkled as he took the cigar and made a bow of thanks. Then he said, huskily, " Bein' as I 'm a hermit, sir, I can't afford cigars. I goes a pipe, and don't allers have terbacker for that."

A hermit ! Well, I *was* astonished. From boyhood I had read of hermits, and taken a deep interest in those mysterious beings. Twice I had made journeys of a number of miles into the depths of forests to find hermits, reported to inhabit certain huts ; but they were not at home, if, indeed, they existed outside the diseased imagination of newspaper paragraphists. And here was a hermit at my door, as I might say, — in Central Park, of all places ! I would as soon have thought to see a boa-constrictor gliding across the Mall, or a whale spouting in the Ladies' Lake.

" Ah ! so you are a hermit," said I, carelessly, to disguise

my emotions, and as if hermits were the commonest creatures on earth. "Excuse me, may I ask where's your
cave?" You see hermits were associated in my mind with
caves primarily.

"Cave? There ain't no cave in the Park, 'cept the one
everybody knows, a mile furder down. That air one's too
wet fo live in. I tried it one night, and got the roomatiz."

"Oh!" said I, offhand-like, "I see, you are a wood-
hermit. Plenty of trees and underbrush round here, where
a fellow could stow himself away. Now, you know, I have
always thought, if I should turn hermit, I'd take to the
woods. It must be glorious to sleep in the open air, these
fine nights, beneath the grand old trees, canopied by the
starry — "

The man interrupted me. "It's cheap," said he. "It
don't cost nothing. That's what I likes it for."

"Exactly, — and healthy. Anybody could see that by your
looks. But how do you manage when it rains?"

The man peered at me out of the corners of his eyes, and
hesitated. I knocked the ash from my cigar, and looked
at him as innocently as I could. Then he said, in his shy
half-voice: "You don't 'pear to be a detective, and I don't
b'l'eve you'd blow on a poor feller like me; so I don't
mind tellin' you how I works it."

Hermit as he was, the man could not repress the social
instincts of humanity. I saw he was bursting for confidence and sympathy.

"My friend," said I, seriously, "your secret is safe with
me. If there is anything I was brought up to respect, it
is the feelings of hermits."

This reassured him. He sidled closer to me. " You know," said he, " the cops don't 'low nobody in the Park after nine clock at night. I don't do no harm here, but I has to be careful, or they 'd nab me." Then he cast his eyes warily about, and pointed upward. " You see that cock-loft ? "

I looked up and saw a large open space between a part of the stonework and the timbers of the bridge. I had often noticed it before, and thought it a mighty fine place for hiding.

" When the weather is good and the grass dry, then you see I sleeps on the ground up in the woods on the hill yonder. But if it 's rainy I gets on the bridge overhead and swings down easy nuf into that air cubby-hole. 'T ain't bad, I tell ye, with straw and leaves up there, and all out of sight."

" And 't is very comfortable, I dare say; but how do you dodge the police? As you remark, they would turn you out or arrest you if they found you here after nine P. M. I know they are not as sharp or strict as the regular city police."

" That 's it. You 've hit it. If they wos the blue-coats they 'd snake me out in no time. But they 're another breed, — them chaps in gray. They takes it easy. I jest minds my bizness and they minds theirs ; but out of re-speck for 'em, I keeps out o' sight arter I hears the fire-bells strike nine. Gi' me the Park perlice for not botherin' a feller — " And the man checked himself as if he were about to say too much.

I saw, by this time, that the man beside me was a vulgar person. Not a sage who had retired from life disgusted to chew on his misanthropy. Not a man once rich and used to luxury, suddenly made poor and reckless. It seemed impossible that such a tough specimen could have been mortally wounded through the affections. Still, he was a *bona fide* hermit,—no better one, perhaps, within a thousand miles. And, in a certain sense, he was *my* hermit. I already began to feel a proprietary interest in him.

"My dear sir," said I, "may I be so bold as to ask how you live? Have you any occupation?"

The hermit glanced suspiciously at me, coughed, and made no reply. I saw his embarrassment, and was sorry the impolite question had escaped me. So I said, jocosely: "Your expenses can't be much. Rent, they say, is one fifth the cost of living. Your rent costs you nothing. Five times naught is naught,—how's that for a calculation?"

He smiled and said, "That's about it." I perceived that I must try another tack.

"Pray, sir, tell me one thing. Don't you find the time heavy, with nothing to do all these hours? It would kill me."

"I don't ketch your idee. Time heavy! How can it be when I ain't at work,—only whistlin' and walkin' about and sittin' down. That's what I calls comfort."

This strange person and myself took widely different views of life; that was clear. So I only said: "It is a matter of taste. But I never could understand how a man could endure life without something to do. I'm afraid I would never make a good hermit."

He looked at me straight in the face, and slowly uttered these words: "*I am broken-hearted.*" There was no emotion visible in his face; his voice did not tremble; but he covered his eyes with his hands.

The remark moved me deeply, for it was totally unexpected, and seemed natural. I had read and heard of broken-hearted men, but it had never been my good fortune (or otherwise) to know one personally. Therefore, I was not conversant, except through the pages of novels, with the external phenomena peculiar to the broken heart in males, but had somehow associated them with cadaverous visages and attenuated frames. Here was my hermit as fat as a buck and red as a lobster. A broken heart had not occurred to me as a part of his damaged general property. But he said he had a broken heart, and it was only civil to believe him.

"The woman! the inevitable woman," I murmured to myself; and I yearned to know what that dear disturber of the Universal Peace had done to my poor hermit, to drive him to lodgings *al fresco*, and a mixed diet of soda-crackers, herrings, and pickles. "Tell me about it," said I, kindly.

Gratefully he looked up. Still no tears in his eyes, no quiver on his lip. He was able to master his feelings, and that pleased me, for I should have been ashamed to see him blubbering like a school-boy.

The substance of his story I will give in a few words instead of the many in which he told it.

The man's name was Winterbottom, — Thomas Winterbottom, — and he lived in the city, and was by trade a picture-frame maker. He once had a good business, a wife not so good, and one child. All was going on happily in the Winterbottom nest, when a gas-fitter named Juggins appeared

on the scene in the familiar rôle of the Demon of the Household, or the Destroyer of Domestic Peace. After the usual
amount of preliminary skirmishing, Mrs. Winterbottom came
to open rupture with her husband, and in his absence left
the house one night, and transferred herself, her child, and
all her portable property to a new home, — a home rented,
furnished, and the running expenses thereof paid by Juggins,
the perfidious gas-fitter. Winterbottom tracked his recreant
partner to the Juggins lair, and would have taken her away
but for the untoward circumstances that she drove him out
of the room with a mop, and Juggins kicked him down stairs
and threatened to shoot him if he showed himself again on
the premises.

My face must have betrayed my disgust at the pusilla-
nimity of the man, for he said quickly, " Mind ye, Mister,
't was n't the mop I wos afraid on. I 'm used to that. But
Juggins is about seven foot high, and carries a six-shooter.
What could I do ? — *I*, a quiet, peaceable feller, what would n't
hurt a mouse."

" Don't ask me," said I, a little impatiently. " I can't med-
dle in family quarrels."

" I thought ter take the law on him. But there ain't no
law."

" Not much," said I.

" I don't see but what he could shoot me, if he wanted ter,
and get off."

" I 'm sure he could," said I. And I volunteered this addi-
tional exposition of existing law (jury law) on the subject :
" Juggins or your wife could shoot you, or you could shoot
Juggins or your wife, or both of them, or, for that matter,

you could shoot me or any other man. There's no punishment for it. But on some accounts, — slight, to be sure, — it is inconvenient to take the law into your own hands, and I would not be understood as advising you to do it. If you really want my opinion — "

"I do, sir," said the hermit, respectfully.

Then I say, "Pick up courage. Let your wife slide. Go to work."

My advice was not very palatable to Winterbottom, especially as I rose to leave, mindful of dinner, which was now quite due, and I three or four miles away.

"My wife may slide, sir. She may slide as much as she pleases, sir. I've done with her. But I can't work. I'm broken-hearted, and I must be a hermit, — allers a hermit. This is where I'll pass the rest of my days, if the perlice don't drive me out, and I sha'n't live long noway."

I had to show the common feelings of humanity, though my hermit was beginning to be a bore, and I said, "But what will you do in winter? You cannot sleep in the Park. If you do you will freeze, or, if not freeze, starve to death."

"Yes, I'll sleep here," he answered, recklessly; "on the snow, on the ice, anywhere. Some day you'll read a story in the paper about a man frozen to death up in that hole thar. That'll be Tommy Winterbottom. I don't mind. But there's one favor I would ask, sir, if you please."

I had put my best foot forward for a quick walk home; but at this point I rested.

"I spoke about my child, sir. Her name is A-Ara-Arabella. As you say, sir, and it's very good of you, let Mrs. W. slide. But I want to save my child from her and from that villain Juggins. She's a bright, pooty gal, sir, 'bout twelve year old ; 't would do your heart good to see her. And she wos allers very fond of her pa. [Here my hermit pulled out a ragged and dirty handkerchief, and wiped his eyes, in which, however, I had not observed any moisture.] What I'd like to do is this, sir. I'd like to get a sight of her, by watchin' round the house, and kinder smuggle her off, sir. Her grandmother, sir, and lots of other relatives, lives in Philadelfy. They'd keep her, sir, and bring her up honest. I'm sure they would, and no fifty Misses W.s could n't tear her away from 'em. That beast of a Juggins, — he'd be glad to be rid of her. My poor Arabella! I hears as how he beats her, and she has n't no shoes to wear, and not a bonnet to her head. If I only had ten dollars, that ud get a ticket for her on the railroad, and a pair o' shoes, and p'r'aps a bonnet. Then I could steal her off some night, sir, and send her to Philadelfy, and I know she'd be safe and happy. As for poor Tommy Winterbottom, he can stay here and die, cos his heart it is broken. Could n't you lend me ten dollars, sir? Fancy how you'd feel if you wos fixed like me." The speaker wiped his eyes (I forgot to note if they were dry this time) elaborately with his musty handkerchief.

His narrative touched me. I tried to fancy how I should feel, as he requested me to, and I confessed to myself I should feel bad. But that did not warrant my giving him ten dollars. And, on a little reflection, I could not credit his story ; and even were it true, I had no business to be mixing myself up in a family quarrel and a kidnapping case to boot. I decided not to give him the sum asked, or to countenance his romantic scheme in the least. But still he was my hermit, and he looked to me for patronage.

Rising hastily, and determined to put an end to this dinner-killing interview, I handed him a small bill rolled up· "That's the best I can do. It is for yourself only. I cannot interfere between you and Mrs. Winterbottom, but I pity you. And now, good by."

"Thank you, sir, for your kindness to a poor hermit, — a hermit broken-hearted, and can't work."

I hurried off to escape a longer outpouring of gratitude; but just before I passed from his line of vision I glanced back over my shoulder. There he was, peeping at the end of the folded bill to see its value, and I could have sworn his mouth curved into a silent laugh. Had I been imposed on? Sweet Charity, forbid!

---

### PART THE SECOND.

CENTRAL PARK has a peculiar and matchless charm on the Fourth of July; for there, and there only, can the city escape the flash and bang everywhere else prevalent that day. Blessed be the Park commissioners for their anti-Chinese and possibly unpatriotic, but decidedly sensible and humane, regulation, forbidding fire-crackers in the territory under their sway! For that reason, if for no other, I betook myself to the Park, July the Fourth, 1872. My hermit had not been much in my mind since that odd adventure with him, other persons and other events having quite jogged him aside. But when I entered the Park I could not help heading towards the Grotto Bridge as an objective point, and wondering if I should meet him there or thereabout.

The Park, in its lower part, was full of people, come like myself for a little surcease from work, and to avoid the pyrotechnic nuisance of a day in town. Women, children, and old persons, besides quiet-loving folk of my sort, occupied the seats, lined the bridges, sailed on the lakes, threw showers of crumbs to the pampered swans, lounged, flirted, and chattered in the bright sunshine and the very ecstasy of carelessness. There was a delightful absence of whooping small boys. They were all adding to the uproar in the city, faint echoes of which I could imagine to reach me.

Stalking over that populous region rapidly, I soon struck into the less traversed ways, and then kept a bright lookout for my hermit. I visited each nook and by-path where I had been accustomed to see him, and finally passed beneath the Grotto Bridge, confidently expecting to find him there. But no Winterbottom! "What a fool!" said I to myself. "He's your debtor now, and of course invisible." Then I laughed as the droll idea occurred to me that Winterbottom had been watching me all this time from some neighboring elevation, knowing me to be in search of him and chuckling over my discomfiture. "My hermit no longer," thought I; "not even a proprietary interest." So musing, I strolled into the open path, and, under the impression that he might be on the watch for me somewhere about, I looked across the Loch to the wooded hill. Sure enough there my good eyesight detected the sturdy figure of my man at an opening in the bushes. I made out his identity all the more easily because he turned away at once and disappeared.

I started after him in my fastest walk, which soon became a run. Crossing the little foot-bridge over the Loch, I bounded up the hillside, and soon reached a spot near which I had seen him ; but he was nowhere in sight. At that point two paths diverged, but I knew that they led by winding ways to the same place ; so I paused not, but trotted along, keeping a close lookout to right and left among the trees and bushes. After going at a rapid pace for about half a mile, I caught a glimpse of my hermit darting into a clump of underbrush.

"Hallo, Winterbottom!" said I ; "I was looking for you."
The man made another forward jump, and then stopped. I knew why he checked himself when I glanced beyond the bushes and saw a gray-coated Park policeman, quietly patrolling the walk on the other side. In another moment Winterbottom would have been in his arms.

"Out of that there," cried the officer, who had heard the noise in the bushes. "You must stick to the walk, Fourth o' July or no Fourth." The policeman said this good-naturedly, as one who must be indulgent to his fellow-citizens on the great holiday.

"Beg pardin, sir. All right," answered Winterbottom, and he softly stepped out into the path where I stood. I never saw a man so changed. He was pale with fright or desperation, — the latter I thought, as I marked his flashing eyes. He had one hand in a coat-pocket, and I could not resist the impression, as I saw the outline of his knuckles through the cloth, that that hand grasped a knife or pistol. His whole aspect was of one at bay and determined to sell his life or liberty dearly. His rough bearded face, half-open mouth, showing two rows of glittering teeth, his square shoulders and broad chest and great girth of loins, made him a formidable animal. I could hardly conceive that the meek and pusillanimous creature of his own story could be transformed into such a fierce-looking ruffian.

" Wot are yer chasin' me fer ? Wot der yer want ? " he muttered, as his eyes blazed upon me, and still keeping his hand in his pocket. It was the worst case of debtor *vs.* creditor that I ever saw.

" I want nothing, my dear fellow," said I, "only to see you and ask how you are getting on. Sit down here and take a smoke. I want company." This I said as amiably as possible, and I am sure I looked kindly at him, for I meant not otherwise.

His set face relaxed and he took his hand out of his pocket. But his glittering eyes were still fixed on my face. I produced the calumet, but to my surprise he declined it.

" Why did you avoid me ? " said I, chidingly, as one might be allowed to upbraid one's own hermit.

" Did n't know 't was you. Thought 't was a gray-coat arter me, fer sleepin' in the Park."

I knew Winterbottom was lying to me, and my steady, reproving gaze spoke as much, for his eyes dropped.

I paused a moment, thinking what to say to this extraordinary person, when he broke in with, —

" Yer say yer want company. Well, I don't want none. Wot 's the use o' bein' a hermit if yer can't be alone by yerself ? "

This was logic undeniably, and it puzzled me to answer him; and before I could do so, Winterbottom growled out,

"Good mornin', sir. I 'm off this 'ere way." And he pushed by me and strode down the path over which I had chased him.

I could not find it in my heart to be cross with the poor outcast. "Good by," said I, quietly; "and forever," I added to myself, for I knew that after this my hermit and I would not be on speaking terms.

Turning to resume my walk in a direction opposite to that taken by Winterbottom, I saw for the first time the figure of a woman, standing on a slight rise or crown of ground about thirty yards from me. She was looking intently at me ; and her face wore a startled expression. Then she strained her eyes towards the fast-vanishing form of the hermit, who in a second more was out of sight. As I neared this woman, I saw two tidily dressed little boys playing together a short distance from her. "Mamma, mamma," one of them called. "In a moment, dear," said she.

"May I speak a word with you, sir?" she said timidly, in a low voice.

"Certainly, madam," in a tone which encouraged her to proceed ; at least, I meant that it should.

A fragile woman, with a thin, pale face, on which care and anxiety were deeply stamped ; poorly but neatly dressed ; looking like a seamstress fighting her solitary, hard battle, to keep herself and children alive ; a poor, half-broken, supplicating creature, touching the pity of every human heart ; — such was my rapidly formed estimate.

Her voice trembled and her whole frame vibrated as she made an effort to control herself. "I beg your pardon, sir," said she ; "do you know that man you were speaking with? I know him, but I fear you do not."

"Well, no, madam, I cannot exactly say that I know him. He is a queer sort of a fellow, — something of a hermit, as he calls himself. I stumbled across him the other day. If you know him, please tell me who he is."

"Ah, sir," heaving a deep sigh; "I do know him to my cost. Alas! I am his wife."

I cannot say I was taken aback by this revelation, for when she first accosted me, I had guessed at the truth. But the coincidence of meeting her so near the spot where I had just parted from the hermit did surprise me.

I told her I was glad to meet her, that I feared that man had attempted to deceive me, that now I should know the truth, with other reassuring phrases. "Take a seat, Mrs. Winterbottom," said I, motioning to one that stood invitingly by, for I saw that the poor woman, after the long holiday walk she had made with her little children, must be tired.

"Winterbottom," she exclaimed; "that is not my name!"

"And you are his wife?"

"I have my marriage certificate, and that man, that bad man's name is Bagfield."

"Another question, Mrs. Bagfield; have you a daughter Arabella?"

"Arabella! No! I have two little boys, — no more children, — and there they are."

"One question more." (This was a test one.) "Do you know a man named Juggins?"

"Juggins? Juggins? I never heard of him before." The candor of her sad face told me she was uttering no falsehood. I had narrowly escaped being duped by a clever rascal.

"This is a very curious case," said I. "Pray tell me why

your husband — if that is he — is playing hide-and-seek in the Park. He sleeps here nights."

"Why, sir, he escaped from Sing Sing about a month ago, — the paper said, — and he must be keeping out of sight of the regular police up here."

"Whew! And that's my hermit, and his yarn to me was a hermit's sell, I may say." And I could not repress a wild laugh at the absurdity of the contrast forced upon my mind, — a melodramatic anchorite changed into a vulgar jail-bird!

"Pardon me, Mrs. Bagfield," said I, respectfully, as the suffering creature looked at me, astonished. "But that humbug, that lying thief, — excuse me for my warmth, for he is your husband — "

"No excuse needed, sir. As you say, he is a liar and a thief, and he is my husband, though no more but in name." I had thought she would have burst out crying a minute before; but now her eyes flashed indignation, and, if I mistook not, revenge.

"That fellow," I continued, "tried to swindle me out of money to help rob you of your only daughter, — your Arabella, a girl of twelve years who loved her pa, and would go to the end of the world with him. I am laughing at myself, madam; but you I pity from the bottom of my heart." Then I briefly related to her the substance of my conversation with the pseudo-hermit. She listened attentively, only interrupting me with exclamations, — "The liar!" "The thief!" "The traitor!" and the like.

"He must be arrested and sent back to prison," she said, firmly. Now I had finished my narrative, I had waited to hear her opinion on that point, before offering my own.

"I agree with you, madam," said I. "It is hard enough to obtain the conviction and punishment of desperadoes in this city, and escape from prison must not be made easy for them. Are you in fear of this man if he is allowed to run loose?"

"I am afraid of him very much, sir. He thinks I caused his arrest, though God knows I did not. I would have shielded him if I could; but not if I had known, as I now do, that he was spending his time and money on another woman, and neglecting me. That I will never forgive him for." And she stamped her foot fiercely on the ground. "He was a decent man once, sir, but that was long ago. Then he got into bad ways,—through that woman, I suppose. He used to be away from me all night, and then he would come home and abuse me and those little children. Sometimes he showed me money, but none of it was for me; and I should 'a' starved, sir, and my children too, if some good friends had not given me work. I wondered how he got his money; for he had quit his trade, and he wasn't earning anything honestly. One day I found out; for a policeman came to the house and arrested him. He had committed a burglary, they said, and almost killed a man. Bad as he was, sir, he was my husband, and it nigh broke my heart to think he should go to prison. But nothing I could do could save him. The proofs were too strong, and he was found guilty, and was sent up to Sing Sing for twenty years. I saw him the morning they took him away, and he called me bad names, and said he would kill me when he got out, for I had betrayed him. I forgave him those cruel words then, but not afterwards, when I found out there was another woman at the bottom of the whole trouble. Then I was glad he was locked up for twenty years; and he must go back there, — he must go back! It was two years ago, sir, that he was sentenced. I saw, by the papers, he had escaped last month, and there . was a reward offered for him. The detectives have been watching round my lodgings, thinking he might come there. But he knew too much; he is a very cunning man, sir" (I nodded affirmatively), "and keeps away, though I believe, if he dared, he would come down some night and kill me. I say, sir, he must go back, and I will tell the police about him. It's my duty, sir."

There was one weak point in this case against Winterbottom *alias* Bagfield. The woman might be mistaken in his identity, though she said she could swear to him positively. It was somewhat singular, too, that he should have chosen for a hiding-place a resort as public as the Central Park. I admitted to myself that under the circumstances it was the place — that is, the north end of the grounds — where he would be least likely to be disturbed by the regular city police; but I deemed it remarkable that the escaped convict should have had the shrewdness to select it. He must be a cunning fox, truly. I made up my mind what to do.

"Madam," said I, respectfully, "I will see to this matter. Do not make yourself uneasy; for if that man is Bagfield, he shall be sent back to Sing Sing in twenty-four hours, — sure, — and locked up safe for the rest of his term, let us hope. Leave the Park at once with your children, and go home, and trust everything to me." I asked for her address, and made a note of it, promising that she should hear of what I had done in due time.

She thanked me most fervently and took my advice without delay. Not a moment should be lost, if Winterbottom, or Bagfield, was to be caught. I had looked about me during this strange interview with the woman who claimed to be his wife, thinking that my hermit might be watching us in the distance ; but there was no sign of him. Bidding her to keep up courage and hope for the best, and enjoining her again to return home immediately and await further news, I hurried on ahead to a police station in the vicinity of the Park. There I knew correct and full information relating to the case could be obtained.

My mission was soon discharged. The Captain of Police heard my story, and as soon as I came to the name of Bagfield, he smiled as if in recognition of it. Then he showed me a handbill which had been issued and distributed at all the station-houses, offering a reward for the arrest of Thomas Bagfield, *alias* " Tommy the Slouch," who had escaped from Sing Sing. The fellow's person was sufficiently described. It was a pen-portrait of my hermit, saving the stubby whiskers grown in his brief absence from prison. He had made his escape through a drain, and gained the woods before the loss was discovered. An accomplice had there supplied him with a change of clothes. There was an active pursuit, but the hunted had a good hour's start, and by wonderful luck and craft had escaped capture, and slowly worked his way to the city.

The worthy Captain knew much more of Bagfield's antecedents than I could impart to him. He was a very desperate character, though, as the Captain said, " only an amatoor," — not one of those gifted beings, the professionals in crime.

He had done a stroke or two in the confidence line, for which I thought him well fitted ; but his crowning achievements were burglaries. He was suspected of having broken into three or four private houses, and of having stabbed (but not fatally) a policeman in attempting to escape. In committing the particular burglary for which he was sentenced to Sing Sing, he had struck down and severely injured the owner of the house with a slung-shot. "One of the worst and most dangerous men I ever knew," added the Captain, with the cautious qualification, "for an amatoor."

"Is it not singular," I asked, "that he should come to the city to hide?"

"They all do," he explained. "Sooner or later we catch 'em — that is, most of 'em — here. But it was a shrewd dodge in the fellow to hide himself in the Park. To my knowledge, the detectives have been watching his wife's house and his old hanging-out places ever since he got loose. It's been a point of honor to bag him, you see, because he stabbed Policeman Q——. But they never thought of looking in the Park for him ; and by playing his game fine I can see how he might have hung round there a long time, till he thought the hunt for him was given up and he could cut away to some other city ; but he'd have been sure to come back here at last. If you'd been fool enough — I beg pardon for saying it — to give him the money he asked for, he'd pushed before this, perhaps." The oddity of Mr. Bagfield's mixed diet — pickles, crackers, and so forth — the Captain clearly explained on the theory that he had broken into some restaurant near the Park and stolen those miscellaneous edibles, or he might have taken the risk of foraging occasionally among the free lunches in the neighborhood, being very careful to avoid the police. Finally, the Captain promised to inquire into Mrs. Bagfield's circumstances, and if she was as respectable and deserving of confidence as I took her to be, he would see that the reward was sent to her, if paid to anybody. No one else could claim it, — certainly not the police, who would be only too glad to pay something themselves for the pleasure of arresting and returning to Sing Sing the man who was believed to have stabbed Officer Q——.

Before the Captain had finished his remarks he had called two of his men, and they had started forth in citizen's dress in quest of the runaway.

I had transacted my part of this unpleasant but necessary business, and did not care to wait and confront my hermit in his deserved misfortune, if they caught him. So I withdrew, having made arrangements with the Captain to learn the sequel promptly.

Within half an hour from that time Bagfield was surprised and seized in the Park, not far from the Grotto Bridge. He was evidently all unsuspicious of his peril; but when the officers pounced upon him, these words burst from his lips with a curse: "Serves me right for talking with that feller t' other day." He was armed with an ugly looking knife, and attempted to stab one of his captors, but they overpowered him. That very night he was returned in safety to Sing Sing.

The good Captain's inquiries proved that Mrs. Bagfield was worthy of all confidence and kindness; and the reward was paid over to her by the practice of a little diplomacy excusable under the circumstances. She was made to believe that it was a testimony of sympathy from a friend who desired to be unknown. Soon after I heard from the Captain that she had moved away with her children to the West, there to begin life anew under an assumed name, and rear her little ones in ignorance of their degraded father. God help her!

# MISS TS'EU.

# MISS TS'EU:

## *A TEA-TASTER'S STORY.*

### By EDWARD GREEY.
(SUNG-TIE.)

I WAS listlessly watching a party of maskers, who were posturing for the amusement of some, to me unseen, ladies, in the court-yard beneath the windows of the apartment in which I was nominally a prisoner," said the Tea-taster, "when I heard the pit-a-pat of a small-footed lady in the corridor leading to my room.

"My curiosity being excited, I turned from the window and peered down the passage, but, seeing the place quite deserted, thought no more of the circumstance, and, throwing myself upon my matted couch, began to ponder over my position. Any hinderance to progress in travel is annoying, but mine was particularly so. I had been despatched by my house to our Chinese agents in Fokeen, with orders to buy up every *picul* of the new crop of black teas harvested in that district, and my *chop*, or passport, directed all officials to see that I was not delayed or molested by turbulent spirits; yet His Excellency, Kee-Foo, Vice-Lieutenant-Governor of Min Shaú-ú, had taken the responsibility of placing me under friendly arrest, and had confined me in one of the rooms of his Ya-mun, ostensibly on the pretence of protecting me from the rioters. It is true that the Chinese are somewhat demonstrative during the time of their New-Year festivities, but the fact was, a rival house in Hong Kong had despatched an agent with a heavy bribe to Mr. Kee-Foo, and the latter gentleman knew full well that, ere I reached the Woo-e Hill, my competitor would have purchased every picul of tea in the district. In vain I wrote to the unmoved official "that my orders were to proceed without delay"; but he merely pencilled, "Impossible; the people are in arms, and I am responsible for your head," across my memorials, and I was forced to submit. True, I could not complain of my accommodations, and, the ladies of the house were evidently interested in my fate, judging by the presents of fruit and flowers I received morning and night; but since the moment that I was introduced to my prison I had only seen one person, the servant who waited upon me, and he was a deaf-mute.

Opposite to the wing in which my room was situated was a portion of the palace that was always kept closely screened. From the tone of the voices which proceeded from this part of the Ya-mun whenever the maskers did anything particularly amusing, I concluded that the ladies' apartments were situated there, and my surmise proved to be correct.

I was wishing that some one would take pity upon me and pay me a visit, when I again heard the pattering noise in the corridor. Cautiously rising, I crept to the open door, when I beheld a sight which at once astonished and delighted me, for there, laughing like a wayward child, just escaped from its nurse, stood a lovely girl about sixteen years old.

She was of medium height, slender as a bamboo shoot, with an exquisitely formed oval face, straight nose, rosebud mouth, and dark, full, liquid eyes, that pierced your very soul in their innocent earnestness ; her charming features being crowned with a profusion of long, raven hair worn *en queue*. Her lower dresses were of colored satin ; each garment shorter than the one beneath, the outer being profusely embroidered with golden chrysanthemums, and her upper robes, of soft tinted crepe, were covered by a long jacket of pale blue brocade, so thickly embroidered as to almost hide the beautiful fabric. The nails of her tiny, dimpled hands were each three inches in length, and cased in jewelled sheaths, while her doll-like shoes shone from beneath her robes like golden foot-notes on an illuminated manuscript.

Instead of screaming or fainting, this charming vision, with imperturbable comic seriousness and grace, opened her coral lips and inquired, in Chinese, —

" Are you the honorable Fankwei ? "

As this meant, " Are you the foreign white devil ? " I felt exceedingly amused, and could hardly retain my self-possession as I replied, —

" *Mei jin,** I am that humble, never-to-be-too-much-execrated animal ! "

Advancing, at first somewhat timidly, yet gradually, assured by my respectful manner, and growing more confident as she neared me, she gazed innocently into my eyes and faltered, —

" Tell me all about — yourself ! "

This was said so naïvely that I was completely conquered, and, although I knew it was totally contrary to Chinese etiquette, I placed my arm around her lithe form and drew her

* Beautiful lady.

towards me. Instead of repelling my advance, she nestled closer and, looking archly into my face, said, —

"There was a rent in the mat which covers our window, and, my mother being below amusing herself by looking at the maskers, — I — I came here! Now tell me about yourself. Do you eat human flesh? — No!"

"Certainly not!" I quickly replied. "We are not tigers, as they represent us to you, nor do we treat our ladies as your men do theirs. In my country, America, women rule everything, and we almost worship them when they are as pretty as yourself!"

"Worship them!" she queried; "how is that possible?"

"Yes, we are their slaves, and do their bidding! Tell me your name, *mei jin!*"

Opening her bright eyes, and laughing at me with them, she slyly answered: —

"Why should I tell you my name? When you go back to Mee-lee-kee you forget it!"

I protested "that as long as memory held," etc., etc., I should never forget her. and that I was really and truly in love with her! Not having a Chinese term by which to describe what we call *love*, I used the word *worship*, when she solemnly shook her head, saying, —

"To the gods, to your parents, to the spirits of your ancestors, to your superiors, you burn incense and pay worship, but not to young girls! O you *sëen jin,* * I would like to go to Mee-lee-kee!"

The look and the proximity of her cherry lips completed it, and I whispered, in English, — for they never use the salute

* A sort of Chinese angel.

in China, and consequently have no word to express the action, —

"Kiss me, *ching neu!*"*

"Ke-e-es?" she queried.

"Yes, — kiss me!" I cried, suiting the action to the word.

She sprang from my arms like a frightened child and ran from the apartment. Fearing that I had offended her, I was about to follow and endeavor to explain her mistake, when she stole softly into the room, and, standing before me, gently clicked her lips, as though she had partaken of something delicious.

"Are you angry?" I asked.

"For what did you do that?" she gravely inquired. "I feared that after all you were a man-eater, but when I found that — I was not injured — I thought you only did it to try my courage!"

"If you tell me your name, I will explain the mystery!" I replied.

"My worthless name is Ts'eu!" she demurely said. "It is an odious appellation!"

As Ts'eu means, literally, "a star," I told her that she had a charming name.

"If you like it so much, tell me about the rite of *ke-e-es me!*" she shyly observed; adding, "Ke-e-es-me! ke-e-es-me!"

"It is thus performed, little Ts'eu! In my country, when a man wishes to show how much he *worships* the lady of his choice, he places his arm around her, — thus, — she looks up

* Innocent one.

at him, — just as you are doing at me now, — you darling, — then he pouts his lips, — as I do mine, — and you are doing yours, — and he presses hers, — so — ! That is the American rite of kissing!"

Miss Ts'eu received the fervent tribute with evident delight, but immediately after sobered down, and, looking sorrowfully at me, pleaded : —

"O *sëén jin*, I do not quite understand! I cannot learn such a difficult rite in one lesson!"

I again pressed her sweet lips, and this time the kiss was returned; however, the pause which succeeded the performance did not augur a repetition of the exercise, but after a few moments she seemed to awaken from her revery and murmured, —

"Tell me again what you call that?"

"Kissing, — little Ts'eu!"

"We have no such ceremony in our Book of Rites! We have no name for such an act! For thousands of periods we poor Chinese women have been ignorant of this delightful rite! — O *sëén jin*, teach me, that I may become perfect in this!"

I repeated the charming task, but soon in magnetic tenderness of expression and delicate sweetness my pupil became my teacher. We felt like children stealing honey. After some moments Miss Ts'eu looked slyly up, and, quoting from an ancient song, chanted, —

"*Jo lew ying fung.*" *

"That is what *I* call KE-E-ESING!" she added; then, after

* "The delicate willow meets the breeze."

glancing round, in order to ascertain if any one were watching, she gently raised her lips to mine and whispered, —

"Ke-e-es me some more, *sëën jin* Mee-lee-kee!"

The sound of her mamma's voice roused us from our dream of happiness, and, after exchanging one long, delicious salute, the fairy Ts'eu vanished from my sight, thus ending her first lesson.

# ANACREONTIC.

# ANACREONTIC.

By CHARLES GAYLER.

FILL the cup!  Fill it up!
   I 'm sad to-night.
Let it sparkle clear and bright;
In it let me drown my pain.
Fill it up!  Again!  Again!
   I 'm sad to-night.  Heigho!


Fill the cup!  Fill it up!
   I 'm gay to-night.
Circle it with flowers of light,
Let me drink deep the witching draught,
My soul 't will to Elysium waft.
   I 'm gay to-night.  Ha! ha!


Fill the cup!  Fill it up!
   I love to-night.
Wine to Love adds double might.
To her! to her of the laughing eyes!
My life, my joy, my paradise!
   I love to-night.  Heigho!

Fill the cup!  Fill it up!
　　　　　I weep to-night.
My tears shall flow by its ruby light.
O'er the daisied sod, above the breast
Of my loved one, where she lies at rest,
　　　　　I weep to-night.  Heigho!


Fill the cup!  Fill it up!
　　　　　I die to-night!
Pledge me once more the goblet bright.
I come, bright spirit!  Ah, joy divine!
Ye conquer Death, O Love and Wine!
　　　　　I die to-night.  Ha! ha!

# THE THEATER.

# THE THEATER.

BY JOHN ELDERKIN.

"THOROUGHLY RESPECTABLE. — ' Well, I think you will suit me. What is your name ? '
" ' Shakespeare, ma'am ; but no relation to the play-actor of that name.' " — *Punch.*

HIS is 1874, and yet the ancient antipathy to the stage exists in the full vigor of ignorant and vulgar prejudice, with a fair prospect of healthy survival until the day of final judgment.

I once heard a brilliant writer, a critic of the drama, assert in a dogmatic fashion, that the stage is a sham from end to end, that all connected with it, from the reigning star to the meanest agent of the manager, know it to be a sham, and in their business act under the influence of the consciousness that they are perpetrating a fraud.

With this as a motive, little, certainly, could be expected of the drama, but the charge is based upon a shallow fallacy which would condemn all art. The drama, in reality, possesses the noblest domain of art, the direct representation of life. It conforms to all the definitions of art. It is the result of contemplation and a study of causes, and is a production in which knowledge and creative power are exercised. It yields in definiteness, depth, subtlety, form, variety, and beauty to no other of the arts, and in its appeal to universal

humanity it excels them all.  The illusions of the stage have
a far greater degree of realism than the work of painter or
sculptor, or that of the poet interpreted from the printed
page.  To produce them, all the arts co-operate, and, as near
as may be, we have the action and passion wrought out with
the heightening effects of personality, poetry, artistic adap-
tation and sequence, costume, scenery, and every available
accessory to give reality and power to the representation.

It is not the art of the drama which is the cause of antipathy and prejudice to the stage, and which has caused it to
suffer condemnation of the Church.  Dramatic art was born
in the service of religion, and so long as it was its exclusive
servant we search in vain for any anathematization of it.  In
order that this may be clearly shown, a brief sketch of the
origin and connection of the drama with religion is necessary.

The mysteries of the ancients, according to the best authorities, were symbolical representations of religious history, and
Greek tragedy in the beginning "was purely a religious worship and solemn service for the holidays; afterwards it came
from the temples to the theaters, admitted of a secular alloy,
and grew to some image of the world and human life."  The
Hindoo drama was based on mythological narratives, and
acted only on solemn occasions.  In China alone, of all nations possessing a national drama, the ancient civilization
has been so overlapped and obliterated by the changes and
deposits of succeeding ages, that it is impossible to trace an
original connection of the drama with religious observance.
But the Roman drama and that of modern Europe was
entirely derived from that of Greece.  "It happened," says
Addison, in the "Spectator," "that Cato once dropped into a

Roman theater when the Floralia were to be represented; and as in that performance, *which was a kind of religious ceremony*, there were several indecent parts to be acted, the people refused to see them while Cato was present. Martial on this hint made the following epigram : —

> " Why dost thou come, great censor of the age,
> To see the loose diversions of the stage ?
> With awful countenance and brow severe,
> What, in the name of goodness, dost thou here ?
> See the mixed crowd, how giddy, lewd, and vain, —
> Didst thou come in but to go out again ? "

The early Christian Fathers were nourished on Greek learning, and, witnessing the effect of the Greek drama upon the multitude, the Apollinarii, A. D. 370, turned particular histories and portions of the Old and New Testament into comedies and tragedies. But previous to the Apollinarii, fearful of the influence of Greek literature and philosophy and the attractions of the Greek drama, the Christians had denounced all heathen learning. Chrysostom, in his homilies, cries shame that people should listen to a comedian with the same ears that they hear an evangelical preacher. About A. D. 378, Gregory Nazianzen, Patriarch and Archbishop of Constantinople, one of the Fathers of the Church and master to the celebrated Jerome, composed plays from the Old and New Testaments, which he substituted for the plays of Sophocles and Euripides at Constantinople, where the old Greek stage had flourished until that time. " If the ancient Greek tragedy was a religious spectacle, so the sacred dramas of Gregory Nazianzen were formed on the same model, and the choruses were turned into Christian hymns." It was in a tragedy of this Patriarch that the Virgin Mary was first introduced upon the stage.

Much of the rapidity with which Christianity supplanted the old faiths of Paganism is due to the facility with which it adapted itself to prevailing tastes and habits. Christian festivals were instituted to supersede the old Bacchanalian and calendary shows and solemnities, and with very little change in the mode of celebration. During the whole of the Middle Ages the acting of mysteries or plays representing the miracles of saints, circumstances from apocryphal story, and subjects from the Old and New Testaments, formed an important part of every religious festival. These were often of a very questionable character, causing, even in those superstitious days, the criticism to be made that there were many portions of the Scriptures unsuitable for representation in a play or mystery. But the mode of celebrating Christian festivals during many centuries of the dark ages bore a nearer resemblance to the Roman Saturnalia than to anything so intellectual as a mystery ; and if mystery-plays at any time declined, it was because they were above the level of priests and people.

The institution of pilgrimages gave a great impetus to the representation of mystery-plays in modern Europe. The pilgrims were accustomed to travel in companies, and in the various cities through which they passed took up their stand in the public squares, where they sang and acted in character, and afterward in public theaters, for the instruction and diversion of the people.

In 1264 a company was instituted at Rome to represent the sufferings of Christ during Passion Week. In 1298, according to Hone, the Passion was played at Friuli, in Italy ; and the same year the clergy of Civita Vecchia performed the play of "Christ, his Passion, Resurrection, Ascension, Judgment, and the Mission of the Holy Ghost," on the feast of Pentecost ; and again in 1304, they acted the "Creation of Adam and Eve," the annunciation of the Virgin Mary, the birth of Christ, and other subjects of sacred history. These pious spectacles were so much esteemed that they formed a part of every great occasion, the reception of princes, coronations and marriages, and extended to every part of Europe. In France these plays were greatly in vogue, and gradually from Scriptural subjects came to represent a great variety of scenes drawn from contemporary life and profane history. This ultimately excited the jealousy of the Church and the active hostility of the clergy. From being the handmaid the theater became the rival of the Church, and the enmity ensuing, like a family quarrel, appears all the more embittered because of the previous connection.

Here we have the key to the hostility and prejudice against the stage in modern times. In a document amongst the archives of the Parliament of Paris, it appears that on the 19th of December, 1541, complaint was made against certain persons who, having undertaken to represent the mysteries of Christ's Passion, and the Acts of the Apostles, " had employed mean and illiterate fellows to act, who were not cunning in these matters, and to lengthen out their time had interpolated aprocryphal matters, and by introducing drolls and farces at the beginning and end had made the performance last six or seven months ; by means whereof nobody went to church, charity grew cold, and immoral excesses were occasioned."

The secularization of the drama was very rapid from this time, and the stage shared in the toleration which resulted from the multiplication of the objects of general interest to the common people, and the lessening rigor of opinion in matters of religious belief. But the distraction of public attention from the churches to the theaters, " so that the preachers finding nobody to hear them left off preaching," and diminished revenues of the Church resulting from their desertion, were sore grievances to the clergy. They complained that the plays " occasioned junketings and extraordinary expenses among the common people," and in France the theaters were made to contribute a certain portion of their receipts to the poor, — a custom which obtains to the present day.

The precursors of the regular drama in England were mystery-plays, and the production of these plays is closely related to the progress of the Reformation. The Scriptures in English had been scrupulously withheld from the people, and the author of the Chester Mysteries, produced in 1328, was obliged to make three journeys to Rome before he could obtain leave of the Pope to produce them in the English tongue. The ecclesiastics were fearful that, once in possession of the Scriptures in their own tongue, the people would exercise private judgment, and their authority be diminished ; all of which fears were justified by the event. But the mystery-plays were in the hands of the priests, who " craftily used them to postpone the period of illumination, and to stigmatize by implication the labors of Wyckliffe." In this way plays became associated in the minds of the English Reformers with the " baleful errors and vain shows " of Papacy, and this led to the condemnation and persecution of the stage at a later day.

After the Reformation, mystery-plays were composed to promote and secure the new order of things; but Hone says, " There is no existing memorial of the representation of mysteries in England since the latter end of the sixteenth century." The English puppet-show was also a vehicle for the production of mystery-plays, but in the adventures of the Punch of the puppet-show there is a complete departure from the mystery. Punch is always a " sensual, dissolute, hardened character, who beats his wife, disregards the advice of the priest, knocks him down, and exhibits a thorough contempt for moral reputation."

That the attitude of Punch in the puppet-show was in a measure that of the early players of the English stage, seems to be probable from the way in which they are characterized in certian decrees for their regulation; but an art which had been for so many centuries the companion and servant of religion had too healthy and strong a constitution to be smothered in the muck in which it might happen for the moment to be cast. In a night it underwent a resurrection, and in its risen glory far outshone its previous estate. Under the dominion of the Elizabethan dramatists the stage became the rival of the pulpit as an eloquent teacher of morals and the vehicle of the most splendid literature given to the world since the days of the ancient Greek. The theatre afforded to Shakespeare and his contemporaries the field for the employment of their genius.

But the stage still had its trials and disabilities. Its legal recognition dates only from 1572, — eight years after the birth of Shakespeare. In the royal license of that year players were assumed to be servants, and were empowered to play wherever it seemed good to them, *if their masters sanctioned their absence ;* and an act of Parliament of the same year suppressed all wandering players unconnected with noble houses, characterizing them in terms of contumely, and providing condign punishment for offenders. The stage thus suffered from the servitude in which, by the barbarism of the age, players were held. It also suffered from severe supervision, legal prohibition of the introduction of subjects drawn from politics and religion, suspensions for indefinite periods, and the persecution of ignorant and bigoted officials. Even when sanctioned by the court, befriended by the noble, and followed by the general public, the players got themselves into trouble by their own imprudence and wantonness. Contemned and tolerated on every hand, recklessness and defiance were begotten in them, which led them to outrage law and custom.

In this condition it is not a matter of surprise that the stage excited the animosity of the English clergy, and drew forth those extraordinary diatribes which cannot now be read without exciting mirth. By the year 1578, according to Mr. Arber, the clergy habitually attacked the stage. The distraction of the people from the churches was still the sore grievance. One of them says, " Wyll not a fylthye play, wyth the blaste of a trumpette, sooner call thyther a thousande, than an houre's tolling of a bell bring to the sermon a hundred." Another, Stephen Gosson, who had himself aforetime written plays, " perceiving such a Gordian's knot of disorder in every playhouse as woulde never be loosed without extremetie," was moved to " bidde them the base at their owne gole, and to give them a volley of heathen writers ; that our divines considering the daunger of suche houses as are set up in London against

the Lord, might batter them thoroughly withe greater shotte."
There is a curious felicity in much of the logic launched by
the worthy divines at the players, which is well illustrated by
the famous syllogism of Master Coldocke, " The cause of plagues
is sinne, and the cause of sinne are playes ; therefore the cause
of plagues are playes." This logic appears to have been conclusive, as licenses for playing, in the reign of King James,
says Dr. Doran, were regulated by the greater or less preva-
lence of the plague.

The players were not unconscious of their power to punish
these adversaries, and that they used it freely we have abundant testimony. The language which Shakespeare puts into
the mouth of Hamlet shows how closely the stage resembled
the press of the present day. Zealous partisans used it as a
means of inflaming their followers, and public characters were
reviled and caricatured, causing great scandal and just indignation. Citizens and justices were represented as " the most
egregious of fools, arrant of knaves, and deluded of hus-
bands." Jeremy Collier, commenting on the liberties taken by
players with persons of quality, asks, " Must all men be handled alike ? Must their roughness be needs play'd upon
title ? And has our stage a particular privilege ? Is their
charter enlarged, and are they on the same foot of freedom
with the slaves in the Saturnalia ?" That the clergy should
come in for a share of the satire and pleasantry of the stage,
considering the very aggressive position which they occupied
toward it, is not a matter to excite any surprise or sympathy.
The assertion of Jeremy Collier that its "aim is to destroy
religion " will not hold good of the English stage of any
period of its history. It is a hard thing to exact that the

priest shall always be treated with the dignity which attaches to his office, regardless of the lack of it which may distinguish his character and manners. And this is the demand which the clergy have always made of the stage. When hit, they have cried out, "Are the poets ordinaries? Is the pulpit under discipline of the stage? And are those fit to correct the Church, that are not fit to come into it?" But there is a ground of justification for the attitude of the clergy in the offences against morality which have flourished so luxuriantly on the boards of the theater.

The stage, from its nature, living upon the breath of popular applause, must please or perish. It is the creature of its patrons, dependent upon the fashion and taste of the period, holding the mirror up to those traits and habits which are regarded with pride or complacency, and reflecting social vices as a foil to social virtues. When there is a confounding of vice with virtue on the stage, it may safely be assumed that they were previously confounded in the mind of the public which patronizes it. But the pictures presented by the stage react powerfully upon the public, by stamping and giving currency to types of character, manners, and modes of life which otherwise would be less widely known and lack the definiteness to induce imitation. The morality of theatrical representations is, therefore, a matter of vast importance, and imposes upon the stage obligations which have been too frequently treated with contempt, giving its enemies an apparent justification for wholesale arraignment and vituperation. The charge of licentiousness which both poets and players have sustained since Plato excluded them from his model commonwealth and Ovid was banished from Rome, to the days of

Dumas the younger, and opera bouffe, is susceptible of too detailed a verification, and is too notorious to render any apology possible.

With the multiplication of interests, increased complexity of relations, and refinement of manners, which characterize modern society, the stage remains unemancipated from the presentation of lust. The appeal to sexual passion may be more veiled in expression, but in personal exposure and suggestive action it would be impossible to surpass the scenes to be witnessed on the modern stage, simply for the reason that " matters have already reached a point beyond which they cannot go."

In place of the gross and indelicate compositions which our ancestors countenanced and admired, we have a lascivious musical medley wrought out by voluptuous *figurantes*, and a drama of adulterous intrigue, in which the moral inculcated is the utter helplessness and therefore innocence of the female party to it. This drama has for its motive the condonation of adultery and unchastity, and by a skilful play upon the passions, and the natural sympathy for a woman in distress, succeeds in confusing the mental perceptions and transforming in imagination a very weak, if not very wicked, sinner to an injured saint.

In this insidious misrepresentation there is a sinister attack upon public virtue far more to be feared than the open assaults of the propagandists of passional freedom. In taking advantage of the phase of sentiment which renders the production of these plays possible, the dramatists have probably no notion of disturbing the present relations of the sexes, but merely look upon it as a means of smuggling the potent element of licentious sexual passion into the theater. There is no palliation of this in the assertion that the drama is necessarily a mirror of the actual life of the time, as in the " actual life of the time " there is always much which must ever be remanded from the stage. The effort to justify such representations by attributing them to humane impulses, is a stretch of sentimentalism fatal to all distinctions of right and wrong, a price at which all the humanity of the age would be dearly bought. " The imitation of an ill thing may be the worse for being exact," but certainly no good can result to the stage or society from the teaching that the pariah is entitled to the position and privileges of purity.

The fascination which attaches to these plays, as well as to the more gross representations of the spectacular drama, is at bottom nothing but that of licentiousness, which is brought forward under cover of a plea for female emancipation from the trammels of duty. It is one of the results of the foolish agitation which has brought the distinctions of sex prominently before the public mind, exaggerated the influence of desire, and thus given an impulse to unlicensed passion. The effect is partly owing to the lack of popular sympathy with high ideals of life, which has rendered audiences insensible to heroic delineations, and driven the theatre to the vulgar sensation which should be the exclusive property of the newspaper. A reform can only be brought about by an exhibition of the real evil, and a popular demand for plays which have a higher aim than to pander to sexual passion. " The stage is respectable only as it is respected "; and in order that it may be respected, it must be preserved from motives that are as inadmissible in art as they are antagonistic to morality.

But the presentation of licentiousness is an abuse, and not an essential feature of the drama. Dr. Channing says, " Poetry has been made the instrument of vice, the pander of the passions ; but when genius thus stoops it parts with part of its power." The appeal to the lower instincts may draw crowds who delight only in sensuality, but the power exerted by the art is far less in degree, as it is lower in character, to that which is exerted when the impersonal and heroic instincts are properly addressed. The field of the drama is as wide as human experience and the sphere of poetic fancy and imagination ; being limited only by those restrictions which the usages of civilization have prescribed in reference to decency. It is not poverty of material which drives the stage to questionable sources, but the weakness of the dramatic genius which is compelled to make up for lack of power in treatment by the morbid fascination of forbidden fruit.

There is no degradation inherent in the stage as there is none in poetry, of which the stage is the interpreter. For a long time it held the same relation to poetry that the printing-press does to modern literature. It was through the instrumentality of the drama that the mass of people got their knowledge of the works of genius, and of history as well. It is by means of the stage that the mighty influence of Shakespeare has been exerted upon all English-speaking men and women, developing and modelling their intellectual structure. A great dramatic poet, said Goethe, if he is at the same time productive and is actuated by a noble purpose, may succeed in making the soul of his pieces become the soul of the people, and this is what Shakespeare has accomplished. The drama is as old as the first story-teller who tried to make his listeners realize his narrative by appropriate rhetoric and mimetic gestures. It is a moving spectacle of life and action, the product of history, imagination, and art, by which a chapter of human experience is realized to a sympathetic audience. But the sympathetic audience is indispensable to the life of the drama, and it naturally seizes upon that which attracts. The stage sinks to the level of its patrons.

> " The drama's laws the drama's patrons give,
> And we that live to please must please to live."

In a purely mercantile community in which little is respected but money, it is not to be premised that managers and dramatists will be over-nice about the matter which they serve up to the public, especially if the worse the mixture the more greedily it is devoured. The conductors of the theater are not artists or moralists, but simply business men determined, if possible, to present a fair balance-sheet, and therefore mainly intent upon first meeting the popular demand. They do not presume to rise above the popular taste, and in deference to a nice sense of propriety shelve pieces which fill their houses and pockets. It is hard to condemn them for not being wiser than the audiences which assist, and no condemnation would be just which did not include the latter. None the less does the representation of immoral plays injure the proper standing and just appreciation of the drama. In reaping the harvest an odium is incurred which drives from the theater many who would otherwise be appreciative and influential patrons, and a stain is inflicted on all connected with it.

The stage is not the only institution which reflects the

infirmities of humankind. Government, politics, diplomacy, the press, the pulpit, and society are all afflicted, and its common origin forbids us to look to the stage for anomalous perfection. The mission of the stage renders it more liable to pander to the weaknesses of human nature, and to excite the censure of moralists. There is a perpetual struggle in the world between duty and desire, work and play ; and it being the object of the stage to minister to human desire and pleasure, it is inevitable that in the conflict it should come in for abundant criticism and condemnation. But pleasure is essential to human well-being, and not even the religion which taught asceticism as the highest form of virtue was able to effect any important change in the conduct and opinion of the world. An institution, therefore, which has labored to lighten the miseries of existence by the cultivation of pleasure, and by diffusing an atmosphere of contemplation in which ideals of beauty and heroism are presented, has rested securely on the favor of the average mass of mankind.

Among the Latin nations, where the functions of government have had more of a paternal character than among the Germans, the idea has obtained that the theatre, like academies and universities, could not rely upon the voluntary patronage of the people. In these countries the influence of vulgar tastes has been deliberately counteracted. Recognizing the power of the stage to elevate the tone of public feeling and as a school of manners, the government in France has always, since the reign of Francis I., with the exception of a brief period during the Reign of Terror, granted a subvention to certain theaters of the capital, insuring the production of the masterpieces of dramatic literature and a high standar,' of histrionic ability.

It is only by the resources and power of the stage that the masterpieces of dramatic literature can ever be adequately interpreted. In regard to his "Iphigenia," Goethe said the printed words were only a faint reflex of the fire which stirred within him during the composition; the actor must bring us back to the first fire which animated the poet. Eloquence, according to the same high authority, is the very life of the stage. The power and meaning of poetry are only half discerned until interpreted by a master acquainted with the resources of manner and expression. Instances will suggest themselves to every one acquainted with the stage and the triumphs of great actors. It still remains the heritage of the stage to reproduce the nobler passions and heroic proportions of humanity. In our day the novel, a form of dramatic composition in which elaborate description supplies in a measure stage accessories, has for a time partially supplanted the art of the theater. But this is only a temporary result of an introspective and reading age, and the return of a more healthy, objective habit of mind cannot but witness a revival of a higher interest in the drama. It will be ascertained that we have overestimated the value of reading, both for the acquisition of knowledge and the appreciation of poetry. In order fully to realize the past, all the accessories of action must be brought to bear on the senses and imagination. "The drama," says Bacon, "is as history brought before our eyes." No critic or commentator has the power which the actor possesses in his voice and action. A great actor takes on the individualities which he personates, and stands to the world as if they actually live in him. In this way the drama reproduces the most precious of human memories, the persons and characters of the men and women of the past.

"The real object of the drama," says Macaulay, "is the exhibition of human character. To this fundamental law every other regulation is subordinate." Herein is the difficult art of the actor. Voice, expression, dress, and action are important as they assist in justly representing character. The finest qualities of mind and feeling conjoined with high culture and careful training are manifestly necessary to an actor fitly to represent the characters delineated in the magnificent literature of the drama. An actor by true and deep feeling has the power of bringing the impalpable before our eyes. "We turn," says Percy Fitzgerald, "to the old portraits of actors, and are amazed at the speaking intelligence, the bustling vivacity, the lines and channels of thought and restless ideas worn into their very cheeks; the roving, brilliant eyes, the lips about to move; and from these character pictures we see how, by sheer training and power of intellect, they forced their features to signify what they represented."

The decline of the stage at the present time may be traced in a measure to the neglect of this primary purpose of the drama to represent character. The demand for dramatic entertainment has outrun the means of our dramatic artists. The number of actors capable of representing character is ridiculously small as compared with the number of theaters. In order to make up for the deficiency of genuine histrionic talent, every available device of spectacle, furniture, dress, slang, grotesque contortion, and commonplace incident of daily life has been seized upon and paraded upon the boards, constituting a ridiculous travesty of the drama. The failure of these permanently to attract and interest might easily have been foreseen and predicted. Every play of enduring interest hinges upon character, for it is character which creates story; and the interest is due to the free and natural development and manifestation of character in varying circumstances. This is the only thing which has inexhaustible interest, and it is upon this rock that the legitimate drama is founded, and upon which all amorphous, parasitical growths will be ground to pieces.

There is a gulf between nature and art which cannot be bridged. Art is essentially imitative, and dramatic art is an imitation of the characters and actions of individuals by individuals, and therefore calculated to provoke comparison of persons. Between one who acts and speaks greatly in a great place and occasion, and one who imitates his action and speech on the mimic stage, there is a vast disparity, to overcome which is the immense task of the actor. The very exaltation of the character and scenes represented provokes an unfavorable parallel. However admirable the acting, the poetry, the stage accessories, the imagination of the auditor, and however perfect the illusion, the afterthought that the whole is an imitation, a counterfeit presentment, comes in to lower the estimation of the assistants in the representation. This imitative character, inherent in the nature of art, must always affect the estimation and regard in which the members of the dramatic profession are held as public characters, but it in no wise detracts from their proper and reputable fame as individual members of the community.

The unmerited disrepute in which actors have been held has exercised an evil influence by habituating the public to regard in them with an indulgent eye offences which have been severely reprehended in others. The strolling life led by actors in the early time, a feature of the actor's life which has not yet quite disappeared, was unfavorable to domestic virtue. In this way a low standard of social morality obtained and was tolerated. In fact, the sentiment that the private character of the heroes and heroines of the stage is a matter of slight concern to the public, and of small weight in the profession, is one of the most depressing influences which the best representatives of dramatic art have to encounter.

The irregular manner in which the profession is recruited has also affected the standard of morality which obtains in it. Whilst excellence is as seldom attained in histrionic art as in any of the fine arts, a minor degree of dramatic power is one of the most common of human possessions ; hence the aspirants to the stage compare in numbers better with the audiences than with the companies of the theater, and the majority have no conception of any training required properly to enter upon the theatrical boards. This latter belief is fostered by the production of spectacular pieces in which personal beauty and voluptuous display are the principal requirements of one portion of the company. Under such circumstances, among numerous aspirants of about equal merits, the most unblushing and unscrupulous are apt to claim public attention. A performance of such persons must be strictly a personal exhibition, a thing which is an offence to nature, and only to be regarded with contempt on or off the stage. The intrusion of amateurs of both sexes is a positive evil which at present there is no means of correcting. There is no school of acting, and barely a tradition of the requirements of histrionic art. Hence we have a class without the ability and training of actors, who have managed to obtain a connection with the theatre, to the incalculable detriment and disgrace of the drama and its genuine followers.

But when all that can be urged against the theater has been weighed, the sum of good which remains far overbalances the causes of censure. The number of plays in which plot, language, and action are decorous and elevating far outnumbers the others, and these have the firmest hold upon public favor. The taste of the day may be low, but it is in the main pure. The majority want to be amused, and offences against decency lose a portion of their noxious effect from the superficial manner in which they are regarded. It is the intention which informs words and actions with immodesty, and that which is perfectly pure and natural may be so construed as to excite lewd attention and gratify a prurient taste. It must ever be remembered that it is always in the power of the public "to restrain the license of the theater, and make it contribute its assistance to the advancement of morality and the reformation of the age."

The actor has to contend with influences which endanger self-control and evade discipline to a far greater extent than the worker in other fields. His profession requires a surrender of individuality, and absorption in the character to be represented. This self-abnegation and a constant vicissitude of emotion have a tendency to unsettle the mind and induce vagaries of thought and conduct. His associations are all personal, and he is by nature peculiarly subject to the magnetic influences of sympathy and passion. We have the authority of Boswell that actors excel in animation and relish of existence. Their profession excites "liveliness and quickness of mind." There is something in the artistic temperament at war with cautious and prudent worldliness. These attractive attributes of the actor prove too often as dangerous to the possessor as they are fascinating to others. They are sought and pressed into society where the free and volatile artist abandons himself to uncontrolled delights, dissipates his energies, and loses that balance without which it is as impossible for actors as others to maintain just relations with the world.

There has always existed a great affinity between authors and actors. Cicero was the friend of Roscius, and modern instances suggest themselves to every mind. The poet is indebted to the stage for the best reading of his verses ; the stage is indebted to the poet for the warp and woof of its productions. The literary knowledge of a well-equipped actor is necessarily extensive, and his perception of ideal and verbal relationships quick and suggestive. It is in the intercourse of these co-workers that we get the best view of the social character of eminent actors. This is especially the case in the history of the English stage ; for it is a curious fact in the social history of theatrical characters, instanced by the late Henry T. Tuckerman, that the English, notwithstanding their prudery and exclusiveness, first recognized actors and actresses of merit as companions. Goethe and Schiller in Germany were foremost in acknowledging their just claims upon society. Goethe interested himself actively to raise the esteem in which actors were held, showing the world that he held them worthy of social intercourse with himself, and securing their admission to the highest circles. Schiller was present at every rehearsal, and after a successful performance of one of his plays it was his custom to celebrate the event with the company of the theater. Of the French actor and poet Molière, Goethe said, "There is in him a grace and feeling for the decorous and a tone of good society, which his innate beautiful nature could only attain by daily intercourse with the most eminent men of the age."

But it is among the authors and actors of England that we have the most copious and pleasing records of mutual appreci- ation and regard. Any account of these reciprocal good offices would exhaust the space allotted to this "Lotos Leaf." It is enough, in conclusion, to cite the indignant answer of the Ettrick Shepherd to the question, " What can ye expec' frae a play-actor ? " " What can I expect, James ? " is the reply ; "why, look at Terry, Young, Matthews, Charles Kemble, and your friend Vandenhoff; and then I say that you expect good players to be good men as men go ; and likewise gentlemen."

We could point this reply with a far longer list of names, but we are still obliged to confess the truth in Douglas Jerrold's sorrowful sketch of the strolling player: " He is a merry preacher of the noblest lessons of human thought. He informs human clay with thoughts and throbbings which refine it ; and for this he was for centuries 'a rogue and a vagabond,' and is, even now, a long, long day's march from the vantage- ground of respectability."

# POEM.

# POEM.

## FROM THE GERMAN.

By C. McK. LEOSER.

WHEN thy slender feet I gaze upon,
Strange it seems to me, O sweetest
maiden,
So much beauty may be borne upon
them !

When thy little hands I gaze upon,
Strange it seems to me, O sweetest maiden,
How they wound, and no scar torn upon them !

When thy rose-leaf lips I gaze upon,
Strange it seems to me, O sweetest maiden,
How my kisses find such scorn upon them !

When thy quiet eyes I gaze upon,
Strange it seems to me, O sweetest maiden,
Love's light seemeth still at morn upon them !

131

There my heart is.  Do not tread upon
My heart again ; such love, O sweetest maiden,
No other souls have ever worn upon them !

Let my longing love-song die upon
Thy heart ; for truer song, O sweetest maiden,
No man's lips have ever borne upon them !

# An Episode of the War

# AN EPISODE OF THE WAR.

By W. S. ANDREWS.

THINK there is but one other person who knows all the facts, — certainly they will never find their way into history unless this account gets into print; had they been known at the time, I have no doubt there would have been a "Congressional Committee" on it, and a "report." I could n't have helped being a witness; I shall tell nothing now, that I might not have told then upon oath.

There are many who will know the story to be true, when they read it here. Some who were actors in it may learn now, for the first time, how it happened that we were so badly beaten.

Perhaps it never occurred to you that the lives of many men, perhaps the fate of a nation, may depend upon such a trifle as the jealousy or dislike of one general for another (instance Fitz John Porter and Pope at the second Bull Run), an attack of dyspepsia, a headache, or a glass of whiskey. You remember we were beaten at the first Bull Run by Johnston, who came up by a forced march just in time to turn the tide of victory.

Beauregard was already beaten; another hour, and his army would have been in full retreat, and the victory ours.

But our wagon-train did not move as soon it was ordered and expected to do, and our army was delayed several hours in consequence. It is said that the delay was caused by a quartermaster who took "a drop too much," and went to sleep when he should have been at work. It was a mere trifle, — only an hour or two lost, just one glass too many, — a mere trifle. Yet how many weary months of warfare did it bring us; how many thousands of lives were sacrificed to regain what it lost us, trifle as it was!

Every soldier knows that the slightest accident may bring defeat upon the ablest general, or victory to the poorest.

But what I'm going to tell you about was n't an accident; if the result was not foreseen, it might have been: but you shall judge for yourself.

The jealousy which always exists, in some degree, between the army and navy, wherever they are called upon to cooperate, is a most fruitful source of trouble, and oftentimes of disaster.

It would not have happened but for that. But I must not get ahead of my story.

I was the officer in charge of the signal-station at General Gillmore's headquarters on Morris Island, where we had taken the Rebel forts Wagner and Gregg, and were waiting for the navy to complete the work.

The monitors had lain for months waiting the order to advance on Charleston, but were detained by one fear and another. (They never did advance until Sherman, having taken the city from the rear, the fleet quietly steamed into the harbor.) Had there been a Farragut, a Rowan, a John Rodgers, or a Boggs in command, it might have been a different story. But Admiral Dahlgren was a timid officer, — not that he did not intend to pass the forts, and take the city ; he planned and issued orders for an attack a dozen times, and as often postponed it. Before we took the forts on Morris Island, they were the excuse. Then it was Fort Sumter, even after that was dismantled. The chief fear, however, was of torpedoes among the harbor obstructions, and probably not without reason.

However, the army, impatient to get into Charleston, and having done all that it could on the land, expected the navy to advance immediately on the fall of the Morris Island forts, as had been promised ; and after about six months of disappointments and delays, General Gillmore determined to attempt the capture of Sumter by assault.

That fort had been reduced to a heap of ruins by continued bombardment, but the lower tier of casements, buried under the *débris*, was intact, and a garrison was maintained there.

It was generally understood that there was not a very friendly feeling between the General and the Admiral, although they were as polite to each other in their official and social intercourse as two Chinese mandarins. Most of their official communication, being conducted by signals, passed through my hands, and I write only from my own knowledge.

One day, early in September, 1863, at about noon, the General directed me to signal to the Admiral the information that he would assault Sumter, by boats, that night. Much to my surprise, there was returned, in a few moments, an answer to the effect that the Admiral had himself planned to assault Sumter that night, by boats from the fleet, and asking "if the General had not heard of his intention to do so."

The General replied that he was "very much surprised, — had no idea that a boat assault was intended by the navy."

Then followed a series of messages to and fro. Each was sorry that he had done anything to interfere with the other; each thought it "very strange that both had hit upon doing the same thing on the same day"; each would gladly withdraw in favor of the other; "but, the orders having been issued, the men being ready," etc., etc. Then it was proposed that both parties should unite under the command of one officer, and, "being an expedition by water, the Admiral thought that the General would at once see the propriety of giving a naval officer the command." The General "would be delighted, certainly; the army forces would be under command of Brigadier-General Thomas Stevenson, who would act under the orders of any naval officer of equal rank that the Admiral might designate." (At that time there was no such officer in the fleet, except the Admiral himself.) The Admiral was delighted; "his force would be under the command of Captain ——, Acting Commodore." "The General was sorry, but an acting commodore was not a commodore, and could not therefore rank with a brigadier-general, and of course General Stevenson could not take orders from an inferior officer," etc. After some further correspondence on this subject, the Admiral admitted that he could not send the ranking officer, but "he had failed, upon research and reflection, to find any precedent for putting a naval officer under the command of an army officer, and so the expedition must go independent as to command, but would co-operate." The General "regretted this, but," etc., etc.; and it was so arranged.

Then it was agreed that whichever party succeeded in capturing the fort should burn from the parapet a red light, seeing which the others would desist.

Other matters remained to be arranged; it was getting late, and for some time past there had been great difficulty in transmitting the signals, owing to the absence of the regular signal officer of the flag-ship from his post. I therefore suggested to the General, that I had better go to the flag-ship, and arrange details verbally. He assented, and having received full instructions, I put off through the surf, in the General's boat.

I found no difficulty in reaching a perfect understanding with the Admiral, a most urbane gentleman, as to the plan of assault. It was agreed that the naval party should leave the flag-ship at 9 P. M., and the army party, having a less distance to pull, about fifteen minutes later. The last words the Admiral said to me, as I left his cabin, were: "Tell General Gillmore that my boats will start at nine, or later should he desire it. If he wishes delay you can signal me to that effect."

It was then after seven o'clock, and I had a good half-hour's pull, bringing me to headquarters at about twenty minutes of eight.

As soon as the General heard my report, he said: "Telegraph to General Stevenson to start as soon as possible." I said, "Why, sir, under that order he will get off by eight, and the Admiral said his boats would not go until nine." For reply I received a very significant look, and a repetition of the order, which I at once transmitted to General Stevenson.

That the intention was to outwit the navy by capturing

the fort in advance of them, was plain; and whatever my opinion of the plan, I had no reason then to doubt its success. But alas for human expectations!

General Stevenson got away soon after eight. He had perhaps fourteen hundred yards to pull, which would take at least twenty minutes. I was therefore not a little surprised, about ten minutes after he started, to hear a brisk fusilade from the fort. Instantly every other Rebel fort in the harbor opened on Sumter, regardless of their own men, and for a few moments it was the centre of a terrible fire, when suddenly a red light was shown from the parapet, and all was still.

It was evident that the assault had been made, and the red light signified its success.

Very soon General Stevenson came back, and reported that he was about midway from the fort when the red light appeared, and supposing the naval party to be in possession, he returned.

I was a little surprised that the navy boats, which were not to have left the flag-ship until nine, should have reached the fort a little after eight. I afterward learned that the moment I left the Admiral he gave orders that his boats should start as soon as it was dark.

General Gillmore and Admiral Dahlgren had designed to outwit each other, each being anxious to take to himself the entire credit of the exploit.

We made a night of it on shore. Our chagrin at being outdone by the navy was forgotten in our joy at having captured the fort, and the sutlers did an unusually large business.

Next morning we learned the truth. The "Rebs" had read our signals. Had we used the "cipher" that would have been impossible, but the signal officer on the flag-ship had never been instructed in its use, owing to the neglect of the senior signal officer, Captain Town, who hated the navy, because he had once been treated with discourtesy on board the new "Ironsides." So we used the common code, easily read by the Rebels. But we didn't know that, until this affair taught us. We kept the secret to ourselves, though. I tell it in the interest of truth, and because no harm can come of it, now.

Many noble fellows lost their lives by it. The Rebels were fully prepared to meet the assault.

It was our boys who were surprised. More than one hundred were captured or killed. Among the former were Porter and Franklin, two young heroes, afterward killed at Fort Fisher.

None of us were proud of the exploit; but the recital of the facts now cannot be out of place, and is a simple act of justice.

NOTE. I find no mention of this assault in the Rebellion records or in any of the official reports of General Gillmore or Admiral Dahlgren. It is, however, mentioned in Bonyton's "History of the Navy during the Rebellion." My official "Record-Book" containing the correspondence by signals was borrowed by General Gillmore at the time, and never returned.

# SUNRISE AND SUNSET.

# SUNRISE.

By C. E. L. HOLMES.

THE curtains of night's murky tent are torn ;
Day's heralds, stealing through the welcome
rent,
Are streaming up the startled orient,
And painting heaven upon the brow of morn.
Aurora hath the poppied Samson shorn ;
And back, amid the caverns of the hills,
His phantom-crew of drowsy sentinels
Are fleeing from Diana's hounds and horn.
Full-orbed along the coronated peaks,
The amorous day-god for young Hebe seeks, —
Fresh pride sits on dame Nature's rotund cheeks ;
The while her bosom quickening with new birth,
Fulfils once more the promise made at first,
When lusty Day espoused the fair young Earth.

# SUNSET.

By C. E. L. HOLMES.

FROM orient to occident once more
The sun has whirled his blazing chariot's rims,
And now his coursers bathe their wearied limbs
In that aerial jasper sea, which pours
Its baptism of golden spray sheer o'er
The crimsoned bastions of that high sea-wall,
Upon the foreheads of the hills to fall.
Day passes outward through the jewelled doors,
And star-eyed Twilight — timorous dusky maid —
Steals in with backward glance and dainty tread ;
E'en of her own sweet shadowy self afraid,
Now half revealed, — now wholly lost to sight, —
She dances coyly through the fading light,
To rest in the enamored arms of Night.

# FAIRY GOLD.

# FAIRY GOLD:

## AN IRISH SKETCH.

### SHOWING HOW TIM DUFF WAS RUINED ENTIRELY BY TOO MUCH GOOD LUCK.

#### BY JOHN BROUGHAM.

"If you coort a dainty maiden,
  You may get nothing for your gains,
But if you catch a Leprachaun,
  Goold, it will reward your pains."

O the romantic and visionary, ever yearning for something beyond the dull tangible realities of every-day life, there is exceeding fascination in the brain-revellings of Faery. The components of Irish character render it peculiarly adapted to receive and cherish such impressions; while the thousand-and-one anecdotes of fairy agency, vouchsafed for in every case as being "Gospel Truth," and related to the wondering youngsters by some old crone, stamp the traditions upon their minds until they have become a portion of their very faith.

The Irish fairies are sufficiently numerous, and all as well classified, their positions assigned, and their duties defined, by *super*-naturalists, as though they were actually among the things that be. The first in order, as well as in usefulness, are *the* fairies *par excellence*, or, as they are usually denominated, "the good people." Their occupations are of the most multifarious description; and here let me call attention to the extraordinary similarity to be found between the imaginings of those simple, unlettered peasants, and the sublimest theories of philosophy. Grave, book-learned men have demonstrated the principle of atomic vitality pervading the universe. The Irish bog-cutter renders the theory into practice, and gives the imagination locality; myriads of fairies, he is taught to believe, are incessantly engaged carrying on the business of universal nature. Troops of them are filching the perfume from the morning air, to feed therewith the opening blossoms; thousands of tiny atomies the while gently forcing the bud into existence; the warm sunbeams are scattered over the chilly earth, borne on fairy pinions; fairy-laden, too, the gentle rain is carried, drop by drop, plunging into the petals of a thirsty flower; the little messenger leaves his welcome load, then flies back to aid his brethren. Thus the whole course of nature's being is supposed to be conducted by this invisible agency; apart from the philosophy of the matter, one must acknowledge that those bright creations contain within them the very soul of poetry.

There are various other individuals of the fairy genus, — the Banshee, the Puckaun, the Fetch, or visionary reappearance of one dearly loved immediately after death, the most touchingly beautiful conception of all. My present intention is to illustrate the position in Fairydom, occupation, and general characteristics of the Leprachaun. He is a fellow of no small importance, as, in addition to his regular trade, that of fairy shoemaker, he is the custodian of all hidden treasure, knows the whereabouts of every concealed hoard, and is, consequently, as much sought after as the gold itself. The tradition goes that if you catch a Leprachaun, — a feat not easily accomplished, as he must be taken when wide awake, — then countless gold may be secured for his ransom ; but if you touch a sleeping Leprachaun, the penalty is to have your cattle bewitched, and your eldest child an *omadhaun* (Anglice, idiot). There is something chivalrous in that same respect for a sleeping antagonist.

However, a Leprachaun once in your power, you may keep him close prisoner until he reveals the place where treasure is concealed ; but you must have your wits about you, or the cunning little rascal will be sure to cheat you. One thing is in your favor, he is bound to answer truly to every question.

Now, having introduced my subject, let me tell you what Tim Duff got by finding a Leprachaun.

When I first saw Tim, his appearance was certainly much more picturesque than elegant. His *tournure* could not be called metropolitan. He was supporting with his shoulder the side of a little sheebeen-house, called, with the usual conflicting combination, " The Duck and Griddle " ; his hands were listlessly " put away," one in his untenanted breeches-pocket, and the other in the breast of what, from its situation only, we must conclude to be his vest ; his coat, a huge frieze, — in the dog-days, remember, — fell negligently off from his brawny shoulders, discovering his " Irish " — I don't think I should be justified in appending " linen " ; corduroy " smalls," patched at the knees with material so different from the original stuff that it must have required considerable ingenuity to procure it ; his thick woollen stockings were minus the entire feet, the deficiency being made up with straw, causing comfort in the wear, and a sort of sliding scale in the article of fit, as a straw or two more or less made all the difference.

One of his stockings had slipped down from under the piece of twine which gartered it, but, with stoical indifference, he let it take its course, justly imagining that if he pulled it up it would, most likely, fall down again ; so there it lay, festooned in easy carelessness around a huge, muscular, and curiously hairy calf. Leisurely and with epicurean gusto he smoked a *dhudieen*, or short pipe, black with service, and in dangerous proximity to his nose, which seemed to have turned itself up to get out of the way ; singing between puffs, for his own immediate gratification, a self-laudatory song, the burden of which went to prove, beyond all manner of doubt, that he was a most extraordinary individual. Here it is : —

### THE SLASHIN' BLADE.

#### TOM'S DITTY.

*Ora ! thin—n—na (a sort of bagpipe drone to begin with).*

Yu nice young maid-ens, where-e'er you be,
Come gather round an' attind to me ;
A sportin' offur I 'm goin' to make,
It 's the heart an' hand iv a rovin' rake.
An' that 's meself that 's come to the fore ;
Me age is twinty, an' a little more.
I won't owe much whin all me debts is paid,
An' I *am* accountid a slashin' blade.

*Ora ! thin—n—na.*

The highest bidder shall have the prize,
The sweetest lips or the brightest eyes ;
I 'll go dirt chape to the twinties, round,
But for each year afthur I 'll have twinty pound.
I 'm strong an' hearty, I 'm sound win' an' limb.
I can fight an' wrassle, too, — dance, drink, an' swim ;
Make love, make hay, an' use both scythe an' spade,
An' the girls all say that I 'm a slashin' blade.

*Ora! thin—n—na.*

Bid, my hearties, iv I 'm to your taste,
I 'll rise the market iv yez don't make haste;
There 's a young heart-breaker wid a rovin' eye,
That I 'd sell my sowl to, iv she 'd only buy.
'T is Molly Rooney is the girl I mane,
If she comes near me, why I 'm bothered clane!
O murther! there, I 've done, you 've spil'd my thrade,
Do what you will wid your slashin' blade!

The easy *nonchalance* of the ragamuffin, and the delicious indifference with which he seemed to regard all sublunary matters, attracted my attention, and urged me to make some inquiries about him.

"Barty," said I to "mine host," with whom I happened to be on terms of peculiar intimacy, for he knew the lurking-places of the "best trout in the stream," and could point out the lodging of a "big fish" with singular accuracy; added to which, he had a "small thrifle" of whiskey, that, between you and me, had never troubled the gauger's stick, and it was n't a bit the worse for that; besides, an uncommonly pretty — But never mind, that don't belong to *this* story. "Barty," said I, "who is that devil-may-care-looking genius outside?"

"I know who you mane widout lookin', sir," replied Barty, winking significantly; "that 's a *karacthur.*"

"A *karacthur!*"

"Divil a doubt ov it. Why, shure an' that 's neither more nor less than Tim Duff himself," said Barty, with the air of a man who had just given a piece of astounding intelligence. Finding that I did not receive the announcement of the fact with the slightest appearance of awe, he continued, in a bless-your-ignorance sort of a tone, "A-thin, don't you know Tim Duff?"

"I certainly have not that honor."

"Not Tim?"

"Not Tim!"

"Duff, that was ruinated horse and foot with too much good luck, by a blaggard Leprachaun! The saints keep us, I did n't mane any offince!"

The anticipation of hearing a fairy adventure aroused me, and, humbly confessing my ignorance both of Mr. Duff and his experience, I solicited an explanation.

"I 'll tell you what I 'll do," said Barty, with what I thought was rather an interested mixing up of circumstances. "I 'll dhraw a half a pint of potteen, to begin wid, and Tim shall tell you all about it himself."

Well, in due time the potteen came, and with it came the renowned Duff, when he gave me the following account of his lucky ruination.

"You must know, sir, that about a matther ov five years ago, come next Michaelmas, there was n't a tidier boy nor meself to be found in the country. I had an elegant farm, wid lashins an' leavins of everything; a hungry man niver entered my doors an' left it wid the same complaint. My rint was niver axed for twice, an' be the same token, I could bate any spalpeen of me age at hurlin', kickin' foot-ball, drinkin' whiskey, thrashin' the flure wid a purty collieen in a jig, or thrashin' the sauce out ov an impident vagabone in a faction fight; an' to crown all, I was miles deep in love wid the bluest eyed, sweetest tongued, tinderest hearted girl in the place. The heavens be her bed, she 's in glory now. Lost, lost to me; an' me own doin'! O Mary!"

There was a slight pause in Tim's narrative. One big tear

stood for an instant in each eye, and I began to tremble for his philosophy, when he suddenly seized the pewter measure, and as the tears, resolving themselves into two large drops, fell into it, took a terrible long pull at the fiery liquid, exclaiming, with an approving smack, as he set the vessel down, —

"Well, any way, there's comfort in that."

Resuming his story, he proceeded : —

"The fact of it was, sir, the divil a one ov me knew how happy I was at all at all, until it was every bit gone; an' so you may aisily suppose that what was left did n't do me much good. You see, I was n't continted wid havin' enough, but I was always wantin' somethin' more ; at last, I had a stroke ov luck that made me fortune, an', more betoken, broke me complately at the same time. Envy, sir, and covetousness, them was my destruction ! I could n't see a betther farm than mine, but I longed for it. I never met a man betther off than myself, but I hated him for it ; everlastingly turnin' an' twistin', an' huntin' about in me own mind to thry an' think ov some way to make money in a hurry, thinkin', like a poor fool as I was, that if I had plenty of riches I should never know a care. It *is foolish thinkin'* *so*, sir, is n't it ? "

"Very," I replied, with as sententious a shrug as I could produce ; the mental conclusion to which I arrived being uninteresting to any one but myself.

"Well, sir," continued he, "to make a long story short, one summer night as I was frettin' myself to fiddle-strings about what was always uppermost in my mind, I fell asleep in a hurry, and was just as suddenly woke up again by the sound of a little tap! tap! tap! an' a weeshy voice, a thrifle louder nor a cricket, singin' away as merry as a taykittle. Hollo! what the puck is that, thinks I. I gave a sideway squint out ov bed, and what do you suppose I saw? What but a Leprachaun atop ov the table, sittin' on a crust of bread and leatherin' away upon a lapstone about the size of a barley-corn. O, murther! what a bump my heart guv, right up agin the roof ov me mouth, when I saw him! There, right forninst me, was what I had so often longed for, or at least the means of gettin' it. His back was towards me, but I was afeard to breathe, lest the sound should start him off, for Leprachauns is mighty sharp at hearin'. Well, sir, as I was puzzlin' myself wid thinkin' how the divil I could manage to invaigle him, I sees him get up from his work, walk quietly across the table, and try to climb up the outside of a jug that had a spoonful of whiskey at the bottom. Bedad, it was as much as I could do to keep from burstin' out, to see the antics of him. He could n't manage it at all. At last, what does the cunning little blaggard do, but he rowls a pitaty over to the side of the jug, and gets atop ov it.

"You may have some idea of the weight of the ruffian, when I tell you that, though it was an uncommon soft pitaty, he did n't even make a dint in the skin.

"He was elegantly fixed then; he could just lean over the top ov the jug, and dive his hat down to the bottom; an' then he began to bail it out, and drink like a hungry herrin'. Why, sir, he must have brought up each time as much as would stan' in the eye ov a sorrowful flay.

"Well, whether it was that the whiskey was above fairy-proof, or that the pitaty slipped from under him, I don't know,

but in he tumbled, body an' breeches, down to the bottom of the jug. The minute I saw that, out of bed I jumped and clapped my hand atop of the jug. 'Ha! ha! you little ragamuffin; I have you,' says I.

"'Let me go,' says he; 'I'm smothering!'

"'Smother away,' says I; 'the divil a toe you stir until you tell me where to find the threasure.'

"'Is it a threasure you want?' says he.

"'It just is, Misther Leprachaun,' says I.

"'You shall have one,' says he. 'But only let me out; I'll be dhrowned here entirely.'

"'Will you promise me that you won't do the shabby thing?' says I.

"'Yes,' says he. 'But make haste, for I'm getting "as drunk as a lord."'

"Wid that, sir, knowin' he could n't go back ov his word, I put in my finger, the bowld Leprachaun made a horse ov it, an' I fished him out. Poor fellow, he was very drunk, to be sure!

"'Here's a pickle,' says he, 'for a dacint Leprachaun to be in.'

"'Sarves you right,' says I. 'What business had you to be stalein' a man's whiskey?'

"'Thrue for you, Tim,' says he. 'Sperrits will be me ruin; av I don't take the pledge, I'm a gone fairy.'

"'But come,' says I. 'About this threasure.'

"'Don't hurry,' says he; 'misfortunes come time enough.'

"'What do you mane by misfortune?' says I.

"'You'll find out soon enough, if you must have this money,' says he.

"'Divil may care,' says I.

"'Well, then, Tim Duff,' says he, 'you have n't far to go. Twelve feet from the kitchen door, dig twelve feet down, and find that which will make you rich, — and *poor!*'

"'Thank you, — long life to you.'

"I looked round an' he was gone; went out like a candle puff. The broad daylight flashed across my eyes, an' I was sitting up in bed starin' at nothin'. 'Twelve feet down,' says I. 'Now or never.' So up I gets, takes a pickaxe and shovel, an' without sayin' a word to anybody, dug away for the bare life. After about an hour's work, seein' no signs of the threasure, I begun to think that it was dreaming I was all the time, when the pick struck something that guv a clink. Hurroo! thinks I, my fortune 's made. With fresh will I shovelled away, and at last, by dint of tremendous exertion, rather than call any one to help me, I succeeded in gettin' a big earthen pot up to the surface, rolled it into the house, and, throwing myself into a chair, pantin' for breath, and the tears rowlin' down my cheeks, I looked at it for as good as an hour.

"I *knew* it contained money, but I could n't bring my mind to smash it open. Just like a cat, the hungrier she is the longer she plays with the mouse. At last I started up, got my shovel, and gave the pot a savage crack. Bash! it flew into a thousand pieces, and out splashed a beautiful yellow shower of guineas. I 'll never forget the shiver of delight the sound of thim guineas sent into my heart. The Leprachaun had redeemed his word, — I was a rich man; but the remainder of his promise had yet to be fulfilled, and it was. The first calamity that befell me began upon the instant. In liftin' the tremendous weight, I twisted somethin' inside of me back, that has nearly driven me crazy ever since, and all the physic in the world can't put it straight again. Then I removed to a larger farm, where, not knowing the land as well as that I was used to all my life, crop after crop failed. But the crowning curse remains to be told. In the pride of my heart, and in the selfishness of increased means, I slighted her for whom I would have died before. I deserted — *killed* my Mary. No, no; it was n't me that killed her; it was the gold, — the accursed gold! Well, sir, after her death an unquenchable thirst came on me, — drink! drink! I cared for nothing else, lived for nothing else. I need n't tell you how that swallows up everything. Worse luck followed bad, until at last the chair my mother nursed me in, *that her mother nursed her in*, was taken from my door by a grasping landlord. And I stood before a cold hearth, and an empty cupboard, a broken-hearted man!

"The world has been a desert to me ever since, but I have learnt to look on rain and sun with the same face."

# THE HAWK'S NEST.

# THE HAWK'S NEST.

## A RIDE IN A STRANGE PATH.

### By GILBERT BURLING.

EFORE these hurrying days of railroads, travellers through Virginia made their journeyings in the slow old conveyance of the stage-coach, and had time, as they passed, to dwell upon the natural beauties of the way. From Kentucky, and the States comprising the then Southwest, the nearest route to the Capitol at Washington was over the old Virginia Turnpike, which runs along the Kanawha River from Charleston, across it at Gauley, over Gauley Mountain, and beside New River for a long distance. Henry Clay and his contemporary lawgivers used to take this road on their annual way to their seats in Congress ; and therefore it happened, in their time, that the magnificent scenery of the region was well known to them, and through their reports celebrated to the nature-loving of that generation. To-day the tide of travel flows elsewhere, and the only visitors to these scenes are the few whose business brings them by the old coach line from Lewisburg to Charleston, or Charleston to Lewisburg, — perchance stray tourists who remember to have heard of the "Hawk's Nest" from their fathers.

At a point just off the road, and some seven miles from the

great Falls of Kanawha, this great rock stands.   It rises more
than a thousand feet straight up from the river-bed to an equal
height with the mountain, of which it is an enormous, grim but-
tress, frowning over the immense extent of country it surveys.
Even with the unimaginative dwellers thereabouts, so remarkable a feature in the landscape cannot wholly fail of romantic
incidents, or legends born of superstition.   Many of their stories
have already found their way into print, but I am not aware
that the veritable incident of its discovery by " curly-haired
McClung " — a startling incident to him — has ever been published.

The exact date of McClung's adventure seems to have been
forgotten, but I have it on the authority of an " oldest inhab-
itant " that it happened on a certain summer's day some eighty
odd years ago.   The old man was following his favorite occupation of hunting with his dogs, when he unexpectedly came upon
a bear, treed at very close quarters.   Being so placed that he
could not " draw a bead " on a vital part of the beast, for the
leaves and branches in the way, and fearing that Bruin might
jump down and make off if he approached too nearly, McClung
was moving cautiously backward, step by step, in order to find
an opening through which to take sure aim, when he chanced
to glance behind him, and find himself close to the edge of an
unsuspected and frightful precipice, over which another step
would carry him, to fall whirling through the blue air, hundreds
of feet down to the dashing stream below.   Terribly startled, he
forgot the bear on the instant, and rushed away from the danger in a state of trepidation no other peril in life could have
caused him.   It is even said that he took to his bed for two
entire days, before he could recover himself; and that for weeks

after he could not muster courage to look again over the precipice from which he came so very near making the dread "last leap."

After McClung's discovery the rock became well known to the hunters of the Gauley, who named it the Hawk's Nest, either from its commanding position and inaccessibility from below, or because of the numerous hawk's-nests yearly built in the convenient caverns which enter its sides a little way below the edge.

Happening, at one time recently, to be making a limited tour of observation in that part of the country, I had an opportunity to make a sketch of this famous rock from the opposite side of the river. It is a new point of view, from which the rock itself appears the most prominent feature of the scene.

I had been riding for several days through Fayette County, back of Cotton Mountain, and was on my way to meet an important engagement at the Kanawha Falls, when I found the road leading me very near the desired spot. The natives told me that by keeping the road to Miller's Ferry until I came in sight of the building there, I would find a mule-path to the left, towards down the river, which would lead me where I could get the best view of my subject, and afterwards to the Falls by a short route.

The mule-path proved to be a very recent one, easily found, and I struck into it with a simple, confident feeling of satisfaction only to be excused by want of experience of the country I was in. My steed was a quiet, well-conditioned animal, which I had hired from a farmer at the Falls a few days previously ; and her knowledge that her head was turned towards home was instantly apparent in her altered gait, — leading me to believe she knew the road we had entered upon.

By the time we (the mare and I) arrived at the best view of the rock, the path had become so bad as to be only just practicable ; and with a mind made up to return by the good road over Cotton Mountain, — on the theory of "the longest way round is the shortest way back," — I dismounted, tied my, or rather Farmer Muggleston's, gray mare to a tree, and sought the most effective point from which to make the sketch. At length I determined upon a seat on a convenient stump, from whence the Hawk's Nest seemed to overhang the sturdier but less graceful cliffs about it. Along its edge, where the light clouds of river mist seemed hanging, were a few trees, ragged and small as seen from below ; and under it great black seams, or scars, divided the ledges of yellow sandstone with openings like caves, at whose yawning mouths lay bands of reddish earths, or pebbly conglomerate, to which cedars clung here and there, grasping the very face of the precipice, and in the effort distorting themselves into various clutching forms, holding on for life. Lower down column-like rocks rested on tremendous masses of whitish limestone, which became smoother and less seamed as it approached the base at the river-bank, where trees, towering nearly two hundred feet, looked only well-grown bushes by contrast with the height above, in front of which, like guardian spirits of the gorge, a pair of large hawks kept watch and ward in airy circlings, on unmoving wings.

Soon, too much interested in this magnificent study to watch the western skies, I found a thunder-squall upon me unawares, — unnoticed until it began to throw its broad black shadows over the scene, and to open thunder-charged columbiads among the resounding echoes of the New River hills. Then the rain put a temporary stop to my work, and so delayed me that by the time my drawing was roughly completed it was half past four o'clock. In consequence of this delay it was hardly possible to get to the Falls before dark by the Cotton Mountain road. The mare could easily travel three miles an hour through the path. There were still three hours of daylight, even if the clouds the squall had left behind did not disperse ; and so, by keeping on, I could reasonably hope to reach my destination in about two hours and a half, if, as I had been told, the distance was only seven miles from where I struck in. If it proved nine miles, it would still be accomplished in time. Besides, I had been reassured, while sketching, by the passing down the path of a ridden mule and a led one. For these reasons I decided to keep on, in spite of the bad road and threatening weather. To prepare for rough riding with my various sketching impedimenta necessitated some further loss of time, but it was not long before I was mounted and on the way, which shortly became very villanous, for the old mare went constantly stumbling over sharp stones, sliding down clayey hills, or walking cautiously in the narrow path as it led along the steep side of a precipitous bank, or surmounted an outlying bowlder of the great piled-up rocks to the left, above. More than once again I thought of turning back, but was always encouraged to go on by seeing the fresh tracks of the mules before me. I must also confess to a certain foolish, pleasurable excitement, at the spice of danger in such rough riding. The old steed, too, was on her mettle, and showed signs of excitement by the way in which she pricked up her ears and snorted with satisfaction at every bit of good road. And then, who could be blind to the new beauty of these woods, so different from the beauty of the Northern forests, to me much better known ?

Great magnolia poplars, with towering stems, grew up from the right-hand side far below, and only put out their luxuriously clothed branches when they could come to a view of the sky on like terms with the growth higher up on the hillside. Through their crowded trunks the river could be seen dashing and foaming with a rush and a roar which continually deceived me with ideas that the Falls themselves were very near at hand. There was but little underbrush, except in places where huge square, green-capped bowlders lay nearly concealed by groups of the great Southern laurels, which thrust up their long glossy leaves, as if in conspiracy with the mosses covering their tops, and drooping about them so as to hide their hard gray sides. These rhododendrons were all in blossom, and seemed further intentioned by displaying their rosy beauty to most advantage, — lavishing their flowers in contrast to the darkest shadows, or against the neutral blackness of the backgrounds of hemlock-trees which stood in clumps through the wood. An hour and a half of such riding brought me to a small opening in the forest, and sharp upon a "branch," or mountain brook, rushing like a river, with the accumulated waters of a dozen streamlets, swollen by the recent rains.

The ford across looked too dangerous for a stranger to attempt, and I should have been obliged to retrace my steps, even then, had not the ringing strokes of an axe told of possible assistance from a short distance above. Leaving the mare "hitched" to a laurel-bush, I sought the wood-chopper, and after much tribulation in scrambling through the under-brush contrived to get sight of him, and of some other workmen who were erecting a shanty on the farther side. The stream brawled so noisily that it was quite impossible for the men to hear what I said or shouted, and it was not until I found a fallen tree on which to cross that they comprehended who I was, or what I wanted. On learning that I was a stranger, one of them kindly volunteered to bring my horse over. When he had ridden through the ford, which he did with enviable address and caution, he commended my prudence in not attempting the crossing at such a time, for he said that one of the mules which had just preceded me to the shanty had been carried off his feet by the rush, and was very nearly swept out into the river. He informed me that the work going on was for the new railroad, and that the mule-path had only been cut for the use of the engineers and surveyors of the corps of construction.

It was now so near night that I left my chance friend with hurried thanks, and rode on so quickly that I forgot to ask him how far I had yet to go, or what sort of riding I might expect. It was grandly picturesque, but even more up and down hill than before. Lofty pines rose in vain attempts to thrust themselves higher than the perpendicular rocks behind them, while creepers and parasitical vines clustered so thick about the tree-trunks, that the hidden roots of them seemed to start from the far depths below. At length we ascended the mountain-side somewhat higher than usual, and came quite unexpectedly upon the most dangerous piece of path I ever saw.

An enormous wall of shaly rock reared itself perpendicularly high up on the left side; before us ran the path, — not a foot wide was it, — the mere edge of a shifting bank of fragments, loose, sliding, and crumbling, built of the fallen scales of the shale. Having come so unwarned upon this perilous spot, concealed as it was by the curve at its approach, the mare had already advanced too far upon the narrow part of it to retreat;

for in an attempt to turn around, she would be certain to push herself off the ledge.

On the right hand was a declivity of unstable fragments slipping to the water's edge ; on the other side, the rock — straight up.

There was no alternative.

We must go on.

I saw that a man could pass to the firm ground on the other side of the cliff safely enough, if his head did not get whirling, and his nerves were steady. There might be room for a horse's feet ; possibly, only possibly, for the projections of the body — the shoulders, the belly, and the thighs — to pass the rock. I dismounted, slung the satchel and sketching-traps over my own shoulders, took off the near stirrup, and fastened the projecting flap of the old saddle down with its leather, that it might not touch the rock, drew the bridle over the old gray's head, and led her along the little ledge with the momentary expectation of seeing her sliding, rolling, bounding, crashing down into the river, three hundred feet below. She was sure-footed, that old mare ; she balanced herself like a gymnast ; the ledge did not give way as she trod it, but, as she lifted each hoof, the path crumbled from the place where it had rested, and the fragments rustled down the bank, detaching other fragments in their course, until the whole mass appeared sliding away, with a sound like stormy wind among the trees.

We had crossed safely, but the path was gone

Ordinary risks seemed as nothing now, and we pushed on rapidly as the woods became more open. When we had passed the mountain, I again thought I heard the distant roar of the Falls, and my spirits rose a bit in spite of the rain, which was coming down briskly.

For the last hundred yards the path had been actually smooth, and wide enough to trot on, when it suddenly went down hill.

At the moment of reaching the bottom, where alder-bushes grew dense on the banks on either side, a most villanous-looking man started out into the path ahead of me.

He was clad in an old overcoat of Rebel gray, and looked a typical bush-whacker as he stood regarding my approach with evil glances. It occurred to me instantly that he might not be alone, — might be accompanied by other desperate fellows, and mean mischief. It was an unpleasant shock ; but the impulse of the moment being to " open the ball " if necessary, I pushed my horse up to him, and asked, —

" How far is it to the Falls ? "

" Dunno, rightly, how fur."

" Is it two miles ? "

" Heap more 'n that. Reckon it 's three. They 'll tell yer down ter the shanty."

There are more of them then, thought I ; and in my nervousness I took my revolver out of its already convenient place in my belt, and put it in the side-pocket of my overcoat, as I rode rapidly on : for the road was again good for a piece. Soon I came upon the shanty the man had spoken of. There were a crowd of laborers gathered about it, — a railroad gang, as I saw at a glance. They were not dangerous, but they were unpleasant and lawless ; so, although they shouted to me to stop, I only dashed along faster, until the path grew as bad as usual.

It was now after seven o'clock ; only half an hour more of daylight, and at least three miles more of this work. I began to feel as if I were lost, and must spend the night in the woods ; which is a very disagreeable thing to do in the rain and alone.

Now, the road led down close by the river, across a bank of sand ; and then in full view of a rough-built house of new boards, with cheerful lights shining through the windows. As I rode up to it, a negro man came to the door. I could get over the bad part of the path, he thought, before it became too dark, if I hurried on, — from there it was only a mile to the Falls, and a good road. From this house the trail was plain for a few hundred yards, when it led out on a flat rock, and was lost in the river, now very high with the freshet. I turned back and cast over the ground, thinking it possible that the true path was up on the hillside, but, failing to find it there, concluded to return to the house of the cheerful lights, and to ask a shelter for the night. The negro again came forward in answer to my summons, and, upon hearing my request for a lodging, referred me to the Captain, who presently appeared at the door from an inner room, to give me a polite but firm refusal. Bright hopes were dashed in an instant ; but, being *in extremis*, I urged my forlorn condition, and presented my card, with an explanation of the circumstances which led me to seek the hospitality of strangers in such a persistent manner. On learning that I was not a " railroad-man," the Captain relented, told the negro, Tom, to look out for my traps, and ushered me into his sitting-room, comfortable with a warm fire and the incense from several pipes of fragrant Virginia weed. The smokers were the associates of the Captain in his surveying corps, and he soon put me at ease by the perfect courtesy of his informal introduction to them, and to a superabundant supper, made ready by Tom in a few minutes.

To my surprise and delight, he seated me at a table furnished in the most highly civilized style.

A damask tablecloth adorned with a service of polished silver, and gold-edged china of a delicate pattern, all laden with choice edibles, of which eggs, nicely fried bacon, creamy wheat-biscuits, and delicious coffee formed the staple articles of what would be a goodly feast at any time, but doubly and thrice welcome to one who, only a few minutes before, had expected to go supperless to bed in the rocky forest under a coverlet of drizzle.

How I appreciated all this, those good fellows can never know! One, not in like straits, can but dimly imagine the sense of real comfort I felt, as I sat in that luxurious chair, with the white-jacketed Tom ready to hand more biscuits, or refill my coffee-cup ; the rain the while pouring down in a great deluge on the sounding roof.

And when bedtime came, instead of letting me take my blanket in a corner, as I proposed, Monseigneur must needs share his bed with me, — a stranger.  Truly my " lines had fallen in pleasant places," and, giving way to the benign fates, I consented to lay me down to sleep between the fair sheets, where Morpheus straightway embraced me, and sent me visions, now and again, of overhanging rocks, narrow paths, gray mares, and blear-eyed fellows in lonely lurking-places.  The night passed thus, very restlessly, as night often does to one whose nerves have been on the strain of novel sights and thoughts.  When the morning came, the rain still fell, and it was late when I took leave, I hope not forever, of the excellent gentlemen into whose pleasant society the mule-path had led me.

I found the trail very difficult to make out, even in broad day, at the place where I had been at fault the night before.  It was confused by numerous blind tracks leading to it, and was only plain when it merged into the unmistakable railroad embankment, which had been pushed from the other end. The road along this was easily passable, until I came to a piece of fresh work, where I was obliged to dismount in order to pass along a steep hillside where there had been a great sand-blast which had filled the way with sharp *débris* not yet levelled off. Trusting in luck to cross it, — luck had so favored me in my ride hitherto, — I attempted to lead the mare over the cruel place. It was not enough that she had stood supperless in the pelting rain all night, that she had carried me all the day before on one feed of oats; but I must put her at this new trial. It was shameful, and I was near getting my deservings; for, in stepping to the farther side of a cut, I slipped and fell, my leg catching in a hole under and between the stones. For an instant I was held motionless, while my horse stood on an insecure piece of rock above me, gathering and balancing herself to step down where I lay, helplessly dreading the descent of her iron-shod feet, of which at least one crushed and mangled limb would be the inevitable result. By a desperate effort I succeeded in dragging myself out of the hole at the very instant the terrible hoofs came down.

Poor old mare! Her forelegs slipped from under her into the same trap where I came to temporary grief; and she came down heavily on the jagged points of the fresh-broken stones, struggled for a moment, groaning sadly, and then, by a great effort, managed to regain her footing and get on safe ground, where she stood, trembling on her gashed limbs, and gazing at her torn flank, as it heaved with pain and fear. She had, however, sustained no disabling injury, and I ventured to remount her, and proceed at a slow pace to the Falls, and thence to Farmer Muggleston's stable-yard.

To this farmer's praise be it said, that he did not make the injury to his property, severe but not dangerous, the excuse for extorting a large sum in damages ; but, believing them the result of a pure accident, accepted so small a compensation as a five-dollar bill with a good grace that many of his Northern superiors in education might do well to emulate in like case. Then he bid me " God speed," and I went my way on foot with rather an exalted opinion of the native " West-Virginian," a determination to ride no more unknown mule-paths, and in my portfolio the sketch of the Hawk's Nest, from which was drawn the little illustration which gives the title to this paper.

# TO A FLOWER.

# TO A FLOWER.

*IN THE STYLE OF HERRICK.*

By C. FLORIO.

O to my love ; and tell her from my heart
    How much I love!
Go to my love ; and tell her should we part
No salve could heal the smart
    I then should know.
    What shall I do
My love to prove?

Go to my love ; and tell her she's more fair
    Than lilies are.
Go to my love ; and tell her all the air
Around breathes perfume rare
    When she doth move ;
    And gales of love
Her tenders are.

Go to my love ; and tell her here I lie
    And weep and sigh.

Go to my love ; and tell her that I die
If she pass coldly by
         And give no chance
         Or pitying glance
    From her bright eye.

Go to my love ; and tell her this, O flower !
     And watch her face.
Go to my love ; and tell her that her power
Enthralls me so this hour
        That, lest I die,
        She must reply
     With loving grace !

# THE PHYSICAL REQUIREMENTS OF SONG.

# THE PHYSICAL REQUIREMENTS
# OF SONG.

By CHARLES INSLEE PARDEE, M. D.

T is frequently said of eminent singers, that "their vocal organs are of exquisite construction."

The remark is so often repeated, that we are led to regard it as the expression of a general belief, that vocalists are endowed with unusual physical attributes, neither inherited nor to be acquired by the masses of mankind.

It cannot in truth be said that this impression is entirely without foundation ; but if by the expression it is intended to convey the idea that the basis of vocalism is a larynx of peculiar anatomical form or of rare functional power, it may mislead us.

Setting aside the singular mental and emotional bias which seems to be essential to the musical artist, and taking into consideration the physical requirements of song only, we have two factors which enter into its production, namely, the vocal organs — i. e. the mouth, larynx, and trachea — and the ear.

The action of the vocal organs is easily explained. The wasted product of respiration, the breath, is forced through a chink in the larynx, and sound is created, while form and expression are given by the mouth. That words are formed by the mouth, without the aid of the larynx, is a fact easily proven, as every one knows that he can distinctly express himself in a whisper.

The larynx is essentially a double-reed instrument, the vocal cords being analogous to the reed of a musical instrument. The vocal cords are thrown into vibration by the breath, and sound is produced, the pitch being determined by the rapidity or slowness of movement. This, in turn, is regulated by the tension of the cords ; sounds of the highest pitch requiring extreme tension, sounds of the lowest pitch extreme relaxation of those organs. The different positions of the cords are caused entirely *by muscular action.* While the parts are at rest, air passes in and out, in the act of respiration, causing no sound, as then their relations are not favorable to its production.

Thus the larynx is the organ of sound ; but the larynx and mouth are the organs of articulate speech.

These organs are susceptible of the highest cultivation, and their functional perfection can only be attained by training. It is gymnastic exercise of the muscles, acting on the parts, which is required, — systematic practice of their functional qualities, subject to the will. That is all. Within the register of his natural voice, any one can attain mechanical precision of vocal expression. Even the register may be increased by the simple expedient of exercise.

What, then, is so essential to the physical requirements of song, that the few who possess it are regarded as phenomena? It is an ear of exquisite function, such as rarely exists. The ear is as important as is the operator to the transmission of a telegram. It is the conductor, — the critic. Witness the person whose deafness is of such high degree that he cannot hear the sound of his own voice, and listen to his harsh, unmodulated tones. Witness the deaf-mute, — mute only because he is deaf, — with vocal organs that are probably anatomically perfect, but with no guide in that process of imitation, which in the general way constitutes man's training, from the imperfect articulation of the words "papa" and "mamma," in babyhood, to the highest form of vocal expression.

Of our special senses, the ear is the organ of tune. Its function is to receive the succession of sounds, musical notes, the various peculiarities of articulate speech, and to measure the periods of silence. It is the register of the properties of waves of sound, — the intensity, quality, and pitch, — conveying to the brain an impression of the relative intensity of the sound created by the firing of a cannon and of a pistol ; of the quality of the sound of a violoncello or of a violin, — the pitch of the soprano and bass voices. If perfect in its functional property, it registers the whole ; but if not, either through irregular development, or because its normal condition has been changed by disease, it may do so but partially, and the unfortunate possessor of such an ear, particularly unfortunate if he desires to sing correctly, ascertains that he is unable accurately to determine the pitch of certain sounds, and that his most careful attempts to reproduce them result in discords. Moreover, he may observe that he cannot appreciate the quality of sound.

Physiologically considered, the human ear is not a homogeneous organ, but the different parts are for the appreciation of the different properties of sound ; and the absence of one part, for instance, that which registers the quality, or the pitch, would cause the disappearance of its peculiar function. In view of this fact, it would be interesting to collate the several opinions of notably just and impartial critics in regard to various vocalists, to know if the tenor of criticism is in a singular groove ; if it has the appearance of being of a certain formula or of particular bias. The singer who is smarting under the infliction of partial and unjust criticism of a performance, that he has perfected through years of careful training, under the guidance of an exquisite ear, may find courage in the reflection that, in all probability, his critic, honest though he be, has imperfect aural perceptions, and is laboring under the disadvantage of performing work requiring the indispensable direction of an ear of faultless physiological attributes, — an ear that he does not possess ; that the author of the criticism is not prompted by any improper motive, nor is he captious, but is functionally incapable of receiving correct impressions.

A human ear of perfect functional attributes is something rare. That competent authority, Von Tröltsch, says : " I shall make too small rather than too large an estimate, when I assert that not more than one out of three persons, of from twenty to forty years of age, still possess good and normal hearing." Good and normal hearing, in the sense of this paragraph, means good enough for ordinary purposes. It does not refer to that exquisite sensibility to all the properties of sound which is indispensable to the accomplished singer. The author, however, touches the point. If his estimate is approximately correct, few of our race may aspire to the distinction of attaining pre-eminence in song.

My friend, have you a wish to become proficient in song ?

Do not concern yourself too much about your voice. In the practice of your life, you have imitated articulate speech with entire success, and now reproduce it in a creditable manner. Your vocal organs show their susceptibility to training and discipline, and doubtless, within the register of your voice, may be trained to song, provided you have the all-important guide. Have you that guide? Can you recognize the distinctive properties of sound? Do you appreciate the intensity, the quality, the pitch? Have you in perfection the three thousand nerve fibres of the cochlear portion of the ear, each one of which vibrates synchronous to the sound of its own appropriate pitch?

If so, you can succeed; otherwise, it would be as reasonable to expect of a blind man the reproduction of color.

# THE TRUTHFUL RESOLVER.

# THE TRUTHFUL RESOLVER.

## A LEGEND OF THE LEVIATHAN CLUB.

### By D. R. LOCKE.

(PETROLEUM V. NASBY.)

**M**R. JOHN UPANDOWNJOHN had the misfortune to be a strictly honest man, in which particular he stood lamentably alone. He was constructed peculiarly, — he was born into an atmosphere of integrity, and his training had added to his natural bent to a degree that made him as incapable of an untruth, or the semblance thereof, as the great George Washington himself. Having this tendency, it was well for him that he was born with a fortune, for his rigid adherence to his principles unfitted him for almost every occupation. He did try journalism, but was dismissed ignominiously for saying of a candidate of the party with which the paper acted, that he was a thief and a trickster. Then he essayed law, but he saw enough of law before he had been in an office two weeks, while medicine lasted him scarcely a week. So he determined to do nothing, but live on his income and be an honest man.

He adopted certain rules by which he lived, and he could no more depart from them than he could rise from the earth and take a place among the stars. He ate exactly so much, at certain fixed hours and of certain kinds of food. He drank so many times a day of certain liquors which he fancied were good for him, measuring the quantity with the accuracy and precision of an apothecary; and so far did he carry rule into his life, that he put on and off his clothing on certain days in certain months, without reference to weather. I saw him shivering one bright but very cold morning in June, and demanded the reason.

"I laid off my woollens this morning," said he.

"Why lay off your woollens in winter weather?" I asked.

"The 1st of June is my day therefor," said he. "The weather *ought* to be warm to-day. I cannot break my rule."

He never neglected to pay a debt, and never told a lie, not even a white one. He was cut out of an aunt's will, by responding to her anxious inquiry as to how she looked in a certain dress which she had set her heart on, with the simple word, "Hideous." And the same devotion to truth barred him no matter what path he took.

He was frightfully unpopular, though, notwithstanding, he held a good position among his fellows. His childlike simplicity and sterling integrity made him valuable, and beside every one knew that his devotion to truth was honest, and had nothing of bumptiousness or malice in it.

Mr. Upandownjohn was a member of the Leviathan Club. I write the word *was* sadly, for he is a Leviathan no more. The cause and manner of his leaving that delightful association of good men is the animus of this paper.

The members of the Leviathan were pleased with the appearance of Mr. Upandownjohn, and made much of him. Had they known him better they probably would have loved him less, for his peculiar virtue was never popular in that Club.

He excited attention, first, by his habit of correcting loose-talking members when their statements were too highly flavored with romance ; as, for instance, when one gentleman asserted that his father owned Flora Temple when she was a colt, using her as a common hack, and selling her finally for fifty dollars, Mr. Upandownjohn quietly put him down.

" I knew your father," he said, " and a worthy, truthful man he was. He died just three years before Flora Temple was foaled. The mare he used as a hack and sold for fifty dollars must have been some other famous animal. Flora Temple will some day be the death of me. Every racing season some man narrates the circumstance of his father having once owned Flora Temple and worked her as a hack, and, what is more exasperating, he always sold her for just fifty dollars. Would that I could find one man whose father sold her for sixty dollars or sixty-two dollars and fifty cents ! You, my dear sir, are the sixty-eighth man this season whose father once owned Flora Temple. She was the most extensively owned mare I ever knew anything about."

On another occasion a gentleman detailed with great minuteness, how in doing the regular thing at Niagara by going under the sheet, the wind parted the torrent and he stepped out upon the shelf outside, when, to his horror, the opening closed, leaving him outside the falling sheet on a narrow ledge of rock. With great presence of mind he darted through the falling sheet and rejoined the frightened party who supposed him lost forever.

Mr. Upandownjohn took pencil and paper, and worked all

night and the next day, without sleeping or eating. The next night he exhibited to the hero of this marvellous adventure the weight of the water in that sheet, and demonstrated to him the fact that, had he got under it, he would have been mashed, though he had been constructed of cast-steel.

"Are you sure it was ˙Niagara?" he asked anxiously. "Was n't it some other fall?"

One day a member died, and the Club did the usual thing by him. A committee of three was appointed to draft resolutions expressing the bereavement of the members, and, as ill-luck would have it, Upandownjohn was put upon the committee.

They met, and, as is always the case, two of the members really had not time to attend to it. One had an engagement at the theater; the other was to take his sister — or some one else's — to the opera.

"Upandownjohn," said the first, "you have nothing to do, and are handy with the pen. There is no earthly necessity for keeping us here. You just write out the usual resolutions, and send 'em down to *The Screamer*, *The Spouter*, and *The Soarer* in time for to-morrow morning."

"How shall I treat the deceased?" asked the obliging Upandownjohn.

"O, in the usual way! Speak of his qualities as a man, the feelings of the Club at his untimely taking-off, the sources of consolation that we have, his qualities as an actor; hurl in something to alleviate the pangs of his family; speak of his general standing; and put in a strong dose of general comfort, you understand, to those who mourn, and so on. It 'll be all right. You 'll attend to it now, won't you?"

"It is a disagreeable duty," replied Upandownjohn; "but I will do it."

And they left him to his work.

Now Mr. Upandownjohn had had no experience in work of this kind, and consequently he was n't exactly clear as to the form. So he sent for the scrap-book in which such utterances of the Club had been posted from its beginning. He was shocked. There were a great many sets of resolutions on deceased members (the liquors were bad at the Leviathan), and they were all precisely alike! They ran as follows:—

*Whereas*, It has pleased Almighty God, the ruler of the Universe, to remove from our midst our esteemed brother and friend, John James So-and-so; and

*Whereas*, It is fit that we, his afflicted survivors of the Leviathan Club, should publicly express their sore grief at this great bereavement; therefore be it

*Resolved*, That in the death of John James So-and-so, this Club has lost a worthy member, society an ornament, his family an affectionate father and husband, the State a pillar and defender, and the world at large one it could illy spare.

*Resolved*, That while we mourn with sorrow that seems to have no alleviation under the great affliction that has fallen upon us, we cannot but bow in humility to this inscrutable decree.

*Resolved*, That we tender our heartfelt sympathy to the family and relatives of the deceased.

*Resolved*, That the Club-house be draped in mourning for thirty days in memory of the deceased.

As he finished, Mr. Upandownjohn brought his fist down upon the table till the glasses jingled.

"What stuff this is!" he said, indignantly. "I knew So-and-so. He was a dishonest and untruthful man, — a tyrant in his family, a trader in politics, a disagreeable man in society, and a curse to humanity generally. And they mourn *him*, do they? And I suppose they want me to mourn Ranter, who is to be embalmed to-night. Ha! ha! I will astonish these people. I will write one set of honest resolutions. I knew Ranter, who has just gone hence, and justice shall be done him sure. I will be as mild as I can be, and do him justice, but I will be honest with his memory."

So Mr. Upandownjohn called for fresh pens and ink and paper, and wrote ; and having made fair copies of what he wrote, took them himself to the offices of *The Screamer*, *The Spouter*, and *The Soarer*, and went home and slept as only he can sleep who rejoices over a duty done and well done.

The next morning the members of the Leviathan were astonished at reading in the journals the following : —

*Whereas*, By a long course of the most outrageous dissipation, of late nights, of late suppers of the grossest food, of perpetual beverages of the most villanous kind, — those that give the stomach no show whatever, — by unchecked and unregulated indulgence in the worst possible sensuality ; in brief, by a long-continued series of the vilest outrages upon the physical, mental, and moral man, our late member, Arthur Simpson Ranter, has been taken to that bourne from which we earnestly hope he may never return ; and

*Whereas*, When a member of the Leviathan Club expires, it is customary to commemorate him, to give him a send-off, as it were, therefore be it

*Resolved*, That when we remember the villanous habit he had of revoking at whist, and also his adroit way of sliding out of paying the score, whenever he lost the rubber, our grief at his departure is severely mitigated, if not entirely subdued.

*Resolved,* That the promptness of our late associate in accepting invitations to slake his thirst, and his intolerable tardiness in reciprocating, did more honor to his head than to his heart.

*Resolved,* That his habitual untruthfulness, his utter disregard of his word, and his blustering and overbearing manner, were the best points in him, as they served as a warning to the younger members of the Club. For this his demise is to be lamented.

*Resolved,* That his habit of getting boozy before eleven A. M., and staying in that condition so long as there was a good-natured man in the Club, gives us his survivors good reason to pause and ask no more that conundrum, "Why was death introduced into the world?"

*Resolved,* That when we remember the success with which our late brother borrowed money, and his utter forgetfulness of such transactions, our hearts are softened toward Adam and Eve (through whose sin death was made a part of the economy of nature), and we publicly thank that lady and gentleman for their investigating turn of mind, and hurl back indignantly the charge that they did not do the best thing possible for posterity.

*Resolve t,* That in the death of our late brother, who was as vile as an actor as he was bad as a man, the long-suffering theater-going public have a boon the sweetness of which cannot be overstated, and upon which we extend them hearty congratulations.

*Resolved,* That we congratulate Mrs. Ranter upon the fact that her private fortune was settled upon herself, and so skilfully tied up that her late husband, our deceased brother, could not get at a cent of it. And we do this, remembering how often we have mourned that it was so, for the reason that, could he have touched it, he would have drank himself into an untimely tomb several years sooner than he did. Death with us buries all animosity and does away with all acrimony.

*Resolved,* That the Club-house be illuminated the night of the funeral, and be draped in white for thirty days in honor of this happy event.

*Resolved*, That this truthful tribute to the memory of our deceased brother be published in *The Screamer*, *The Spouter*, and *The Soarer*.

---

To say there was an uproar in the Club the next morning, as these resolutions were read, would be to convey a very faint idea of the case. In the midst of it, when it was at its height, entered Upandownjohn, cleanly shaved, and as serene as a June morning.

"Did you write and publish this miserable mess, — this ghastly concoction of infernalism?" demanded a score of indignant men.

"Did I write those resolutions, you mean. I did. I was appointed a committee to embalm the memory of the late Ranter in the daily papers. I did it. Do you find anything objectionable in them?"

"Why, you assert that he was a sponge!" exclaimed one.

"Unhappily it is the truth. I have myself paid for gallons of liquor for him."

"You say he was a bad actor?"

"The worst I ever suffered under."

"What will his wife think of what you have said of him?"

"She will recognize the portrait, and with us thank Heaven for her release."

"You give it as the sense of the Club that he was — "

"Everything that was bad, mean, and disreputable. Very good. It is true, every word of it. He owes me this day thirty-seven dollars sixty-three cents and a third, which he has owed (it was borrowed) since July 9, 1871, at twenty-seven minutes past ten o'clock in the evening. And every man of you is also his creditor. If there is a mean thing that he has not done, it has escaped my notice."

By this time Mr. Upandownjohn saw that his fellow-members were angry, and for once he lost his balance and became angry too.

Brandishing his umbrella (it was not raining, but as it was the time of month when it should have rained he carried it), he exclaimed : —

"Gentlemen, you have had one set of resolutions written which contained nothing but the truth ; not the whole truth, for my time was limited, and it was impossible to get in all that I could have said, and besides, I desired to be as lenient and mild as possible. Having written nothing but truth, you are offended. It is well. I will have nothing whatever to do with a club where the truth cannot be told. Truth, if not the immediate jewel of the soul, is very close to it. Gentlemen, adieu. You have seen the last of John Upandownjohn. Should I stay, I might be called upon to resolve over some of your inanimate remains, and as I cannot tell a lie, it would be unpleasant."

And that afternoon the directory received his resignation, and he was seen there no more.

There is no particular moral to this. There are very few men in the world of whom it would be pleasant, as the world now goes, to tell the exact truth. Therefore may all who read these lines live, as does he who writes them, so that when Azrael waves his dark pinions over them, they may lie down and die, feeling certain that the committee on resolutions, though they be as truthful as Upandownjohn, will say nothing that will call a spirit-blush to their cheeks in the hereafter.

# TRANSLATIONS.

# TRANSLATIONS.

By C. FLORIO.

## "*DIE LORELEY.*" — (Heine.)

KNOW not what it presageth
    That I am so heavy of heart,
A tale of old times comes o'er me,
    And will not be forced to depart.

The air is cool, and the twilight
    Shadows the calm-flowing Rhine;
While red, in the fading sunlight,
    The tops of the mountains shine.

A maiden, wondrous and lovely,
    Sitteth in beauty there;
Her jewels glitter and sparkle;
    She combs her golden hair.

With golden comb she combs it,
    And sings — 'neath the dark'ning sky —
A song, with a magic, resistless,
    All-powerful melody.

A boatman who glides beneath her
Is seized with wild affright ;
He sees not the rocky ledges,
He sees but her on the height.

The waves surround, ingulf him,
He sinks with the setting sun !
And this, with her wondrous singing,
This hath the Loreley done.

-------

"*KENNST DU DAS LAND.*" — (GOETHE.)

### 1.

KNOWEST thou the Land where the pale lem-
ons grow,
Where golden oranges mid dark leaves glow,
Where, ceaseless breathing from blue heaven,
a breeze
Kisses the myrtle, and tall laurel-trees ?
Knowest thou it well ?
Ah ! there would I fly with thee, O my Belovéd !

### 2.

Knowest thou the House ?  Its roof high pillars raise ;
Its spacious halls with matchless splendors blaze ;
Pale statues stand and eye thee sleeplessly.
Ah, thou poor child ! what have they done to thee ?
Knowest thou it well ?
Ah ! there would I fly with thee, O my Protector !

### 3.

Knowest thou the Mountain, up whose cloudy way
The mule seeks footing, led by fogs astray?
In craggy caverns dwells the Dragon's brood;
Rocks crashing fall, and o'er them roars the flood.
    Knowest thou it well?
Ah! thither leads our way.  O Father, let us go!

---

### BACCHANAL.

 ET graybeards preach of temperate bliss,
  And the pains endured by a toper;
 We 'll drink, boys, drink! and the red
   wine's kiss
  Shall kill grief, — the interloper.

Drink to the eyes of her you love!
 Drink to her lips of coral!
Drink to her kisses, — her stolen glove!
 Drink! Let the old be moral!

Time to repent when passion 's cold,
 And the bloom of life 's bereft us;
When the hair is white, and the heart is old,
 And no enjoyment 's left us.

Time to repent in years to come!
 Our young day knows no morrow: —

Drink!   Bid those preaching fools be dumb, —
What do we know of sorrow?

Give us another goblet here!
  Hurrah, for jolly Bacchus!
Drink on! 't is now no time to fear
  The pains that yet may rack us.

Drink! let us spend a jovial night;
  'T is time, when pains oppress us,
To dream of nights that *have been* bright,
  And murmur a meek, "God bless us!"

Time enough then; but, till it 's here,
  Let 's drink the night into morning;
Drown — in your brimming cups — old Care,
  And with him the dotard's warning!

# A FATAL FORTUNE.

# A FATAL FORTUNE.

## By WILKIE COLLINS.

ONE fine morning, more than three months since, you were riding with your brother, Miss Anstell, in Hyde Park. It was a hot day; and you had allowed your horses to fall into a walking pace. As you passed the railing on the right-hand side, near the eastern extremity of the lake in the Park, neither you nor your brother noticed a solitary woman loitering on the footpath to look at the riders as they went by.

The solitary woman was my old nurse, Nancy Connell. And these were the words she heard exchanged between you and your brother, as you slowly passed her:—

Your brother said, "Is it really true that Mary Brading and her husband have gone to America?"

You laughed (as if the question amused you) and answered, "Quite true!"

"How long will they be away?" your brother asked next.

"As long as they live," you replied, with another laugh.

By this time you had passed beyond Nancy Connell's hearing. She owns to having followed your horses a few steps, to hear what was said next. She looked particularly at your brother. He took your reply seriously: he seemed to be quite astonished by it.

"Leave England, and settle in America!" he exclaimed. "Why should they do that?"

"Who can tell why?" you answered. "Mary Brading's husband is mad, — and Mary Brading herself is not much better."

You touched your horse with the whip, and, in a moment more, you and your brother were out of my old nurse's hearing. She wrote and told me, what I here tell you, by a recent mail. I have been thinking of those last words of yours in my leisure hours, more seriously than you would suppose. The end of it is that I take up my pen, on behalf of my husband and myself, to tell you the story of our marriage, and the reason for our emigration to the United States of America.

It matters little or nothing, to him or to me, whether our friends in England think us both mad or not. Their opinions, hostile or favorable, are of no sort of importance to us. But you are an exception to the rule. In bygone days at school we were fast and firm friends; and — what weighs with me even more than this — you were heartily loved and admired by my dear mother. She spoke of you tenderly on her death-bed. Events have separated us of late years. But I cannot forget the old times; and I cannot feel indifferent to your opinion of me and of my husband, — though an ocean does separate us, and though we are never likely to look on one another again. It is very foolish of me, I dare say, to take seriously to heart what you said in one of your thoughtless moments. I can only plead in excuse, that I have gone through a great deal of suffering, and that I was always (as you may remember) a person of sensitive temperament, easily excited and easily depressed.

Enough of this! Do me the last favor I shall ever ask of you. Read what follows, and judge for yourself whether my husband and I are quite as mad as you were disposed to think us, when Nancy Connell heard you talking to your brother in Hyde Park.

## II.

It is now more than a year since I went to Eastbourne, on the coast of Sussex, with my father and my brother James.

My brother had then, as we hoped, recovered from the effects of a fall in the hunting-field. He complained, however, at times of pain in his head; and the doctors advised us to try the sea air. We removed to Eastbourne, without a suspicion of the serious nature of the injury that he had received. For a few days, all went well. We liked the place; the air agreed with us; and we determined to prolong our residence for some weeks to come.

On our sixth day at the seaside, — a memorable day to me, for reasons which you have still to learn, — my brother complained again of the old pain in his head. He and I went out together to try what exercise would do towards relieving him. We walked through the town to the fort at one end of it, and then followed a footpath running by the side of the sea, over a dreary waste of shingle, bounded at its inland extremity by the road to Hastings and by the marshy country beyond.

We had left the fort at some little distance behind us. I was walking in front; and James was following me. He was talking as quietly as usual, when he suddenly stopped in the middle of a sentence. I turned round in surprise, and discovered my brother prostrate on the path, in convulsions te. rible to see.

It was the first epileptic fit I had ever witnessed. My presence of mind entirely deserted me. I could only wring my hands in horror, and scream for help. No one appeared, either from the direction of the fort or of the high road. I was too far off, I suppose, to make myself heard. Looking ahead of me, along the path, I discerned, to my infinite relief, the figure of a man running towards me. As he came nearer, I saw that he was unmistakably a gentleman, — young, and eager to be of service to me.

"Pray compose yourself!" he said, after a look at my brother. "It is very dreadful to see ; but it is not dangerous. We must wait until the convulsions are over, and then I can help you."

He seemed to know so much about it, that I thought he might be a medical man. I put the question to him plainly.

He colored, and looked a little confused.

"I am not a doctor," he said. "I happen to have seen persons afflicted with epilepsy ; and I have heard medical men say that it is useless to interfere until the fit has worn itself out. See!" he added, "your brother is quieter already. He will soon feel a sense of relief which will more than compensate him for what he has suffered. I will help him to get to the fort ; and, once there, we can send for a carriage to take him home."

In five minutes more, we were on our way to the fort ; the stranger supporting my brother as attentively and tenderly as if he had been an old friend. When the carriage arrived, he insisted on accompanying us to our own door, on the chance that his services might still be of some use. He left us, asking permission to call and inquire after James's health the next day. A more gentle and unassuming person I never met with. He not only excited my warmest gratitude; he really interested me at my first meeting with him.

I lay some stress on the impression which this young man produced upon me, — why, you will soon find out.

The next day the stranger paid his promised visit of inquiry. His card, which he sent up stairs, informed us that his name was Roland Cameron. My father — who is not easily pleased — took a liking to him at once. His visit was prolonged, at our request. In the course of conversation, he said just enough about himself to satisfy us that we were receiving a person who was at least of equal rank with ourselves. Born in England, of a Scotch family, he had lost both his parents. Not long since, he had inherited a fortune from one of his uncles. It struck us as a little strange that he spoke of this fortune with a marked change to melancholy in his voice and his manner. The subject was, for some inconceivable reason, evidently distasteful to him. Rich as he was, he acknowledged that he led a simple and solitary life. He had little taste for society, and no sympathies in common with the average young men of his own age. But he had his own harmless pleasures and occupations; and past sorrow and suffering had taught him not to expect too much from life. All this was said modestly, with a winning charm of look and voice which indescribably attracted me. His personal appearance aided the favorable impression which his manner and his conversation produced. He was of the middle height, lightly and firmly built; his complexion pale; his hands and feet small and finely shaped; his brown hair curling naturally; his eyes large and dark, with an occasional indecision in their expression which was far from being an objection to them, to my taste. It seemed to harmonize with an occasional indecision in his talk; proceeding, as I was inclined to think, from some passing confusion in his thoughts which it always cost him a little effort to discipline and overcome. Does it surprise you to find how closely I observed a man who was only a chance acquaintance, at my first interview with him? Or do your suspicions enlighten you, and do you say to yourself, She has fallen in love with Mr. Roland Cameron at first sight? I may plead in my own defence, that I was not quite romantic enough to go that length. But I own I waited for his next visit, with an impatience which was new to me in my experience of my sober self. And worse still, when the day came, I changed my dress three times, before my newly developed vanity was satisfied with the picture which the looking-glass presented to me of myself!

In a fortnight more, my father and my brother began to look on the daily companionship of our new friend as one of the settled institutions of their lives. In a fortnight more, Mr. Roland Cameron and I — though we neither of us ventured to acknowledge it — were as devotedly in love with each other as two young people could well be. Ah, what a delightful time it was! and how cruelly soon our happiness came to an end!

During the brief interval which I have just described, I observed certain peculiarities in Roland Cameron's conduct which perplexed and troubled me, when my mind was busy with him in my lonely moments.

For instance, he was subject to the strangest lapses into silence when he and I were talking together. They seized him suddenly, in the most capricious manner; sometimes when *he* was speaking, sometimes when *I* was speaking. At these times, his eyes assumed a weary, absent look, and his mind seemed to wander away, — far from the conversation and far from me. He was perfectly unaware of his own infirmity: he fell into it unconsciously, and came out of it unconsciously. If I noticed that he had not been attending to me, or if I asked why he had been silent, he was completely at a loss to comprehend what I meant. What he was thinking of in these pauses of silence, it was impossible to guess. His face, at other times singularly mobile and expressive, became almost a perfect blank. Had he suffered some terrible shock, at some past period of his life? and had his mind never quite recovered it? I longed to ask him the question, and yet I shrank from doing it, — I was so sadly afraid of distressing him; or, to put it in plainer words, I was so truly and so tenderly fond of him.

Then, again, though he was ordinarily the most gentle and most lovable of men, there were occasions when he would surprise me by violent outbreaks of temper, excited by the merest trifles. A dog barking suddenly at his heels, or a boy throwing stones in the road, or an importunate shop-keeper trying to make him purchase something that he did not want, would throw him into a frenzy of rage which was, without exaggeration, really alarming to see. He always apologized for these outbreaks, in terms which showed that he was sincerely ashamed of his own violence. But he could never succeed in controlling himself. The lapses into passion, like the lapses into silence, took him into their own possession, and did with him, for the time being, just what they pleased.

One more example of Roland's peculiarities, and I have done. The strangeness of his conduct, in this case, was noticed by my father and my brother as well as by me.

When Roland was with us in the evening, whether he came to dinner or to tea, he invariably left us exactly at nine o'clock. Try as we might to persuade him to stay longer, he always politely but positively refused. Even *I* had no influence over him in this matter. When I pressed him to remain, — though it cost him an effort, — he still persisted in retiring exactly as the clock struck nine. He gave no reason for this strange proceeding ; he only said that it was a habit of his, and begged us to indulge him, without asking for any further explanation. My father and my brother (being men) succeeded in controlling their curiosity. For my part (being a woman), every day that passed only made me more and more eager to penetrate the mystery. I privately resolved to choose my time, when Roland was in a particularly accessible humor, and then to appeal to him for the explanation which he had hitherto refused, as a special favor granted to myself.

In two days more I found my opportunity.

Some friends of ours, who had joined us at Eastbourne, proposed a picnic party to the famous neighboring cliff called Beachy Head. We accepted the invitation. The day was lovely, and the gypsy dinner was, as usual, infinitely preferable (for once in a way) to a formal dinner in-doors. Towards the evening our little assembly separated into parties of two and three, to explore the neighborhood. Roland and I found ourselves together as a matter of course. We were happy, and we were alone. Was it the right or the wrong time to ask the fatal question? I am not able to decide, — I only know that I asked it.

## III.

"Mr. Cameron,". I said, "will you make allowances for a weak woman? And will you tell me something that I am dying to know?"

He walked straight into the trap, — with that entire absence of ready wit, or small suspicion (I leave you to choose the right phrase), which is so much like men, and so little like women.

"Of course I will!" he answered.

"Then tell me," I asked, "why do you always insist on leaving us at nine o'clock?"

He started, and looked at me, so sadly, so reproachfully, that I would have given everything I possessed to recall the rash words that had just passed my lips.

"If I consent to tell you," he replied, after a momentary struggle with himself, "will you let me put a question to you first? and will you promise to answer it?"

I gave him my promise, and waited eagerly for what was coming next.

"Miss Brading," he said, "tell me honestly, do you think I am mad?"

It was impossible to laugh at him : he spoke those strange words seriously, sternly I might almost say.

"No such thought ever entered my mind," I answered.

He looked at me very earnestly.

"You say that, on your word of honor?"

"On my word of honor."

I answered with perfect sincerity; and I evidently satisfied him that I had spoken the truth. He took my hand, and lifted it gratefully to his lips.

"Thank you," he said simply. "You encourage me to tell you a very sad story."

"Your own story?" I asked.

"My own story. Let me begin by telling you why I persist in leaving your house, always at the same early hour. Whenever I go out, I am bound by a promise to the person with whom I am living here, to return at a quarter past nine o'clock."

"The person with whom you are living?" I repeated. "You are living at a boarding-house, are you not?"

"I am living, Miss Brading, under the care of a doctor who keeps an asylum for the insane. He has taken a house for some of his wealthier patients at the seaside; and he allows me my liberty in the daytime, on the condition that I faithfully perform my promise at night. It is a quarter of an hour's walk from your house to the doctor's; and it is a rule that the patients retire at half past nine o'clock."

Here was the mystery, which had so sorely perplexed me, revealed at last! The disclosure literally struck me speechless. Unconsciously and instinctively I drew back from him a few steps. He fixed his sad eyes on me with a touching look of entreaty.

"Don't shrink away from me!" he said. "*You* don't think I am mad?"

I was too confused and distressed to know what to say; and, at the same time, I was too fond of him not to answer that appeal. I took his hand and pressed it in silence. He turned his head aside for a moment. I thought I saw a tear on his cheek; I felt his hand close tremblingly on mine. He mastered himself with surprising resolution: he spoke with perfect composure when he looked at me again.

"Do you care to hear my story," he asked, "after what I have just told you?"

"I am eager to hear it," I answered. "You do not know how I feel for you! I am too distressed to be able to express myself in words."

"You are the kindest and dearest of women!" he said, with the utmost fervor and at the same time with the utmost respect.

We sat down together in a grassy hollow of the cliff, with our faces towards the grand gray sea. The daylight was beginning to fade, as I heard the story which made me Roland Cameron's wife.

## IV.

"My mother died when I was an infant in arms," he began. "My father, from my earliest to my latest recollections, was always hard towards me. I have been told that I was an odd child, with strange ways of my own. My father detested anything that was strongly marked, anything out of the ordinary way, in the characters and habits of the persons about him. He himself lived (as the phrase is) by line and rule; and he determined to make his son follow his example. I was subjected to severe discipline at school, and I was carefully watched afterwards at college. Looking back on my early life, I can see no traces of happiness, I can find no tokens of sympathy. Sad submission to a hard destiny, weary wayfaring over unfriendly roads, — such is the story of my life, from ten years old to twenty.

" I passed one autumn vacation at the Lakes ; and there I met by accident with a young French lady. The result of that meeting decided my whole after-life.

" She filled the humble position of nursery-governess in the house of a wealthy Englishman. · I had frequent opportunities of seeing her. Her life had been a hard one, like mine. We took an innocent pleasure in each other's society. Her little experience of life was strangely like mine : there was a perfect sympathy of thought and feeling between us. We loved, or thought we loved. I was not twenty-one, and she was not eighteen, when I asked her to be my wife.

" I can understand my folly now, and can laugh at it or lament over it, as the humor moves me. And yet, I can't help pitying myself, when I look back at myself at that time, — I was so young, so hungry for a little sympathy, so weary of my empty, friendless life! Well, everything is comparative in this world. I was soon to regret, bitterly to regret, that friendless life, wretched as it was.

" The poor girl's employer found out our attachment, through his wife. He at once communicated with my father.

" My father had but one word to say, — he insisted on my going abroad, and leaving it to him to release me from my absurd engagement, in my absence. I answered him that I should be of age in a few months, and that I was determined to marry the girl. He gave me three days to reconsider my resolution. I held to my resolution. In a week afterwards, I was declared insane by two medical men ; and I was placed by my father in a lunatic asylum.

"Was it an act of insanity for the son of a gentleman, with great expectations before him, to propose marriage to a nursery-governess? I declare, as God is my witness, I know of no other act of mine which could justify my father, and justify the doctors, in placing me under restraint.

"I was three years in the asylum. It was officially reported that the air did not agree with me. I was removed, for two years more, to another asylum, in a remote part of England. For the five best years of my life I have been herded with madmen, — and my reason has survived it. The impression I produce on you, on your father, on your brother, on all our friends at this picnic, is that I am as reasonable as the rest of my fellow-creatures. Am I rushing to a hasty conclusion, when I assert myself to be now, and always to have been, a sane man?

"At the end of my five years of arbitrary imprisonment in a free country, happily for me, — I am ashamed to say it, but I must speak the truth, — happily for me, my merciless father died. His trustees, to whom I was now consigned, felt some pity for me. They could not take the responsibility of granting me my freedom. But they placed me under the care of a surgeon, who received me into his private residence, and who allowed me free exercise in the open air.

"A year's trial in this new mode of life satisfied the surgeon, and satisfied every one else who took the smallest interest in me, that I was perfectly fit to enjoy my liberty. I was freed from all restraint, and was permitted to reside with a near relative of mine, in that very Lake country which had been the scene of my fatal meeting with the French girl, six years since.

"In this retirement I lived happily, satisfied with the ordinary pleasures and pursuits of a country gentleman. Time had long since cured me of my boyish infatuation for the nursery-governess. I could revisit with perfect composure the paths along which we had walked, the lake on which we had sailed together. Hearing by chance that she was married in her own country, I could wish her all possible happiness, with the sober kindness of a disinterested friend. What a strange thread of irony runs through the texture of the simplest human life! The early love for which I had sacrificed and suffered so much was now revealed to me, in its true colors, as a boy's passing fancy, — nothing more!

"Three years of peaceful freedom passed ; freedom which, on the uncontradicted testimony of respectable witnesses, I never abused. Well, that long and happy interval, like all intervals, came to its end ; and then the great misfortune of my life fell upon me. One of my uncles died and left me inheritor of his whole fortune. I alone, to the exclusion of all the other heirs, now received, not only the large income derived from his estates, but seventy thousand pounds in ready money as well.

"The vile calumny which had asserted me to be mad was now revived by the wretches interested in stepping between me and my inheritance. A year ago, I was sent back again to the asylum in which I had been last imprisoned. The pretence for confining me was found in an act of violence (as it was called) which I had committed in a momentary outbreak of anger, and which it was acknowledged had led to no serious results. Having got me into the asylum, the conspirators proceeded to complete their work. A Commission in Lunacy was issued against me. It was held by one commissioner, without a jury, and without the presence of a lawyer to assert my interests. By one man's decision, I was declared to be of unsound mind. The custody of my person, and the management of my estates, was confided to men chosen from among the conspirators who had declared me to be mad. I am here through the favor of the proprietor of the asylum, who has given me my holiday at the seaside, and who humanely trusts me with my liberty, as you see. At barely thirty years old, I am refused the free use of my money and the free management of my affairs. At barely thirty years old, I am officially declared to be a lunatic for life."

## V.

HE paused; his head sank on his breast; his story was told.

I have repeated his words as nearly as I can remember them; but I can give no idea of the modest and touching resignation with which he spoke. To say that I pitied him with my whole heart, is to say nothing. I loved him with my whole heart, — and I may acknowledge it now!

"O, Mr. Cameron," I said, as soon as I could trust myself to speak, "can nothing be done to help you? Is there no hope?"

"There is always hope," he answered, without raising his head. "I have to thank *you*, Miss Brading, for teaching me that."

" To thank me ? " I repeated. " How have I taught you to hope ? "

" You have brightened my dreary life. When I am with you, all my bitter remembrances leave me. I am a happy man again ; and a happy man can always hope. I dream now of finding, what I have never yet had, a dear and devoted friend, who will rouse the energy that has sunk in me under the martyrdom that I have endured. Why do I submit to the loss of my rights and my liberty, without an effort to recover them ? I was alone in the world, until I met with you. I had no kind hand to raise me, no kind voice to encourage me. Shall I ever find the hand ? Shall I ever hear the voice ? When I am with you, the hope that you have taught me answers, Yes. When I am by myself, the the old despair comes back, and says, No."

He lifted his head for the first time. If I had not understood what his words meant, his look would have enlightened me. The tears came into my eyes ; my heart heaved and fluttered wildly ; my hands mechanically tore up and scattered the grass around me. The silence became unendurable. I spoke, hardly knowing what I was saying ; tearing faster and faster the poor harmless grass, as if my whole business in life was to pull up the greatest quantity in the shortest possible space of time !

" We have only known each other a little while," I said. " And a woman is but a weak ally in such a terrible position as yours. But useless as I may be, count on me now and always as your friend — "

He moved close to me before I could say more, and took my hand. He murmured in my ear,

" May I count on you, one day, as the nearest and dearest friend of all ? Will you forgive me, Mary, if I own that I love you ? You have taught me to love, as you have taught me to hope. It is in your power to lighten my hard lot. *You* can recompense me for all that I have suffered ; *you* can rouse me to struggle for my freedom and my rights. Be the good angel of my life. Forgive me, love me, rescue me, — be my wife ! "

I don't know how it happened. I found myself in his arms, and I answered him in a kiss. Taking all the circumstances into consideration, I daresay I was guilty, in accepting him, of the rashest act that ever a woman committed. Very well. I did n't care then : I don't care now. I was then, and I am now, the happiest woman living !

## VI.

IT was necessary that either he or I should tell my father of what had passed between us. On reflection, I thought it best that I should make the disclosure. The day after the picnic, I repeated to my father Roland's melancholy narrative, as a necessary preface to the announcement that I had promised to be Roland's wife.

My father saw the obvious objections to the marriage. He warned me of the imprudence which I contemplated committing, in the strongest terms. Our prospect of happiness, if we married, in our present position, would depend entirely on our capacity to legally supersede the proceedings of the Lunacy Commission. Success in this arduous undertaking was, to say the least of it, uncertain. The commonest prudence pointed to the propriety of delaying our marriage until the doubtful experiment had been put to the proof.

This reasoning was unanswerable. It was, nevertheless, completely thrown away upon me. When did a woman in love ever listen to reason? I believe there is no instance of it on record. My father's wise words of caution had no chance against Roland's fervent entreaties. The days of his residence at Eastbourne were drawing to a close. If I let him return to the asylum an unmarried man, months, years perhaps, might pass before our union could take place. Could I expect him, could I expect any man, to endure that cruel separation, that unrelieved suspense? His mind had been sorely tried already; his mind might give way under it. These were the arguments that carried weight with them, in my judgment! I was of age, and free to act as I pleased. You are welcome, if you like, to consider me the most foolish and the most obstinate of women. In sixteen days from the date of the picnic, Roland and I were privately married at Eastbourne.

My father — more grieved than angry, poor man! — declined to be present at the ceremony, in justice to himself. My brother gave me away at the altar.

Roland and I spent the afternoon of the wedding-day and the earlier part of the evening together. At nine o'clock, he returned to the doctor's house, exactly as usual; having previously explained to me that he was in the power of the Court of Chancery, and that until we succeeded in setting aside the proceedings of the Lunacy Commission, there was a serious necessity for keeping the marriage strictly secret. My husband and I kissed, and said good by till to-morrow, as the clock struck the hour. I little thought, while I looked after him from the street door, that months on months were to pass before I saw Roland again.

A hurried note from my husband reached me the next morning. Our marriage had been discovered (we never could tell by whom), and we had been betrayed to the doctor. Roland was then on his way back to the asylum. He had been warned that force would be used if he resisted. Knowing that resistance would be interpreted, in his case, as a new outbreak of madness, he had wisely submitted. "I have made the sacrifice," the letter concluded, "it is now for you to help me. Attack the Commission in Lunacy, and be quick about it."

We lost no time in preparing for the attack. On the day when I received the news of our misfortune, we left Eastbourne for London, and at once took measures to obtain the best legal advice.

My dear father — though I was far from deserving his kindness — entered into the matter heart and soul. In due course of time, we presented a petition to the Lord Chancellor, praying that the decision of the lunacy commission might be set aside.

We supported our petition by citing the evidence of Roland's friends and neighbors, during his three years' residence in the Lake country as a free man. These worthy people had one and all agreed that he was, as to their judgment and experience, perfectly quiet, harmless, and sane. Many of them had gone out shooting with him. Others had often accompanied him in sailing excursions on the lake. Do people trust a madman with a gun, and with the management of a boat?

As to the "act of violence," which the heirs at law and the next of kin had made the means of imprisoning Roland in the madhouse, it amounted to this. He had lost his temper, and had knocked a man down who had offended him. Very wrong, no doubt ; but if *that* is a proof of madness, what thousands of lunatics are still at large ! Another instance produced to prove his insanity was still more absurd. It was solemnly declared that he put an image of the Virgin Mary in his boat when he went out on his sailing excursions ! I have seen the image, — it was a very beautiful work of art. Was Roland mad to admire it, and take it with him ? His religious convictions leaned towards Catholicism. If he betrayed insanity in adorning his boat with an image of the Virgin Mary, what is the mental condition of most of the ladies in Christendom, who wear the Cross as an ornament round their necks ? We advanced these arguments in our petition, after quoting the evidence of the witnesses. And, more than this, we even went the length of admitting, as an act of respect to the Court, that my poor husband might be eccentric in some of his opinions and habits. But we put it to the authorities whether better results might not be expected from placing him under the care of a wife who loved him, and whom he loved, than from shutting him up in an asylum, among incurable madmen as his companions for life.

Such was our petition, so far as I am able to describe it.

The decision rested with the Lords Justices. They decided against us.

Turning a deaf ear to our witnesses and our arguments, these merciless lawyers declared that the doctor's individual assertion of my husband's insanity was enough for them.

They considered Roland's comfort to be sufficiently provided for in the asylum, with an allowance of seven hundred pounds a year ; and to the asylum they consigned him for the rest of his days.

So far as I was concerned, the result of this infamous judgment was to deprive me of the position of Roland's wife ; no lunatic being capable of contracting marriage by law. So far as my husband was concerned, the result may be best stated in the language of a popular newspaper which published an article on the case. "It is possible," (said the article, — I wish I could personally thank the man who wrote it !) " for the Court of Chancery to take a man who has a large fortune, and is in the prime of life, but is a little touched in the head, and make a monk of him, and then report to itself that the comfort and happiness of the lunatic have been effectually provided for at the expenditure of seven hundred pounds a year."

Roland was determined, however, that they should *not* make a monk of him ; and, you may rely upon it, so was I !

But one alternative was left to us. The authority of the Court of Chancery (within its jurisdiction) is the most despotic authority on the face of the earth. Our one hope was in taking to flight. The price of our liberty, as citizens of England, was exile from our native country, and the entire abandonment of Roland's fortune. We accepted those hard conditions. Hospitable America offered us a refuge, beyond the reach of mad-doctors and Lords Justices. To hospitable America our hearts turned as to our second country. The serious question was, — how were we to get there ?

We had attempted to correspond, and had failed. Our letters had been discovered and seized by the proprietor of the asylum. Fortunately, we had taken the precaution of writing in a "cipher" of Roland's invention, which he had taught me before our marriage. Though our letters were illegible, our purpose was suspected, as a matter of course ; and a watch was kept on my husband, night and day.

Foiled in our first effort at making arrangements secretly for our flight, we continued our correspondence (still in cipher), by means of advertisements in the newspapers. This second attempt was discovered in its turn. Roland was refused permission to subscribe to the newspapers, and was forbidden to enter the reading-room at the asylum.

These tyrannical prohibitions came too late. Our plans had already been communicated : we understood each other, and we had now only to bide our time. We had arranged that my brother, and a friend of his on whose discretion we could thoroughly rely, should take it in turns to watch every evening, for a given time, at an appointed meeting-place, three miles distant from the asylum. The spot had been carefully chosen. It was on the bank of a lonely stream, and close to the outskirts of a thick wood. A water-proof knapsack, containing a change of clothes, a false beard and a wig, and some biscuits and preserved meat, was hidden in a hollow tree. My brother and his friend always took their fishing-rods with them, and presented themselves as engaged in the innocent occupation of angling, to any chance strangers who might pass within sight of them. On one occasion the proprietor of the asylum himself rode by them, on the opposite bank of the stream, and asked politely if they had had good sport !

For a fortnight, these stanch allies of ours relieved each other regularly on their watch, and no signs of the fugitive appeared. On the fifteenth evening, just as the twilight was changing into night, and just as my brother (whose turn it was) had decided on leaving the place, Roland suddenly joined him on the bank of the stream.

Without wasting a moment in words, the two at once entered the wood, and took the knapsack from its place of shelter in the hollow tree. In ten minutes more, my husband was dressed in a suit of workman's clothes, and was further disguised in the wig and beard. The two then set forth down the course of the stream, keeping in the shadow of the wood until the night had fallen and the darkness hid them. The night was cloudy : there was no moon. After walking two miles, or a little more, they altered their course, and made boldly for the high road to Manchester ; entering on it at a point some thirty miles distant from the city.

On their way from the wood, Roland described the manner in which he had effected his escape.

The story was simple enough. He had assumed to be suffering from nervous illness, and had requested to have his meals in his own room. For the first fortnight, the two men appointed to wait upon him in succession, week by week, were both more than his match in strength. The third man employed, at the beginning of the third week, was, physically, a less formidable person than his predecessors. Seeing this, Roland decided, when evening came, on committing another "act of violence." In plain words, he sprang upon the keeper, waiting on him in his room, and gagged and bound the man. This done, he laid the unlucky keeper (face to the wall) on his own bed, covered with his own cloak, so that any one entering the room might suppose that he was lying down to rest. He had previously taken the precaution to remove the sheets from the bed ; and he had now only to tie them together to escape by the window of his room, situated on the upper floor of the house. The sun was setting, and the inmates of the asylum were at tea. After narrowly missing discovery by one of the laborers employed in the grounds, he had climbed the garden enclosure, and had dropped on the other side, a free man !

Arrived on the high road to Manchester, my husband and my brother parted.

Roland, who was an excellent walker, set forth on his way to Manchester on foot. He had food in his knapsack, and he proposed to walk some twelve or fifteen miles on the road to the city, before he stopped at any town or village to rest. My brother, who was physically incapable of accompanying him, returned to the place in which I was then residing, to tell me the good news.

By the first train the next morning, I travelled to Manchester, and took a lodging in a suburb of the city well known to my husband. A prim smoky little square was in the immediate neighborhood ; and we had arranged that whichever of us first arrived in Manchester should walk round that square, between twelve and one in the afternoon, and between six and seven in the evening. In the evening I kept my appointment. A dusty, footsore man, in shabby clothes, with a hideous beard, and a knapsack on his back, met me at my first walk round. He smiled as I looked at him. Ah ! I knew that smile through all disguises ! In spite of the Court of Chancery and the Lords Justices, I was in my husband's arms once more.

We lived quietly in our retreat for a month.

During that time (as I heard by letters from my brother) nothing that money and cunning could do towards discovering Roland, was left untried by the proprietor of the asylum and by the persons acting with him. But where is the cunning which can trace a man, who, escaping at night in disguise, has not trusted himself to a railway or a carriage, and who takes refuge in a great city in which he has no friends? At the end of one month in Manchester, we travelled northward; crossed the channel to Ireland, and passed a pleasant fortnight in Dublin. Leaving this again, we made our way to Cork and Queenstown, and embarked from that latter place, taking steerage passage in a steamship bound for America.

My story is told. I am writing these lines from a farm in the West of the United States. Our neighbors may be homely enough, but the roughest of them is kinder to us than a mad-doctor or a Lord Justice. Roland is happy in those agricultural pursuits which have always been favorite pursuits with him; and I am happy with Roland. Our sole resources consist of my humble little fortune, inherited from my dear mother. After deducting our travelling expenses, the sum total amounts to between seven and eight hundred pounds; and this, as we find, is amply sufficient to start us in the new life that we have chosen. We expect my father and my brother to pay us a visit next summer; and I think it just possible that they may find our family circle increased by the presence of a new member in long clothes. Are there no compensations here, for exile from England and the loss of a fortune? *We* think there are. But then, my dear Miss An-stell, " Mary Brading's husband is mad ; and Mary Brading herself is not much better."

If you feel inclined to alter this opinion, and if you remember our old days at school as tenderly as I remember them, write and tell me so. Your letter will be forwarded, if you send it to the enclosed address at New York.

In the mean time, the moral of our story seems to be worthy of serious consideration. A certain Englishman legally inherits a large fortune. At the time of his inheritance, he has been living as a free man for three years, without once abusing his freedom, and with the express sanction of the medical superintendent who has had experience and charge of him. His next of kin and heirs at law (who are left out of the fortune) look with covetous eyes at the money, and determine to get the management and the ultimate possession of it. Assisted by a doctor, whose honesty and capacity must be taken on trust, these interested persons, in this nineteenth century of progress, can lawfully imprison their relative for life, in a country which calls itself free, and which declares that its justice is equally administered to all alike.

---

Note. — The reader is informed that this story is founded, in all essential particulars, on a case which actually occurred in England, eight years since.

W. C.

# IN ECHO CAÑON.

# IN ECHO CAÑON.

## By NOAH BROOKS.

E had been several days in Echo Cañon. This picturesque defile in the Wahsatch range of mountains is not so extensive that one need long tarry there if in haste. Nowadays the passenger-trains of the Pacific Railroad are whisked through it so rapidly, that the wondering tourist hardly gets a sight of the striking panorama on either side of him. But in the early times of California emigration, of which I shall write, Echo Cañon was a favorite place for the rest and refreshment needed by men and beasts weary with a long tramp through dust and heat and over stony trails and alkaline deserts, all the way from "the States." The cañon was filled with verdure ; along the banks of a small stream that wound through it were graceful birches, alders, and box-elders, with many a silvery cottonwood and sturdy young sycamore. The undergrowth was a tangle of sumach-bushes, wild vines, and flowering shrubs. Here and there were sunny patches of rich grass ; and in the rocky edges of the winding defile grew salmonberries, gooseberries, and wild currants in great profusion.

The walls of the cañon are precipitous ; the beetling cliffs rise three or four hundred feet on either side in fantastic shapes, resembling castles, turrets, spires, and airy domes. The prevailing tint of these mimic architectural wonders is a mellow yellow. The walls and flying buttresses are flecked with red and orange. The crumbling mass, broad in its effect of light and color, is clouded with all hues of buff drab, pale umber, and saffron. I have seen the rich heart of a Cheshire cheese present the same tones and melting shades. This figure is not a lofty one, but it will occur to the unromantic observer. Shut in by these glorious cliffs, abundant in water, fuel, and pasturage, — three things most desired by the overland emigrant, — Echo Cañon detained our little party many days. We rested luxuriously in the midst of the cool herbage. Wagons were mended, clothes once more patched up, cattle were allowed to wander at their own sweet will, wild berries from the vines about us refreshed palates weary of the unvarying fare of bread and "side meat," and, above all, we were secure from Indian alarms.

In my day I have been in many charming places enriched by the hand of Nature or Art, have enjoyed lotos-eating in great content, and have sat at costly feasts ; but above all the pleasures that have ministered to the senses in all my years, I still give chief place to those two or three days of camp-life in Echo Cañon. The wild world of disappointment was months behind us ; the wilder world of struggle was weeks before us ; and we four brawny youths, jaded and footsore, bearing upon us the marks of long marches in alkali dust, midnight adventures in the Indian country, and perilous climbings in the Rocky Mountains, flung ourselves down in the lush grass, and, eying the blue vault that bent over thicket, stream, and cliff, murmured, " This is heaven ! "

To the California emigrant in those far-off days the world was comprised in the thread along which desultory travel passed to and fro across the continent. Four months were usually consumed by an emigrant train passing from the Missouri to the Sacramento. With the last newspaper was dropped, not unwillingly, the last link that bound the gold-seeker to the life that he had known. Henceforth, without impatience, he stretched his hands and eyes towards the golden west. Tidings of that far-away land came to him in fragments, rumors, and vague whispers. But mainly was he occupied with the gossip and slow-travelling reports that slid backward and forward on his line of march. Outside this narrow channel of communication the world might go to wreck ; he would not know it. He would not greatly worry about the concerns of empires, kingdoms, and republics, so long as tidings of them were as completely beyond his reach as if he were travelling in the moon. He left civilization and the Missouri River behind him ; the Sacramento and something else were before ; all between was his present world, in which the things which concern the majority of mankind had no possible representation.

Little by little, after we were fairly launched upon the continental waste, we knew our companions ; not those who sat at our camp-fires and slept under our tent, but the mighty multitude before us and behind us. Motley they were, and divers their names. Each party had its individuality. There were the Boston Chaps, the Jennesses, the Swearing Brothers, Big Jake and his Boy, the Kewanee Fellers, the Man with the Go-cart, the Brown Boys, the Wises, Old Missourah, Toothpicks, and innumerable other little communities, nightly pitching their moving camps a day's march farther westward, but each more truly individual than your next-door neighbor is to you. These all stretched along the sinuous line that marked the trail across the continent.

Passing and repassing each other, day after day and week after week, they learned the antecedents, characteristics, and adventures of each, so far as these were communicable. A helpful, neighborly set of fellows were those rough pioneers of a new civilization. They made common cause of each other's difficulties when they met at dangerous fords, steep trails, and other trying passages by the way. Common perils brought wayfaring groups into common sympathy for the time ; then, the emergency passed, each went toiling, rejoicing, sorrowing, cursing, or singing on its way. We knew the dispositions and fortunes of those who were ahead of us, as well as those who followed hard after us. The men by whom we camped at Independence Rock were before us at Church Buttes ; we passed them at Green River, but they crossed the Sierra Nevada before we left Honey Lake. This weaving of human shuttles to and fro carried the thread of news, — a kind of intelligence that had no great world gossip in it. There were neighborhood reports of quarrels, fallings-out by the way, exploits in hunting, condition of camping-places ahead, depth of streams to be forded, and the prices of whiskey, flour, and bacon with those who had such rations to sell. All these items of daily news were colored by the hopes and fears, passions and prejudices, of the reporters. I suppose our straggling and long-drawn public was not, after all, much unlike any other.

One sunny Sunday morning in Echo Cañon we were surprised by a visitor from a camp beyond us. Before we were astir, he rode noisily up to our tent and bawled, "Hillo! house!" in mild derision of the effeminacy that deterred us from sleeping in the open air or under wagons, as was the manner of most journeyers. We scrambled to the tent-flap with a rude "Hillo! hoss!" which rejoinder so tickled our morning caller that he grinned as he said, "I allow you've got a shovel?"

"Yes, we have. Want it?"

"Ef you'll lend it to our crowd (we're the Sandy Hill Boys), we'll have it back by sundown. We want to bury a man."

"Bury a man! Who's dead up your way?"

"Well, he ain't adzactly dead yit. It's Old Missourah. He's bin a-stealin'. We're goin' for to hold a court onto him at noon, and hang him on the divide at four o'clock, sharp. Whar's yer shovel? Come down and see fair play?"

Shocking as was this information, it was not novel, though borrowing a shovel to dig a grave for a man not yet on trial for his life had in it an element of grotesque newness to us.

The rude announcement of our visitor, who was not altogether a stranger, dispelled the calm repose of Sunday in Echo Cañon. The serene, pastoral stillness was gone, and, though the ringing echoes of departing feet died away as Blue Pete rode down the Cañon, we felt that with him had gone the brief idyl of our days of rest. The tender sky looked down on mimic tower and spire just as before; there were the golden light on the leaves and the sober twinkle on the stream, but human crime and violence were just ready to stain the sylvan purity of the little paradise.

Breakfast over, we walked down the trail to the mouth of the cañon where the Sandy Hill Boys were camped. The cañon widens out into the valley of the Weber River. On the right the ground is broken by a ridge or divide that pushes into the undulating valley from the main chain here cleft by Echo Cañon. Dotted over the grassy meadows bordering the river were four or five camps, each distinguished by its cluster of wagons, ox-yokes, and camp furniture, with here and there a weather-stained canvas tent. Thin smoke curled up from the smouldering camp-fires. Slatternly women and tow-headed children hovered about two of the wagons; and some little attempt at old-time decency was solemnly making by a few of the men who seemed to realize the impressive importance of the approaching "trial."

We knew Old Missourah, the culprit in this little tragedy. He was not more than sixty years of age, perhaps; but his face was dry and wrinkled, and his thin long hair was as white as snow. He was a solitary traveller, journeying to find his sons, who had gone to California with the first rush for gold. He had a little two-wheeled canvas-covered cart, drawn by a very small mule, or *burro*, so small that when the diminutive equipage came in sight anywhere along the road, the rough emigrants were ready with their jokes. Old Missourah was usually advised to put his "hoss" in his pocket lest he should lose him; or he was asked the price of rats; or some reference was made to the length of his legs and the size of his go-cart. All along the trail, Old Missourah and his poor little team were as well known as Big Jake, who killed four men while running a-muck at City Rocks, or Bush the Fiddler, with his one song of "Lather and Shave."

No more fun now for Old Missourah. His tall, gaunt form lashed to a wagon-wheel, his head bowed upon his breast, he was the image of helpless and guilty despair. A useless keeper stood over him, offering him a ration of bread and coffee; but the old man, his thoughts apparently far away, painfully waved his pinioned hands in refusal.

It was a short story. Old Missourah was charged with stealing seventy-eight dollars and fifty cents, in gold and silver coin, from Shanghai, a simple fellow, one of the Vermillion County Boys. These were a small party of men whom we now met for the first time, though we knew them well. Shanghai was cook for the mess, and kept his money in a buckskin purse in the "grub-box" of his company's wagon. This box was, as usual with emigrant-wagons, carried in the rear end of the vehicle, easily accessible from without. It had a close, but unlocked lid; and the men, trudging along behind, could take a bite of luncheon as they marched. Down among the humble table furniture, bits of food, small stores, and miscellaneous dunnage, poor Shanghai had kept his little store of worldly wealth.

On Saturday night, when they camped with the rest, Shanghai's gold was secure. He had gone to it for money enough to buy a hand of tobacco from a neighbor. In the morning, when he took out his breakfast things, it was gone. Andy Snow, one of the Vermillion County Boys, had seen Old Missourah, the night before, go to the grub-box, take something therefrom, and hide it in his shirt. Thinking it was a cake of bread, good-natured Andy looked another way and pretended not to see anything. The old man was known to be miserably poor. But when the money

**was** missed, and simple Shanghai, bereft and woebegone, made great lamentation through the camps, Andy remembered. and told what he had witnessed. Then Blue Pete, one of the Sandy Hill Boys, reinforced the evidence. He swore, with a great many large oaths, that he saw Old Missourah coming away from Shanghai's grub-box, hiding something in his bosom ; he said he was cock-sure it was a bag, a yellow buckskin bag.

Blue Pete was a pretty good fellow ; he had a low forehead, and a great shock of blue-black hair, and a blue welt or scar across his cheek. But, for all that, he had a good, honest face ; we always liked him. His evidence was conclusive. But for the sake of precedent and appearances, the accused should have fair trial.

No trace of the missing purse was found. The principal prosecutor, when questioned as to this part of the case, said that he " 'lowed that Old Missourah had got shut of that thar pouch just as quick as he found thar was a-goin' to be a row."

My heart went out to the friendless old man. But then, everybody was sure he was guilty, circumstances were all against him ; and if this sort of thing was to go on, whose property was safe ? Men could usually take care of their lives ; with property it was more difficult. Hangings for murder were very few ; those for theft, particularly horse-theft, were numerous. I do not know if the fact that murders were more common than robberies has any connection with this statement. But it was the fact. And, in truth, the prevailing sentiment of the time was that Lynch-law was especially designed to protect personal property.

Usually a Lynch-court on the road was a very informal affair. There was no time to spare for needless ceremony; a *viva voce* vote on the question "Guilty or not Guilty" was all that was required to settle the case. I do not recollect that the oral traditions of those days mention an instance of an accused person being acquitted. The fatal tree was selected before the prisoner was brought to the bar. But in this case there was leisure enough for the necessaries, if not for the luxuries, of a formal ceremonial. Here were more than twenty men willing to "lay over" for the Sunday, and give Old Missourah a full trial. Indeed, the emigrants entered into the performances with a calm satisfaction which came of a consciousness that they were doing "the square thing" by Old Missourah, and providing themselves with a dignified diversion for the day. The trial and execution were an impromptu drama, which most of the performers enjoyed very much.

Twelve men were duly chosen as the jury by drawing twelve previously designated cards from a well-thumbed pack. No man who drew anything higher than a ten-spot was competent to serve; and the drawing was continued until the panel was complete. This formality over, the jury proceeded to appoint a prosecuting attorney and a counsel for the defendant. There was no judge; the jury thenceforward, in a somewhat disputative way, taking sole direction of the proceedings.

The public prosecutor was Bill Ballard, a stalwart Arkansian, whose grammar was confused, but whose heart was thought to be in the right place. He had proposed blowing off the top of Old Missourah's head early in the debate. The counsel for the accused was Royal Younkins, a gentleman from Pike County, and of great physical beauty. Blond, full-bearded, blue-eyed, and standing six feet in his moccasons, Younkins was likened by the historical painter in our party to young Edward of York, as he is pictured by the chroniclers of the Wars of the Roses. A Saxon prince in comeliness and bearing, Royal was well named. I regret to add here that he was subsequently hung in Siskiyou County, California, for several murders. He confessed five of these before the hangman's noose was put over his beautiful blond head.

There is not much to say about the trial. The jury sat together on a rocky ledge that cropped out of the turf in the midst of the camp. The prisoner, with an odd perversion of judicial etiquette, was put in charge of Bill Ballard, the prosecutor, who contended that this " was the fa'r thing by the Vermillion County Boys," as he would take care "that Old Missourah did n't break for tall timber." Ballard's revolver was special constable.

The witnesses were examined ; they were Shanghai, Snow, and Blue Pete. Shanghai testified as to the fact of his money being in the grub-box on Saturday evening ; Snow told how he saw Old Missourah taking something therefrom ; and Blue Pete finished the chain of evidence by swearing that he saw the accused take from the box something that looked like a buckskin bag and hide it in his shirt-front. It was a clear case ; and angry murmurs went around as the shameful story was related once more, with some imperceptible additions. Jake Wise, who, by virtue of having his wife and mother with him, had the right to be spokesman for the jury, said sternly to the old man, "Guilty or not Guilty ? "

Old Missourah, for the first time lifting up his white head, tremblingly pleaded: "O, pity, kind gentlemen! I have n't got Shanghai's money; 'deed, I have n't. I 've two boys in Yuby County, Californy. They 'll be master sorry to hear of this; 'deed, they will. I ain't right peart myself to-day. My head 's kind of unstiddy-like; I 'low you 'll put in a good word for me. I was born in Arkansaw, I was."

This somewhat inconsequent appeal of the poor old man was looked upon with profound disfavor by Royal Younkins, to whom it was addressed. The court, that is to say, the jury, ruled that the prosecuting attorney had "the first say."

Ballard, putting his special constable in his belt, blushed with confusion and made his brief plea: "I say, boys, this yere old man 's been and stole this yere money. Shanghai 's told yer so; Andy Snow 's told yer so; and Blue Pete, he seen him take it. So what 's the use o' jawin' any more? As fur me, I want to git shut o' this bizness and git up and git." The prosecuting attorney sat down with great relief, and one impatient juror remarked, "You bet yer."

Here the foreman of the jury, who was filling his pipe, pointed the toe of his big boot at Royal Younkins, and said, "Unyoke yer jaw, Younk, and waltz in."

Thus admonished, our Edward of York, in rude but forcible language, begun his plea. It was chiefly personal at first. For his part, *he* "had nothin' agin the old man." *He* had "lost nary scad sence he had struck the plains." This amused the jury; but it had no other effect. Presently, however, with a natural fondness for rhetorical display, he assumed the accused to be innocent. With considerable skill, he pictured "the boys" waiting on the banks of the Yuba for the old man. He alluded to the prisoner's great age, his white hair, and the unlikelihood that such an aged man could be a thief. He roughly analyzed the evidence, which he showed to be purely circumstantial. He was proceeding to work on the sympathies of his audience, when one of the jury, beginning to weaken, bawled, " O, dry up, dry up! You 've played that."

Royal's face flushed in a moment, and, whipping out his revolver, he said angrily, " *You* dry up, or I 'll — "

He did not finish his sentence, for he saw the impropriety of his remark ; and the jury had scattered in all directions when they saw his pistol come to light. He turned away with a cunning smile, remarking to me as he passed, " I 'm dog-oned if I hev n't a mind to believe the old man 's innocent, after all." Young Edward of York had almost convinced himself for the moment.

The jury retired to an alder thicket with a small black bottle of whiskey. They returned when it was empty, with a verdict of, " Guilty of stealing in the first degree."

Jake Wise announced the finding of the court, and added that the prisoner should be hanged forthwith. Some of us who had conscientious objections to this summary trial and execution made every possible effort for the old man's release. It was offered to pay Shanghai twice the amount of money he had lost, if Old Missourah might be let go in peace. Poor Shanghai showed signs of relenting at the prospect of recovering something ; but the crowd was determined on a stern vindication of justice. They firmly believed Old Missourah guilty ; they would accept no atonement or reparation short of his life.

The rude procession was formed; it was a pitiful and sickening spectacle. The miserable condemned man was set on his little steed, his feet tied under the animal's belly, his hands pinioned behind him, and his face turned to the tail of the beast, — an additional mark of contumely usually bestowed in such cases.

Bill Ballard walked by the side of the old man to steady him as the group struggled up the ridge where grew a tall sycamore, — the fatal tree. At the mouth of the cañon, the rocky walls break off abruptly, and, on the right, the sloping divide leans up against a mass of richly colored rock resembling some grand old cathedral. This towered far above our heads, and, westward, the eye glanced over the lovely valley of the winding Weber now spread out like a map below us.

There was little said. The men were determined and very bitterly in earnest. The old man would not say whether he was guilty or not. He seemed sunk in utter abstraction. Once only he lifted his head. As the little procession mounted the brow of the hill, Old Missourah straightened himself up and looked off over the panorama below. The sunny vale, belted with trees and laced with glittering streams, wound afar into the distant hills; and around the western horizon there were purple peaks fretted with silvery snow. It was the poor wretch's last gaze at a beautiful world. His pale blue eyes gazed far over the horizon, westward, where his boys were digging on the banks of the Yuba. His white hair blew about his face as the rude west-wind met him on the summit of the hill, and he stood under the gallows-tree. Even this mute sycamore seemed to pity him. It bent down its long branches as if in voiceless compassion for his infinite woe; and the clustered leaves stirred in the breeze with a low and sooth-ing death-song.

But there was no softness in the scene for the stern men who stood about. The simple preparations were made. I turned away, and saw only the group of jury, counsel, and witnesses pulling at the long rope that ran from the neck of the con-demned man over a stout limb above. This joint action at the rope was a formal assumption of joint responsibility for the hanging. No one man could be called to account. Blue Pete led the file of executioners, and, as he pulled with the rest, he chanted in a strange, sad monotone, " Hail, Columby, Hail, Columby, Hail, Columby!" This rude song was all the cere-monial. Old Missourah was hanged by the neck until he was dead.

That night, at sundown, our shovel was returned to us. Old Missourah was buried. His little cart was left by the trail ; its poor contents were divided among the Vermillion County Boys, each of whom thereafter threw his share into the river ; the small mule was confiscated to the benefit of Shanghai. This ill-fated animal was afterwards stolen by the Mormons near Box Elder ; and so all trace of Old Missourah disappeared from the emigrant road across the continent.

We reached Salt Lake City a few days after this occurrence, and in that strange capital of the wilderness refitted while we rested and wrote letters home. Passing once more westward, on the fifth day out of the Mormon hive, we crossed the Malad, a deep and narrow stream on the edge of the Valley. Camping for the night on the farther bank, we met a fever-and-ague-rid-den Missourian,• who, with his wife and numberless small chil-dren, was bound to Oregon. A sad-faced, dejected pair were husband and wife; but their white-headed babies, lively as crickets, swarmed in and out of their wagon as if they were contented with their travelling home and had never known any other. Perhaps they had not. The canvas cover of their four-wheeled mansion bore, in rude black letters, this lament :—

> "O Missouri, O Missouri, I much regret to see
> You so much altered for the worse
> From what you used to be.
> Time was when all the people were
> All happy and content.
> But now they are so very poor,
> Scarce one has got a cent."

The self-satisfied author of these lines informed us that we should see a sorrowful sight in the cañon through which the road wound after leaving the Malad. He had been down to see. The Vermillion County Boys had hanged a man there last Friday night.

"What! another man? They hanged one in Echo, about two weeks ago!"

"Yaas, so they did. He was the wrong man, though. I 'low they hung the right one this time."

"But who was he?"

"Don't know. The Sandy Hill Boys found the stole money on him; and they waited till the Vermillions came up, and they strung him up to oncet."

"And is he still hanging?"

"Sure pop. Seen him myself. They would n't plant him, cause he was an uncommon hard case."

No questioning could bring out of the languid Missourian any further information; so, in the dusk of the evening, to satisfy

ourselves who "the right one" might be, two of us mounted
and rode into the gorge.

A tall, dead tree, writhing its leafless branches against the
twilight sky, bore this evil fruit. The form of the convicted
thief twirled solemnly in the wind that sighed down the cañon.
It was Blue Pete, the man who had sung "Hail, Columby,"
at Old Missourah's execution. Next day, we buried him with
the shovel he borrowed of us in Echo Cañon.

# A Fragmentary Hint.

# A FRAGMENTARY HINT ON A FAULT OF THE ENGLISH LANGUAGE.

BY CHAMPION BISSELL.

O write a page of Saxon like this, is an easy thing, but it is not so easy to make it bear your thoughts to the man who reads it. This page is a sore trial, for when I try to talk only in Saxon, I try thereby to talk in another tongue than my real mother-tongue, if indeed we Western-World sons of Englishmen can be said to have a mother-tongue. Once we had the good roots of a great tongue, but, just at a time when men in England began to think and to call for a way to make their thoughts known, a body of men, called wise, reached out to a dead tongue for help, instead of reaching down into the deep rich ground among the roots of their own mother-tongue. Then was built up the now English speech, made up of a few short, strong words, and a great many longer words, lifted out of the dead speech of the race whom the Goths overthrew. Thus it comes that our speech is large but not rich ; like a great farm with a shallow soil, on which you may work hard and reap small crops, though to the eye alone it is fair and wide-spreading, and makes its owner seem like a rich man, when he is not.

See how short and stunted are the words with which I

hedge myself in when I try to write all Saxon, and only Saxon. These Goths were children indeed, with deep enough thoughts, but scant breath to utter them. But what a pity that the men who made our tongue did not think it worth while to plough their own ground, but must needs go and borrow from the burying-places of dead people.

Our speech now is like Frankenstein's man, built up of bones and dead things, and gifted with a kind of weird life, by which it walks over us and crushes us, while we cannot hope to make it bend to us. Had we grown our speech from its own roots, as a gardener grows a shrub, it would have been a sweet and kindly thing, fit for use always, and would keep on growing forever, and in whatever shape we might wish to bend it. Now instead of this, we have Frankenstein's made-up man.

How hard it is with such a tongue to make other people see things as we do! When I talk to my neighbor with my best words, I do not always bring his soul alongside of my own, so that our souls' eyes look out on the field of thought from the same window. It is apt to be quite the other way, so that we look crosswise, and he says " Yes " to what I say, or I say " Yes " to what he says, out of sheer good-will only.

Can we help this? I fear not. We are wedded to our tongue, and have lived together so long, we would find it hard to change each other. So we must do the best we can with what we have.

The above effort to express ideas rising above one's wants for daily food wholly in words underived from Latin and Greek, shows clearly the poverty of our *root*-language, and the immense dependence under which we have brought ourselves to the Latin element introduced into the English language.

While we borrowed so much Latin, it was a fatal mistake that we did not borrow the case-declination of that noble language. By this omission alone, we robbed our tongue forever of the possibility of growth from within. Accessions to it must always be mere accretions from without. We can build on, and build on, but whatever we build on the present structure is inorganic and lifeless, and has the further fault that it hides and covers up something else.

Thus, we ruined the prospects and possibilities of the growth of our language from its own root, and we nailed on dead twigs from another full-grown tree, instead of grafting on the live scions, which perhaps might have been found, by careful search, somewhere among the hoary and storm-beaten branches of the old Latin tree.

I envy with inexpressible longing those who spoke Greek, and those who spoke Latin, and those who now speak German. The French language is good enough to write contracts in ; and Italian and Spanish are good enough to express the day-dreams of indolent races ; but no language other than a self-growing and a case-declination language can ever serve as a fit and full channel for the highest human thoughts.

One instance. Take the German word " Wahlverwandtschaft." It is a long word, yet Goethe made it the title of a novel designed for the public. *Any* German can see the growth of the word ; how " Wahl " naturally grows on "Verwandtschaft," and how " schaft " grows on " verwandt," and how " verwandt " grows out of " Gewand," and " Gewand " out of "winden."* The whole word is a blaze of light to him, and if it were twice as long, it would be twice as luminous. The nearest we can get to the word in anything like elegant English is "Elective Affinities," and, so titled, the translated work stands in our libraries. And yet it requires a very well-educated person to comprehend the phrase "Elective Affinities," and it is a chance if any two readers affix the same meaning to it. These two words are simply two dead Latin words nailed on to the trunk of the English language, and have to be studied from without, just as fossils have to be picked up, or picked off, and studied from without.

Conscious of no remedy for this sad condition of the language of a great people, I commend it to the attention of the members of our literary and progressive club.

* "Winden" means to wind or twist: in early times the Germans wound their garments about their bodies, in default of pins and buttons; the imperfect tense of "winden" is "wand": hence comes "Gewand," a drapery, or a garment. something wound about. As a family would naturally be clothed in garments of the same stuff, the family relation was indicated by the word "verwandt" Our verb has now produced us a very rich noun, which, when united with two other nouns, as we see it, becomes a word of great depth and beauty; obvious to the comprehension of the uneducated German, and full of suggestive meaning to the scholar.

In going outside of the Latin or Greek languages to find a synonyme for "Wahlverwandtschaft," I have not been able to light upon anything better than the very ugly word "Friendship-choosing." This would certainly carry a clearer idea to the mind of a teamster than the phrase "elective affinities." but it is awkward and barren of meaning. If we could use the word "sympathy" or its adjective, we would do better, but that lands us in Greek, which is contrary to the problem. In this case, as in thousands of others, the educated mind retreats into the cloisters and catacombs of the dead languages, to find means for the contemplation of an active and living idea. What a commentary upon the incredible misfortune that befell our language at its critical period !

C. B.

# LIBERTY.

# LIBERTY.

### By JOHN HAY.

HAT man is there so bold that he should say,
"Thus and thus only would I have the sea"?
For whether lying calm and beautiful,
Clasping the earth in love, and throwing back
The smile of heaven from waves of amethyst;
Or whether, freshened by the busy winds,
It bears the trade and navies of the world
To ends of use or stern activity;
Or whether, lashed by tempests, it gives way
To elemental fury, howls and roars
At all its rocky barriers, in wild lust
Of ruin drinks the blood of living things,
And strews its wrecks o'er leagues of desolate shore; —
Always it is the sea, and all bow down
Before its vast and varied majesty.

So all in vain will timorous men essay
To set the metes and bounds of Liberty.
For Freedom is its own eternal law.
It makes its own conditions, and in storm
Or calm alike fulfils the unerring Will.
Let us not then despise it when it lies

Still as a sleeping lion, while a swarm
Of gnat-like evils hover round its head ;
Nor doubt it when in mad, disjointed times
It shakes the torch of terror, and its cry
Shrills o'er the quaking earth, and in the flame
Of riot and war we see its awful form
Rise by the scaffold, where the crimson axe
Rings down its grooves the knell of shuddering kings.
For always in thine eyes, O Liberty !
Shines that high light whereby the world is saved ;
And though thou slay us, we will trust in thee !

# How We hung John Brown.

# HOW WE HUNG JOHN BROWN.

BY HENRY S. OLCOTT.

T will be conceded that the first act in the bloody drama of the American Conflict had its climax on the 2d of December, 1859, when John Brown of Ossawatomie was hung at Charlestown, Virginia. Thirty years of agitation of the question of African slavery culminated in that direful event, which was at once the prelude to one of the most terrible wars of modern times, and the harbinger of a new era of equal rights and true republican government. Looking back now over the intervening fourteen years, it seems incredible that so much should have happened in so short a time. The rapid rush of events, the upheaval of our whole national system, the changed relations between the two sections of country, and especially between the black and white races, make the tragical end of John Brown appear as something that occurred at least a generation ago ; and the true story of his hanging, by an eye-witness, will perhaps be read with as much interest as any other thing I could contribute to the present volume. It is time the story was told ; for with negro ex-slaves sitting on the bench, in the gubernatorial chair, in legislatures, in Congress, serving as State treasurers, as cadets, as surgeons, as consuls, and as foreign ambassadors, it reads like fiction that the life of an editor should have been put in peril so recently, within the limits of this country, in the peaceful performance of his duty. And I am sure that if these lines should be read by any of the men whom I met at the exciting time of which I write, he will confess to mortification that such should have been the fact.

In 1859 I was one of the two agricultural editors of the *New York Tribune*, having as little to do with politics as any man in the city, and perhaps as unlikely as any to see or care to see the execution, the preparations for which agitated the whole American people. Although connected with the leading Abolitionist journal, I was scarcely an Abolitionist, but rather what might be called a congenital Whig. That is to say, I came of a Whig ancestry, and, caring far less for politics than scientific agriculture, I was content to let others fight their full of the slavery question, while I attended to the specialty whose development was my chief care.

But events at last happened which aroused all my interest in the topic of the hour. The people of Virginia, led away by a blind fanaticism, and by blind fanatics like Wise, declared war upon the *New York Tribune* as the representative of the principles John Brown held most dear. One after another, three gentlemen were driven out of Charlestown and Harper's Ferry on suspicion that they were the correspondents who supplied that journal with its vivid accounts of the local occurrences ; and when, in spite of all this, the letters still continued to appear, they gave out that they would hang the mysterious unknown to the nearest tree, on sight. Then the liberty of the press was for the first time practically destroyed in this country, and mob rule asserted itself. Our correspondent, who had sent his letters, under the guise of money-packages, by express, at last found things so hot that he was forced to leave the neighborhood of Charlestown, and from Baltimore send such reports as he could gather upon the arrival of the train.

The fatal 2d of December was now fast approaching, and it seemed as if the paper would be forced to let the day pass without having a correspondent on the ground, to tell John Brown's friends how he met his doom. Distressed to see the perplexity of my dear friend Horace Greeley, I went to the managing editor, and volunteered to undertake the job if he would allow me to do it in my own way. With some remonstrance about the risks I would run, he at last consented, and gave me *carte blanche* to go and come and do as I chose.

Things were decidedly lively at Charlestown just then. Wise had poured cavalry and infantry into the place until it was a very camp; sentries were posted in the streets, to stop every one at will; a provost-guard boarded every train, a sum of money was privately offered for the *Tribune* man, the medical students had hung up the preserved skeleton of John Brown's son in a museum, and the people were on the *qui vive* for shadowy legions of rescuers, expected from over the mountains. I had n't the remotest wish to figure in the Book of Martyrs, nor the slightest disposition to have my tanned hide tacked to the door of the jail, and so it was with me a problem of the most serious nature how to get to the place, how to move about while there, and how to get away with a whole skin. After considering many expedients, I finally concluded to go to Petersburg, and make that my base of operations. So, taking passage by steamer, I found myself, late one night, safely landed in the house of a dear old friend in that ancient city. He was a fire-eater of fire-eaters, an uncompromising, rank, out-and-out Secessionist, in whose mind Divine right and State rights were convertible terms, and who, as I soon found, hated John Brown with the perfect hatred that the Devil is said to bear to holy water. Tired and sleepy as I was, he would not let me go to bed until he had cursed the hoary old Abolitionist from crown to sole, heaping a separate and distinct malediction upon each particular hair of his head and each drop of blood in his veins. He talked so fast and swore so hard as to leave him little time before daylight to ascertain my own sentiments, although, for the matter of that, I was quite ready to express my honest conviction that John Brown's raid was an inexcusable invasion of a sovereign State. I was Whig enough then to be quite willing to have Virginia hang him if she chose, and those at the North who thought otherwise were in a decided minority. See how we trimmed and shuffled and paltered with the South, until the first cannon-ball smashed against the walls of Sumter, and so smashed through our dough-faceism upon the patriot adamant beneath!

At this night session with my fire-eating friend, I learned that some recruits for the company of Petersburg Grays, then doing duty at Charlestown, were to go forward the next day, and, expressing my desire to assist at the hanging of the great agitator, I received permission to join the party. Behold, then, the agricultural editor of the *Tribune* transformed into a Virginia militia-man, his editorial plowshare, so to speak, turned into a sword, and his pruning-hook into a spear. And just here, for fear of being misunderstood, let me say that in joining the Virginia soldiers I meant to do my duty, to fight if there should be occasion to fight, and not turn my back upon my new comrades. I can't say that I thought there would be any opportunity for us to display our valor, for, in common with all New York, I discredited the absurd idea that any organized body of Pennsylvanians would attempt John Brown's rescue. Nevertheless, I took service in good faith, and all the chances with it. This matter being satisfactorily settled, my friend at last showed me to my room, and I slept the sleep of the weary.

At the appointed time our party of recruits met at the railway station, and I was put in charge of the chief surgeon on General Taliaferro's Staff as a true-blue Northerner. I found him to be a brother Mason, and our trip was made most agreeable by the close friendship that sprang up between us. As we reached the last station before coming to Charlestown, our train was boarded by the provost-guard, and every passenger subjected to a rigid examination. My friends of the Grays vouching for me, I was enabled to pass muster, and the place of our destination finally came in sight.

Looking out of the car-window, I saw something that was the reverse of assuring to one in my situation, — a crowd of a thousand or more unsavory, lounging Virginians, every man of them with his two hands stuffed in his pockets, and his two eyes fixed upon the train, as if it were some nondescript monster about to vomit an enemy. Next to the track stood a provost's party, wearing uniform caps and other insignia of brief authority. The captain ordered us to form a line outside the cars, and front face. The doctor and I, being the only ones of the passengers dressed in citizen's clothes.

naturally attracted a greater share of the public attention than was at all gratifying, to myself at least, — being naturally of a modest and retiring disposition. However, there I was, and there were the fifteen hundred, and, as I could n't get away, I put as good a face on it as possible, and returned stare for stare. It was n't long before my equanimity was cruelly disturbed, for who should come poking through the throng but my old Washington acquaintance, Colonel Blank, the great sheep-breeder, — an impulsive, good-natured, amiable fire-eater, one of your sort who clap you on the back, and shout out your name, and wonder what the deuce you are doing there. The mild face of my bucolic friend seemed for the moment to threaten like that of Nemesis, the cold sweat started on my forehead, and in about a second I counted my chances of being pointed out as Mr. Wurzel of the *New York Tribune*, and thereupon gently stretched at the end of an inch rope, from the swaying bough of a neighboring tree, that caught my eye at the moment! My fate came nearer and yet more near, and my brain went faster and faster, until, just as the old fellow got within easy eyeshot of me, I formed and executed a *ruse*. I was suddenly attacked with strabismus of the most pronounced type, my mouth got a shift to leeward, and a general expression of vacancy settled over my usually vivacious countenance. The transformation probably was not as artistic or wonderful as any one of those with which Garrick amused his friends in the hack, but it served a good purpose, for the terrible man passed on down the line, and I heaved a sigh of relief. Then we right-faced and forward-marched, and filed this way and that, and finally came to our quarters. It was a one-story little build-ng, used as a law office, comprising one small. cramped room, where perhaps a half-dozen fellows might manage to bunk on he floor, by each man swallowing his neighbor's feet ; but as to giving our party of twenty or thirty the least chance to do more than stand up and sleep, like Dickens's fat boy, it was out of the question.    The dear old doctor, however, being of the General Staff (and by this time my sworn brother and companion-in-arms), concluded to forage about for better quarters and take me with him ;  so we went to Taliaferro's headquarters, at the principal hotel.    I let him enter alone, as I had no disposition to intrude upon the general's privacy, nor seek an introduction, and I stopped outside until my ally should come with our billet.    There was a porch to the hotel, and men sitting there talking ; and as my eye ran over the group, I experienced a second shock, even worse than the first ; for there, in his bodily presence, long gray hair and all, sat Edmund Ruffin, with whom I had only a short time before passed some weeks on the lordly plantation of one of the most violent of the South Carolina senators.    It is needless to say who and what Mr. Ruffin was, — the old man who offered to hang John Brown with his own hands, who afterwards fired the first cannon-shot at the walls of Fort Sumter, and who was by all odds the bitterest hater we Northern men had in Dixie.

I thought my time had come then, sure enough, for I knew that this man had had as much as, if not more than, Wise himself, to do with exciting the fears and passions of the people of their native State.    He was another of your impulsive sort, strong in his likes as in his hates, and, friendly as he was to me beyond doubt, on account of our mutual interest in

Agriculture, he would n't have listened a moment now to anything I might have said by way of explanation, but have insured my destruction by announcing my professional affiliation. I got out of this scrape easily enough by simply turning my back and walking leisurely off; although the image of that stern, implacable face followed me all the while I was in that village.

Our billet was far better than I could have anticipated, no less, in fact, than in the house of one of the principal functionaries of the court, and with the whole Staff of the commanding general. While my comrades of the Grays fared wretchedly, the doctor and I had a comfortable room to ourselves, a wide French bedstead to sleep in, bountiful meals to eat, and, luxury of luxuries! a full-blooded blackie to polish our shoes.

I found the fellows of the Staff a jolly, good-natured lot, fond of smoking, honest whiskey-drinkers, courteous towards the ladies of the household, and very cordially disposed towards the New York gentleman who had come down there to help hang John Brown. I scarcely think it would have made much difference in our relations if they had known the terrible secret that I was going to write a plain unvarnished account of the execution, for I made no bones about expressing my surprise, and something stronger, at the farcically great preparations they had made to hang one poor wounded old man.

You may believe that all the old stock of merry tales, stowed away in odd corners of my head, were brought out of the lavender of memory, and refurbished and passed around ; and that I sang my comic songs (always with one eye on the

company and the other on the door) and smoked pipes and
drank whiskey with the best of them ; and was generally
voted a capital sort of fellow, and — learned a good bit
about John Brown, you may be sure. Yes, I got all the
wonderful sayings and doings, the comings-in and goings-
out of this terrible Ossawatomie Brown, who, as Mr. Gid-
dings expressed it, "with a force of fifteen men, had taken
Virginia with his right hand, and Maryland with his left, and
shaken them, till every corner of the Union resounded with
their shriekings!" And all this time, the mysterious *Tribune*
man vexed the peace of the whole South ; and the Charlestown papers indignantly repudiated the idea that any such
person was in the place ; and Colonel Taylor, the puffy
militia-man, notified Frank Leslie's artist that he was suspected and must clear out ; and General Taliaferro proclaimed
that all strangers should report themselves to the provost for
examination ; and the papers of the Gulf States were calling
upon the Virginians to clean out the reptile! The fact is,
that my predecessor had so faithfully chronicled the events
at Charlestown, had so set the sensible people of the whole
country to laughing at the cowardly behavior of the villagers,
and had so pertinaciously stuck to his post, concealed his
identity, and rubbed vitriol into the wounds his keen lance
inflicted, that the community were wellnigh distracted. I
recollect how, the night before the execution, I opened up
this matter to my generous host, and with charming *naïveté*
asked him to tell me candidly how this *Tribune* man continued to elude the vigilance of the people! He drew his
chair up to mine, and, leaning over, whispered confidentially,
"I 'll tell you how it is. You see our local papers publish

accounts of what is transpiring here, and somebody connected
with the *Tribune* gets hold of these papers in New York City,
and then writes a letter at the *Tribune* office and dates it
from Charlestown.   Of course I need n't tell you that, in
their present state of excitement, our people would be more
than likely to hang such a person to the nearest tree.   You
know some hot-headed fellows have even offered a reward for
him."   I laughed with all my heart, slapped my host on the
knee, and protested that that was a Yankee trick I had n't
thought of.

But I must not forget my wretched trunk, for, as Mrs.
Gamp says, " It giv me sich a turn ! "   On the morning after my
arrival, something was said about the lot of trunks and things
they had down at the provost-marshal's office, and it flashed
across my mind that, in the excitement of my encounter with
that bloodthirsty old sheep-breeder at the railway station, I
had quite forgotten my luggage, and that it had undoubtedly
gone to the provost's with other unclaimed or suspicious property.   It was marked with my initials, and the words " New
York " ; and in the temper in which the Charlestown people
then found themselves, this was enough to place its owner in
no little personal jeopardy.   It occurred to me that perhaps
at that moment they were searching, or even, to use a Southern
expression, "gunning," after the person in question.   I did n't
know what to do ; it was a real dilemma.   I got away by
myself and cudgelled my brains for an hour to no purpose.
To be able to get it away myself without imminent danger
of discovery and the defeat of my mission, was a sheer im-
possibility, and it was equally dangerous to leave it unclaimed ;
for as it came up with the Grays' reinforcements, its owner

would be certainly hunted up. I considered it a matter of
life and death, and so I determined to try what my Masonry
would do. I picked out a fine, brave young fellow of the
Staff, a perfect gentleman, and, under the seal of Masonic
confidence, told him who I was, and directed him to go to
the Court House, and claim and bring away the trunk. He
did it, and I was safe.

But for the terrible strain on my nerves that my situation involved, and the melancholy business that was going
on about us, I should recall the days I passed under the
hospitable roof of our host, in the companionship of so rare a
lot of good fellows, as among the pleasantest of my life. I
was particularly charmed with Mr. Colyer, a white-haired lawyer, whose name has since figured prominently as that of a
Rebel Congressman and an officer of the Rebel army, and
the dear old doctor, my bedfellow, whom I have never set
eyes on since, much to my regret; and when all was over,
and the brave-souled Brown's spinal cord was broken, and we
were all ready to turn homeward, and my fellow-guests refused to let me subscribe towards a service of silver for our
hostess, merely because I was a Northern man, — albeit, as
they were so kind as to say, a deuced good fellow, — I felt
really hurt, and sorry enough to part with them. What made
me feel worse than all was to go through the town, arm in
arm with some of my new friends, cheek by jowl and all that
sort of thing, and think how shameful, how pitiful and cowardly it was that, in this "land of the free and home of
the brave," I was walking those streets with the specter of
Death stalking lock-step behind me, never leaving me day or
night, because I dared to write an honest letter to a great

newspaper, and tell how a brave, if perhaps fanatical, man behaved and talked.

The morning of that memorable 2d of December dawned at last, and the first gray streak saw us stirring. Wise had seized the Winchester and Potomac Railroad on the 29th November for military purposes, and issued his proclamation to the people of the State. He cautioned them to remain "at home and on guard or patrol duty on the 2d of December, and to abstain from going to Charlestown. Orders," said he, " are issued to prevent women and children, and strangers are hereby cautioned that there will be danger to them in approaching that place, or near it, on that day. If deemed necessary, martial law will be proclaimed and enforced." These are his very words, and I submit if they don't show how badly scared the great State of Virginia was! The field of execution — a plot of about forty acres, half in sod and half corn-stubble — was directly opposite our house, and the gallows stood on a rising ground not one hundred yards away from the porch. A military force of between two and three thousand troops — artillery, cavalry, and infantry — had been concentrated at the place ; the whole country for fifteen miles around was guarded by mounted and foot soldiers ; all intercourse between town and country was stopped. A field-piece loaded with grape and canister had been planted directly in front of and aimed at the scaffold, so as to blow poor Brown's body into smithereens in the event of attempted rescue ; other cannon commanded the approaches to the modern Aceldema ; and all Virginia held breath, until the noontide should come and go. The most stringent precautions had even been taken to prevent the townspeople from approaching the outermost

line of patrolling sentries, for the authorities were determined
to choke their prize malefactor, without giving him a chance
to make any seditious speeches.

The December sun had risen clear and bright, but soon
passed into a bank of haze, and I was afraid we should have
a stormy day of it. By nine o'clock, however, as beautiful an
azure sky hung over us as man ever saw, and, winter as it
was, the sun became so hot, that doors and windows were
flung wide open. The ground had been staked the day before, and fluttering white pennons all around the lot marked
the posts of the sentries, who came on the scene at the hour
above named. Then a strong force of volunteer cavalry, wearing red flannel shirts and black caps and trousers, rode up
and were posted, fifty paces apart, around the entire field ;
and then the guns and caissons of the artillery rumbled up ;
then more cavalry and infantry came ; and then a solemn
hush settled over the awful scene, and no sound was heard
but the twittering of some birds, the sigh of the south-wind
among the tree-branches, and the occasional impatient stamp of
a horse's hoof on the greensward. All eyes were turned to the
jail, a scant half-mile away down the road ; but nothing could be
seen but the glint of bayonets, and gilt buttons and straps, in the
bright sunshine, until, of a sudden, the mass opened right and
left, and a wagon, drawn by two white horses, came into view.
In it, seated on a long box of fresh-cut deal, was an old man,
of erect figure, clad in a black suit, with a black slouch hat on
his head, and blood-red worsted slippers on his feet. The
melancholy *cortége* formed and advanced towards us. There
was the one helpless old man, suffering from five saber and
bayonet wounds, going to his death under escort of : —

MAJOR LORING'S "BATTALION OF DEFENSIBLES."
CAPTAIN WILLIAMS'S "MONTPELIER GUARD."
CAPTAIN SCOTT'S "PETERSBURG GRAYS."
CAPTAIN MILLER'S "VIRGINIA VOLUNTEERS."
CAPTAIN RADY'S "YOUNG GUARD."

Now, is n't that pitiful? Is n't it enough to make a stone image blush, to think of all this great army, with its flying flags, and its brass guns, and its videttes and patrols all the way up to the foot of the Blue Ridge Mountains, haling one wounded Kansas farmer to execution? I could n't help thinking of all this, as the head of the column filed into the field, between the loaded howitzers, and I looked upon the majestic face of the Man of Destiny. For an instant our eyes met. Whether he read anything in mine of the thoughts that crowded my mind I cannot say, but an expression of intense inquiry came into his, and he gave me a glance I shall never forget. As his wagon turned in from the dusty road, and the whole array of military was presented to his view, the old man straightened himself up on his coffin, and proudly surveyed the scene. He looked to me more like Cæsar passing in his triumphal chariot through the streets of Rome, than like Jack Sheppard going to Tyburn Hill. He bore the searching gaze of the soldiery with a kingliness of manner, as if he were receiving homage that was his due, and did not cower under it, as if he were a malefactor about to be punished for some crime he had committed. He fully appreciated the effect of all this display of military upon public opinion, for you will recollect he said one day in prison, " I am not sure but the object I have in view will be better served by my dying than by my living ; I must think of that."

The *cortége* passed through the triple squares of troops, and over the hillock ; and wound around the scaffold to the easterly side, and halted. The body-guard — our company of Grays — opened ranks, and John Brown descended, with self-possession and dignity, and mounted the gallows-steps. He looked about at earth and sky and people, and remarked to Captain Avis, his jailer, upon the beauty of the scene. It was beautiful indeed. The sun shone with great splendor, and the gleaming guns and sparkling uniforms were strongly relieved against the somber tints of sod and woods. Away off to the east and south, the splendid mass of the Blue Ridge loomed against the sky, and shut in the horizon. Over the woods towards the northeast, long, thin stripes of clouds had gradually accumulated, foreboding the storm that came in due time that evening ; while, looking towards the south, there lay an undulating, fertile country, stretching away to the distant mountains. Brown's eye lingered wistfully upon the few civilians who had been permitted to gaze from a distance upon the tragedy, as if, so it seemed to me, he longed for a glimpse of one friendly face ; then, with another glance at the sky and the far-away Blue Ridge, he turned to the sheriff, and signified that he was ready. His slouch hat was removed, his elbows and ankles pinioned, and a white hood was drawn over his head. The world was gone from his sight forever, and he and Eternity were face to face. . . . . One would have thought that, after all their indecent haste to get him tried, convicted, sentenced, and hung, they would have despatched the poor old man as quickly after that as

possible ; but not a bit of it. There was still the shadow of
a possibility that some Cadmus-sown soldiers might spring
out of the dull sod of that field, and stampede the prize, so
there must be movements of troops hither and thither, march-
ings and countermarchings ; and I stood there, watch in hand,
for eight minutes, that seemed centuries, before Colonel Scott,
losing patience, gave the signal. Then Sheriff Campbell cut
the rope, the trap fell, with a wailing screech of its hinges,
and John Brown's body hung twirling in the air. You could
have heard the sigh of satisfaction that passed over the whole
armed host, so dead was the stillness that brooded over it.
There was but one spasmodic clutch of the tied hands, and
a few jerks and quivers of the limbs, and then all was still.
. . . . After the thing had dangled in mid-air for twenty
minutes, the Charlestown surgeons went up and lifted the
arms and dropped them like lead, and placed their ears to
the dead thing's chest, and felt the wrists for a pulse. Then
the military surgeons had their turn of it ; and then, after a
consultation, they stepped back, and left the body to dangle
and swing by its neck eighteen minutes more ; while it turned
to this side or that, swinging, pendulum-like, from the force
of the rising wind. At last the lion was declared dead, and
the body, limp and horrid, with an inch-deep groove cut
into its neck by the Kentucky hemp halter, sent as a special
donation for the occasion, was lowered down, and slumped
into a heap. It was then put into a black-walnut coffin, lifted
into the wagon again, the body-guard closed in about it, the
cavalry took the right of the column, and the mournful procession moved off. Then, if you could have heard some of
the brutal remarks that I did, you would have blushed for

your kind.   Some said that his head ought to be cut off and preserved in the Winchester Medical College, along with the dissected body of his son ; some, that instead of a fall of eighteen inches, they ought to have had the body fall ten feet, so as to snap his head off ; and others, that after he was hung, they ought to stuff a dose of arsenic into the corpse's mouth, so as to effectually prevent his Abolition friends from resuscitating him.   But then, on the other hand, there were some gentlemen, and among others, a captain on Taliaferro's Staff, who expressed their admiration for Brown's splendid pluck.   The latter person sat next me at table that night, and when I asked him what he thought of the affair, he turned a sparkling eye upon me and said, " By God, sir, he 's the bravest man that ever lived ! "

# THE WEED THAT CHEERS.

# THE WEED THAT CHEERS.

## By J. HENRY HAGER.

"NICOTIA, dearer to the Muse
Than all the grapes' bewildering juice,
We worship, unforbid of thee ;
And, as her incense floats and curls
In airy spires and wayward whirls,
Or poises on its tremulous stalk
A flower of frailest revery,
So winds and loiters, idly free,
The current of unguided talk,
Now laughter-rippled, and now caught
In smooth, dark pools of deeper thought.
Meanwhile thou mellowest every word,
A sweetly unobtrusive third ;
For thou hast magic beyond wine
To unlock natures each to each ;
The unspoken thought thou canst divine ;
Thou fillest the pauses of the speech
With whispers that to dream-land reach,
And frozen fancy-springs unchain
In Arctic outskirts of the brain ;
Sun of all inmost confidences !
To thy rays doth the heart unclose
Its formal calyx of pretences,
That close against rude day's offences,
And open its shy midnight rose."

AS it ever occurred to the reader that "the long result of Time" has failed to displace Tobacco as a narcotic in the popular esteem ?   That in spite of the "Counterblaste" of the "Defender of the Faith" ; the rage of Amurath IV., of Turkey ; the edicts of the Emperor Jehan-Ghir ; the excommunications of Popes Urban VIII. and Innocent XI., and the repressive measures of other potentates, who have assailed the liberties of mankind in forbidding the use of Tobacco, — that much-reviled herb has invaded every civilized and many barbarous countries, and stands to-day victor over all adversaries !

Surely when its opponents remember how bitterly its introduction into Europe was fought, step by step, — how in Turkey smoking was punished by thrusting the pipe through the nose ; how in Russia the unlucky wight caught using snuff was kept perpetually in mind of the heinousness of his crime by the summary amputation of the offending member ; how in the Swiss Canton of Berne the use of tobacco in any form was ranked in the table of misdemeanors next to adultery, and that even so late as the middle of the last century, an especial court for trying delinquents was held ; how, that armed with scourges, halters, and knives, and with gibbets painted on their banners, the Anti-tobaccoites of those days denounced death to all found inhaling the fumes of the plant through a tube, or detected with a pellet of it under their tongues, — it must be confessed that during the nearly four hundred years that have elapsed since the two sailors sent by Columbus to explore the island of Cuba first discovered the (to them) novel method of self-fumigation, the use of the Indian herb has extended with a rapidity and inhered among the customs of civilization with a tenacity that all must acknowledge to be remarkable.

In truth, the despised plant is in greater favor at the close of this good year of our Lord eighteen hundred and seventy-our than it has ever been. In Great Britain, the increasing consumption has compelled the manufacturers to have partial recourse to the inferior varieties of Tobacco grown in China and Japan, since the better qualities raised here are so much in demand on this side the Atlantic as to largely prohibit their exportation. And this, while every year witnesses the extension of the tobacco-producing area in these United States into sections where, until recently, its culture was unknown.

In view of these undeniable facts, we put it to the ingenuous Anti-tobaccoite to say whether the crusade against the weed has been a success?

If candid, he must admit its utter and universal failure.

The sincere contemners of Tobacco, from King James downward, have not lacked eloquence, learning, scientific attainments, nor a specious show of sound logic and pure morality.

Had their arguments not been based on a fallacy, could they have failed?

Against all the preachments of the last four hundred years, the irresistible logic of facts and the universal practice of mankind may very properly be left to make answer.

To the attacks based on the various physical and moral grounds that have been assumed, we are content to respond, on the part of those who believe in the use of the weed in moderation, that the movement against it has not taken any deep root in popular sympathy, nor been indorsed by the common-sense of the masses. It is quite true that many are found who avoid the use of Tobacco in any form from personal and physical reasons, but they are satisfied with being "a law unto themselves," and rarely seek to make converts to their peculiar practices, or join the ranks of the aggressive

opponents of the weed.   In fact, the latter have rarely succeeded in doing more than exciting the general and deserved
derision of mankind.

When we call to mind the reform movements against the
different abuses of the day, and the earnestness and intelligence with which many of them are carried forward, this
absence of hearty sympathy on the part of the people, and
the want of practicality that inevitably characterizes the
schemes of the Anti-tobaccoites, furnish food for thought, and
lead irresistibly to certain conclusions.

We find that the reasoning powers of the masses teach
them that of the charges made by the opponents of the
weed, those not absolutely false could be brought with equal
force against the use of certain other so-called luxuries.   When
gentlemen who assume to speak in the name of Science,
assure us of the deadly qualities of the pipe, we may very
appropriately ask, how it happens that mankind, after smoking over three hundred years, manage to attain to so tolerable
a degree of health?

And in this connection, an interesting subject of inquiry
for our scientific friends would be, the hygienic condition of
the native Cubans when Columbus surprised them engaged in
the deleterious practice of smoking?   Or, still more feasible,
the general health of Europe before and after the introduction
of Tobacco.

Unless the savans can approach the inquiry satisfactorily
from this standpoint, and demonstrate beyond cavil how some
particular nation has steadily receded in the scale of moral
and physical well-being in consequence of the use of the
weed, their theories, based on one-sided experiments and scien-

tific half-truths, will continue to be as powerless to convince in the future as they have been in the past.

Any hypothesis based on the experience of individuals, or observations of exceptional cases, are, for the purposes intended, simply worthless. It must be shown, not that Tobacco has proved injurious under certain conditions of the human organism, but that the human organism, during a series of years, and in the case of entire communities, has sensibly and decidedly deteriorated!

This proved beyond a doubt, the savans might justly claim the victory ; that they may be led to enter upon the inquiry, we challenge them to the demonstration.

The difficulty is, that the Anti-tobaccoites, considering the actual facts established by them, go too far.

Universal condemnation never convinces, especially when contradicted by every-day experience.

Besides, our Tobacco reformers are the most inconsistent of men. While protesting against the abused plant, they quietly allow the object of their anathemas to pay a large proportion of their taxes and thus contribute to their income.

Perhaps it has never occurred to the Rev. Trask and his *confrères* that Tobacco, imported and domestic, pays nearly forty millions of dollars annually towards the support of " the best government on which the sun ever shone " ; while, across the water, the British Constitution is preserved intact by a yearly contribution of over thirty-five millions on the part of the (involuntarily) patriotic chewers and smokers of that benighted and expensive isle.

Yet how much of these eighty millions would our Anti-tobacco friends be willing to assume, in case it were possible to make the use of the weed in both countries a criminal offence, and thus to drop it from the list of sources of national income ?

"We pause for a reply !"

But is it consistent for these earnest gentlemen to live without protest under the protection of institutions that may be said to be in part reared on the ashes of a much-reviled herb ?

If the use of Tobacco is morally wrong, — and we never met an Anti-tobaccoite who claimed less, — it is certainly wrong to participate, however indirectly, in the profits accruing from traffic in the "accursed thing !"

Can the honest Anti-tobaccoite, either in England or America, truthfully assert that he is not sinning against his conscience in this respect ?

Nor, indeed, is his co-believer on the Continent in much better case.

In Austria, France, Italy, Spain, — nay, even in Turkey, — the weed is deemed so precious a commodity that its sale is regulated and the profits largely shared by the government ; while in Russia, Germany, Holland, and Belgium an import duty is imposed on all packages of Tobacco entering those countries, so that the resident Anti-tobaccoite is equally, though indirectly, interested in the gains arising from the commerce in the article he so greatly detests.

The alternative thus presented to the opponent of the weed is either a change of country or of creed.

And may we not sooner or later look for the latter consummation?

Will there remain any so beclouded as to their mental vision — we speak with all reverence — when the millennial sun dawns upon a regenerated world?

Cannot we reasonably look forward to that promised season of fruition, as to a period when the voice of the Anti-tobaccoite shall no longer be heard in the land?

Surely in the full blaze of Truth, those reformers who see partially and draw exceedingly lame and impotent conclusions from premises very much awry, cannot remain unconvinced!

Our belief in "the eternal fitness of things" forbids any different conclusion.

Let us, then, in the mystic brotherhood of the Lotos, continue to keep the pipe undimmed. Let its steadfast light illume the shadows, and kindle anew the fires on the altar of friendship.

In our especial realm where "it is ever afternoon," we may smoke the calumet even with the repentant Anti-tobaccoite, whose hoped-for conversion might possibly be succeeded by his elevation in the social and moral scale until he became "one of us!"

Meantime we commend to him the following quaint lines by a writer of the last century as suited to his present stage of development, and as proof that, despite his prejudices, the soundest morality may be fairly derived even from a pipeful of Tobacco: —

> "Come, lovely tube, by Friendship blest,
> Beloved and honored by the wise :
> Come filled with honest 'Weekly's best,'
> And kindled from the lofty skies.

" While round me clouds of incense roll,
    With guiltless joys you charm the sense,
And nobler pleasure to the soul,
    In hints of moral truth dispense.

"Soon as you feel th' enlivening ray,
    To dust you hasten to return ;
And teach me that my earliest day
    Began to give me to the urn.

" But though thy grosser substance sink
    To dust, thy purer part aspires ;
This when I see I joy to think
    That earth but half of me requires.

" Like thee, myself am born to die,
    Made half to rise and half to fall ;
O could I, while my moments fly,
    The bliss you give me, give to all ! "

# THE ASPERITIES OF TRAVEL

# THE ASPERITIES OF TRAVEL.

By COLONEL THOMAS W. KNOX.

T has been said, many times, that travel wears off the rough edges of an individual and gives him a polish that he cannot obtain in any other way. He acquires a knowledge of men and their manners and customs more thoroughly than when remaining in one place, and he learns to regard with a tolerant eye the social, moral, political, and religious beliefs at variance with his own. He accepts the correctness of the maxim that all men are brothers, and that their thoughts, impulses, and passions are not altogether unlike in the main, though differing in detail. He finds that enmity and friendship, love and hatred, honesty and depravity, hope and fear, joy and sorrow, are the same among all nations and tribes of the human race, from the Equator to the Poles and from the Poles back again to the Equator. Born under the flag of the United States, and cherishing an undying affection for a republican form of government, he learns to respect a monarchy for whatever good qualities it possesses ; and, born and reared within the limits of a despotism, and taught to regard it as of divine origin, he learns by travel and observation to look upon the republic as not unblessed with advantages of its own. Broader views of humanity and a respect for the opinions of others are generally the result of travel, provided, always, the traveller is capable of mental enlargement, and enters upon his journeys with a willingness to be instructed. Some men there are who might visit all the ground ever trodden by Livingstone, Kane, Ledyard, and Marco Polo, and return to their homes more narrow and bigoted, if possible, than ever before. But such as these are exceptions that only prove the correctness of the rule.

Most men are taught through adversity, rather than through good fortune, and do not sympathize with suffering until they themselves have suffered. And the traveller who has a hard time of it is quite as likely to be benefited by his wanderings as the man whose path is strewn with roses and whose journeys are a succession of unvarying delights. The skilful artist makes the light in his picture effective by reason of its contrast with the shadows. Light and darkness are relative, and, strictly speaking, there cannot be the one without the other. Velvet feels softer than otherwise when contrasted with haircloth or India matting; and an individual who has been clad in a suit of tar and feathers, and treated to a ride upon a fence-rail, finds a blanket covering and a seat in an ox-cart a luxurious contrast to the clothing and locomotion of indignity. Serene happiness follows the withdrawal of the pain of an aching tooth; and plain soda-water, ordinarily unattractive, is welcome as the nectar which Jupiter sips when brought to one's bedside the morning after a late supper on champagne and broiled quail. Pleasure and discomfort, joy and sorrow, happiness and misery, are things of contrast, and none of us can ever know one of these feelings to its fullest extent without some acquaintance with its opposite. If all travel were in palace-cars and luxurious steamers, and every

traveller halted only in hotels which contain all the comforts
of this or any other age, one would be little better off than
if he remained at home. But happily we must make acquaintance with many kinds of vehicles and caravansaries, and submit to a thousand discomforts and vexations, if we would emulate the example of Rosin the Bow, who narrates, in his
autobiographical poem, that he had travelled this wide world
all over. Like Queen Dido, we are schooled through our misfortunes; we remember them, and generally to our subsequent good. Those that can be avoided we learn to shun,
and those which are inevitable we undergo with moral philosophy and greater mental serenity. Contrasts are of constant
occurrence, and we look back over a course of travel as we
would recall the thousand combinations and changes of a re-
volving kaleidoscope.

Some years ago, it was my fortune to make a ride of
nearly two hundred miles on the back of a powerful horse
in less than four days. He was a trotter; not a fancy animal, but a good sound roadster, whose trot would have roused
the digestion of a dyspeptic of forty years' standing. His
back rose and fell like the walking-beam of a North River
steamboat, and his legs seemed to have been made for at
least four horses of different sizes and attached to a body
which was intended for a fifth beast. When I finished my
ride, I felt as if I had been put through a patent clothes-
wringer, and every joint in my body had started loose from
active wear, or had become so swollen as to be immovable.
My ride on this wonderful piece of horseflesh ended at a
railway station. Half an hour after I alighted, a freight-
train arrived, and I secured a place in a box-car. Seated on

a pine box, and leaning against the rough side of the car, I continued my journey. No Pullman palace or English first-class was ever half as luxurious as that vehicle; the box on which I sat was like a Turkish ottoman, and the board where my back rested, occasionally touching a protruding nail or screw-head, was like the most elegant sofa from a Parisian shop. I reclined, and speedily fell asleep, lulled by the gentle motion of the car along the rails. The track was unballasted, and the rails were laid with none of the fish-joints and other improvements which add so much to the comfort of railway travel. Months afterward I travelled the same route in an ordinary passenger-car, and found the rough jolting almost unendurable. But I had been resting in the mean time, and had not preceded the excursion with a rough ride on horseback.

Travel, like poverty or politics, makes one acquainted with strange bedfellows, both literally and metaphorically. A traveller may sleep with a prince or a beggar according to circumstances, though he is much more likely to share his dormitory with the latter than with the former. Beggars are much more numerous than princes, and, moreover, the princes have a practice of exclusiveness that is not generally observed among mendicants. Your prince is shy of strangers, and has a regard for his aristocratic position, but the beggar does not emboss himself with any such pretensions. He fastens to you, and oftentimes the surroundings are such that he cannot be shaken off with ease. If he be a genuine, low-down beggar, he may be sent away with a small contribution, and that is the end of him so far as you are concerned ; but if he belongs to the upper or swindling class of beggary, the case may be different. The swindler will adhere to you as long as there is a prospect of obtaining a dollar or a fraction of one ; and sometimes, when he considers the financial prospect hopeless, he remains at your side for the sake of your society.

I have in mind several of these personages whose abilities would have gained them comfort, if not affluence, in any honest enterprise. The most artistic of the lot was a French adventurer who entered a car with me when I left Strasburg on a journey down the Rhine.

Before we reached Kehl, he had told me his history, or a goodly portion of it, and offered to assist at the opening of my baggage, and its examination at the custom-house. We changed cars twice before reaching Baden-Baden, and each time he remained with me ; he went to my hotel, supped at the table with me, ordered a bottle of wine, which I afterwards found on my account, and would have forced himself into my room had I not negatived any such arrangement. He disappeared after supper, but when I went to the *Conversation-Haus*, I found him at one of the tables ; he informed me that he was always lucky at *rouge-et-noir*, and offered to bet my money for me ; but in consequence of various prejudices which I entertained about the man and the game, his kindness went unappreciated and unaccepted. By this time I was amused with the fellow and loaned him five francs by way of encouragement. An hour before I left the place I confided to him my intention of remaining a week or two, and found that he intended staying about the same length of time. He lost sight of me at my departure, but made up for it by catching me a couple of days later at Frankfort. He adhered to me as closely as possible, and took the train with me to

Mayence. We agreed to go to a certain hotel, and while he was looking for his baggage I slipped away to another, and made a wager to myself that he would find me within an hour. The wagering half of me was victorious, as he was with me in just forty-nine minutes by my watch, and as smiling as a prize-fighter, coming up at the end of his third round.

I tried to deceive him about my departure from Mayence, but he was too sharp for me, and when the boat was well under way he appeared on deck, as if shot up from below like the harlequin in a pantomime. Here he had me fairly cornered, and most energetically did he endeavor to inveigle me. He had sent his baggage to Cologne by rail in order to be rid of the encumbrance, and, *quel bêtise*, he had forgotten to take his money from his trunk, and there he was penniless, or, rather, sous-less. He wanted five francs to pay his fare to Coblenz, and I cheerfully accommodated him; then he wanted more, but just then I was out of money, and depressed him with the information that I must call on my banker.

I stopped at Coblenz and he continued to Cologne, where he proposed to secure rooms for me, and meet me at the landing next day. I thought I was rid of him; but next day there he was, delighted to see me, and sorry to say that his baggage had not arrived, and thát he should be forced, much as he regretted it, to depend upon the kindness of his dear American friend. Could I lend him a hundred francs, which he would repay me in Paris, whither both were travelling; and if I would do so, he would be my friend forever, and would remain with me as collateral until we arrived in the city of luxury. I saw that he would no longer amuse me as a social study, except at heavy expense; he had cost me only three dollars up to that point, and I naturally considered that that sort of thing had gone on long enough. Henceforth he would be a burden, and if I desired the pleasure of his company I must pay for it. So I told him, in the best translation I could make of American slang, that the game was played. "*Je ne le vois pas*," I said; "*vous êtes un bête mort*." I could not think just then of the exact expression in French for "fraud," but am satisfied that he understood me. Under the shadow of the Cathedral of Cologne, whence the centuries look lovingly down, I gave him a valuable lesson in Gallic phrases culled from the American tongue,—a lesson which probably proved of value, as he took down some of the phrases in his note-book.

I never saw him again. He went away sorrowing, for he had not great possessions, and thought, when he made my acquaintance, that he had found somebody who would be his comfort and support.

The strange bedfellows which a traveller meets are not all of the human sort. He associates at times with most of the animals that figure in zoölogical works, and especially with those that have been domesticated. He may sleep in a stable, and be thankful that he is admitted there; the society of horses, mules, and cows may not be entirely congenial to him, but he endures it with quiet philosophy, albeit he departs with a strong smell of stable about his garments, and sometimes with a few footprints of his quadrupedal companions on various portions of his body. The cow and the horse have many excellent qualities, but they cannot be commended as bosom friends, while the mule, especially the one that kicks, is to be shunned when shunning is possible. The mule has no paternal instinct, and consequently can never develop affection, like the cow or horse. The dog will do to sleep with, especially if he is your dog and is not overborne with fleas. But unfortunately, the flea has for the dog an affinity that shapes his ends, rough indeed for his human associates, and wretched is the man whose couch is with a flea-haunted canine. In many parts of the world fleas abound and make the traveller miserable. My first intimate knowledge of them was on the Amoor River, where the cabin of a small steamer seemed to be full of them. They bit me from head to foot, and at the end of my first night in their society my body looked as if it had been tattooed with red ink and croton oil. I was worse off the next night, and set my genius at work to devise a means to be rid of them. I obtained some bad brandy from the steward of the boat, and before retiring the next night I rubbed myself with the liquid, and then wrapped snugly in a sheet. That fixed them. They must have belonged to a temperance society, as they did n't disturb me afterwards so long as I took my daily bath of brandy. The captain of the boat expressed a desire to know how to drive away the fleas, but said he could not. I told him it was his duty to utilize them, and suggested that he might set up a treadmill for them, and by using them to run his machinery he could dispense with engines and steam. He did not again refer to the subject.

It has never been my fortune to find snakes in my boots, though persons of strictly temperate habits have been known to do so in India and Java. On two occasions I have found snakes — or, strictly speaking, a snake — in my bed. Once while camped out on our Western Plains, I waked in the morning, and made my usual attempt to turn over in my blankets for another nap. There was something lying close against me; it felt like a coil of rope, but developed the unropy characteristic of life. I thought of snakes, and that thought was followed by an emphatic and unusual fondness for early rising. It was not quite sunrise, and all my companions were asleep; there were no camp duties to bring me out at that time, but nevertheless I was determined to get up. I rose from my blankets with less grace than Venus rose from the sea, but with far greater rapidity. I made a remark in rising that waked a friend lying near me, and caused him to be equally unceremonious in abandoning his couch. One after another the rest of our party were waked, and in less than two minutes about twenty half-dressed and dishevelled beings were gathered around my blankets, and gazing upon them with all the eagerness of a group of scientists, examining a newly discovered trilobite.

There was something moving under the blankets, and it was speedily decided that the something was a snake. A club was held in readiness, and as the reptile showed his head at the edge of the blanket he received a tap that would have broken the skull of a buffalo. He was unceremoniously killed and stretched on the grass where all could see and admire him. He was a cheerful creature, about five feet long, and belonged to the race known on the Plains as the "bull-snake," a sort of first-cousin to the rattlesnake. We hanged him on a tree and left him as a warning to his friends who might come that way. For several days I thought almost constantly of snakes, and for an equal number of nights I dreamed of them. But, after a while, I became convinced that snakes and lightning do not generally strike twice in the same place, and gradually ceased to keep this incident uppermost in my mind.

The other snake which I found in my blankets was an insignificant affair, quite unworthy a prominent place in this narrative. I will dismiss him as summarily as on the occasion when I discovered him. Rats and mice have found comfort and food at my side in several instances, but I cannot say that I particularly desired their friendship. It is not at all pleasant to wake in the night, as has been my luck, and find rats and mice using you for a parade-ground or race-track, without so much as asking your permission, and I hereby enter a protest against the practice. I have in mind an occasion when I waked in the morning and found a mouse seated on my nose and contemplating the scenery around him. He was not a large mouse, else he would have found the nose too small for a resting-place, and I was glad on his account that he was not thus incommoded. But he was so near my eyes, that he appeared as large as an elephant, and I did not know his genus and species until my movements sent him scampering away.

The characteristics of hotels form a pleasing subject of contemplation, and to a thoughtful traveller they are an unfailing source of instruction. From the great hotels of Paris and New York, the eye looks down an imaginary avenue of hostelries, diminishing in more senses than one, as they recede and are lost in the distance. The Grand Hotel of Paris stands at the end of the avenue nearest the spectator, and beyond it are the — Well, you may name a dozen or two of the first-class hotels that are your favorites outside of the French capital. Then you come to less commodious, though not always less pretentious establishments, and so you go into the distance until you find a hostelry of the most primitive character. You may be reminded by this imaginary avenue of the road somewhere out West, that began most magnificently with fine pavements, broad sidewalks, and rows of shade trees, and gradually diminished, until it terminated in a squirrel-track, and ran up a scrub-oak. The hotel avenue may terminate in the same way, as many travellers can tell you. I have had the pleasure of sleeping in a hollow tree, and thought my accommodations were far preferable to staying out of doors. When the Calaveras Grove of trees in California was first made a public resort, an enterprising American fitted up a hollow *Sequoia* as a hotel, and hundreds of persons were entertained there. A neighboring log was used as a stable, so that the landlord could boast of accommodations for man and beast.

I could tell many stories of funny experiences in hotels, but the limits of this article forbid, and I can give only a few of them. Years ago, on my first trip to the West, I arrived one evening at a rural hotel, and was shown to a room. When about to retire, I found there was but a single sheet on the bed, and, supposing a mistake had been made, I descended to the bar-room, and found a son of the landlord. Explaining the situation, I was told that no bed in the house was furnished with more than I had found on mine, and the youth muttered something about my being " mighty particular." I insisted upon a more complete dressing for my couch, and the son went for the father. Through the open door from the bar-room to the kitchen I heard the statement that " a stuck-

up cuss from New York wants an extra sheet on his bed."
The landlord intimated that I could go to a locality where
even one sheet would be a superfluity, and for a while my
wants were treated with the greatest contempt. Only by
making a row did I obtain what I desired.

I have lodged in a hotel which consisted of a fence drawn
around the space covered by the branches of a large elm-
tree, and divided by imaginary lines into parlor, kitchen, and
bedroom. The patrons slept on the ground in the bedroom, and each patron supplied his own blankets. To make
our toilets in the morning, we went into the kitchen; i. e.
we stepped behind the tree. In a hotel in Tennessee I once
found a printed placard over the wash-stand as follows:
"GENTLEMEN wishing towels in their rooms will please leave
fifty cents at the office for security." The emphasis on the
first word would seem to imply that there were gentlemen
who have no use for towels. In another establishment I
found the injunction, "Guests who do not wish their boots
stolen will not put them outside the door." A man suffering
from ill-fitting boots of which he wished to be rid was thus
kindly informed how he could dispose of them. Whether the
landlord kept a servant whose special duty it was to steal
boots ejected from the rooms, I did not venture to inquire.

I will close with a story told by a traveller in Texas. "I
was on foot," said he, "and came to a river where the only
bridge was a log stretched across the stream. Like the Irish-
man's blanket, it was too short at both ends, and was secured
by a stout grapevine. At either end of the log there was
an aching void of five or six feet; it took me two hours to
bring brushwood to make a raft to ferry myself from the

bank to the log; and when I got upon it, the confounded thing rolled and twisted so, that I had hard work to keep my footing. I managed to get to the other end, and there I was obliged to jump. I fell short and into the river, but caught hold of the grapevine and pulled out. When I mounted the bank and stopped to let the water drip from my clothes, I found a sign-board announcing in bold, savage letters, "FIVE DOLLARS FINE FOR PASSING THIS BRIDGE FASTER THAN A WALK!"

# EDGAR A. POE AND HIS BIOGRAPHER.

# EDGAR A. POE AND HIS BIOGRAPHER, RUFUS W. GRISWOLD.

By WILLIAM F. GILL.

FROM the fact that "Lotos Leaves" contained no other paper of a similar character to the article which I have prepared with what care a somewhat brief notice would permit, I have thought it best to consult the exigency presented by this fact in offering my contribution to this volume. A banquet, too largely composed of toothsome confections, however excellent their quality, would prove palling to the appetite. The gem must have its setting, which, if claiming naught of beauty or rarity, still holds a useful, necessary place. The brightest limnings in the painter's choicest landscape are not the less effective in that they stand out relieved by the contrast of a most somber background.

So in this "leaf," which may serve the humble purpose in lending, by its harder tone and deeper shadow, a useful contrast to the brilliant color of the brighter and more gladsome petals with which it is surrounded.

"Dr. Griswold's biography of my Eddie is one atrocious lie," writes Mrs. Clemm, the mother-in-law of Edgar Allan Poe, in a letter to an intimate friend; and after careful researches, extending over the space of three years, I have come, from the cumulation of corroborative documentary evidence, to give an unequivocal indorsement to Mrs. Clemm's statement. Intense admiration of Poe's writings and of his genius, mingled with deep sympathy for the exceptional misfortunes of his career, first prompted me to the arduous task of investigating the story of his life, and verifying or disproving the statements of the Griswold biography of Poe, which, for nearly twenty-five years, has been permitted to preface the authorized editions of his works ; also forming the basis of several of the biographies that have been written to preface the English editions of the poet's works. As a matter of fact, Poe's poems are fivefold more popular in England than in America, and his prose writings, which have never secured the recognition of extended popular currency in America, are even more admired in England than are his poems. I cannot refrain from feeling and expressing the conviction that Griswold's mendacious biography, preluding the American editions of Poe, and, as it were, forming a chilling wet-blanket, most repelling to the warmest admirer of the poet, is in a degree responsible for the comparatively limited circulation enjoyed by his works in America. I measure the effect of the Griswold biography upon the intelligent reader precisely as does an English reviewer the biography of Poe by James Hannay, based upon Griswold, to wit, — should any man of taste and sense, not acquainted with Poe, be so unfortunate as to look at Mr. Griswold's preface before reading the poetry, it is extremely probable he will throw the book into the fire, in indignation at the self-conceit and affected smartness by which the preface is characterized.

As a matter of fact, the demand for the complete edition of

Poe's works containing the Griswold memoir is so limited, that within a few months, calling for this edition at two of the largest book-houses in Boston, I was unable to obtain a copy, and was informed that the calls for it were so few that they, the dealers, were not encouraged to keep this edition of Poe in stock.

Yet no one will deny that among the *collections* of poems by various authors published, Poe is among the most popular and the most admired of the authors represented.

My purpose in this paper being to offer an impartial statement, or a series of statements, duly authenticated by documents, controverting the statements of Dr. Griswold, rather than to attempt any eulogium of the poet, I shall devote my allotted space, so far as it will allow, principally to meeting the misstatements of the reverend vilifier. Some of Dr. Griswold's statements are properly attributable to malicious and vengeful mendacity, others to gross and inexcusable carelessness. Imprimis, the biographer states that Edgar A. Poe was born in Baltimore, January, 1811. Mr. Poe was not born in 1811, in Baltimore; this is on the authority of the records (still in existence) of the University of Virginia, at Charlottesville.

In 1816, writes the biographer, he accompanied Mr. and Mrs. Allan to Great Britain, and afterwards passed four or five years in a school kept at Stoke Newington, near London, by the Rev. Dr. Bransby. "Encompassed by the massy walls of this venerable academy" (writes the poet in "William Wilson"), "I passed, yet not in tedium or disgust, the years of the third lustrum of my life."

Had he not been born until 1811, as Dr. Griswold states, he would not have attained his third lustrum during his sojourn at this place. Of this school and its play-ground Poe writes in the same sketch : " The extensive enclosure was irregular in form, having many capacious recesses. Of these, three or four of the largest constituted the play-ground. It was level and covered with hard gravel. . . . . But the house ! how quaint an old building was this ! to me how veritably a palace of enchantment ! There was really no end to its windings, to its incomprehensible subdivisions. It was difficult at any given time to say with certainty upon which of its two stories one happened to be. From each room to every other there were sure to be found three or four steps either in ascent or descent.

" Then the lateral branches were innumerable, inconceivable, and so returning in upon themselves, that our most exact ideas in regard to the whole mansion were not very far different from those with which we pondered upon infinity. During the five years of my residence here, I was never able to ascertain with precision in what remote locality lay the little sleeping-apartment assigned to myself and some eighteen or twenty other scholars."

" In 1822 " (continues Dr. Griswold) " he entered the University at Charlottesville, Virginia, where he led a very dissipated life ; the manners which then prevailed there were extremely dissolute, and he was known as the wildest and most reckless student of his class ; but his unusual opportunities, and the remarkable ease with which he mastered the most difficult studies, kept him all the while in the first rank for scholarship, and he would have graduated with the highest honors, had not his gambling, intemperance, and other vices induced his expulsion from the University."

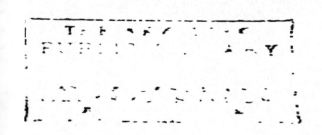

This is all false from beginning to end, and is absurd, like-wise, on the biographer's own showing. If Poe was born in 1811, he would at this time (1822) have been *eleven* years of age, — rather a precocious age, is it not, for one to whom is ascribed the rôle of a rake and a gambler? As a matter of fact, Poe did not enter the University until 1826, being then just seventeen years of age. He was never, according to reliable evidence, intoxicated while there, nor was he expelled.

Following the death of his foster-father, there came to Poe a period of great, although probably not of his greatest, suffer-ing. He had not at that time secured attention as a writer, and his condition and location up to the time of his appear-ance as a competitor for the Baltimore prizes are veiled from his biographers. It is not improbable, however, that he made his headquarters at the time with his aunt, Mrs. Clemm, who afterwards became his mother-in-law. Dr. Griswold, not having a fact at hand to mortise into this gap, comes to the rescue of his impotent researches, and as usual placidly *in-vents* another bit of defamatory fiction. "His contributions," says Dr. Griswold, "attracted little attention, and, his hopes of gaining a living in this way being disappointed, he enlisted in the army as a private soldier. How long he remained in the army I have not been able to ascertain. He was recog-nized by officers who had known him at West Point, and efforts were made privately, but with prospects, to obtain for him a commission, when it was discovered by his friends that he had deserted." The facts are, on the written testimony of Mrs. Clemm, that at this time his friends were seeking for him a commission, and it is folly to believe, when the prospects were favorable for his securing a higher position, that he would have enlisted as a private, and thus deliberately and unnecessarily have incurred the penalty and disgrace of desertion. That Mrs. Clemm, at least, was in full knowledge of his whereabouts at this time, is evident from her statement made in this regard, that Poe never slept one night away from home until after he was married. It is futile to say that such an audacious rumor should never have obtained admission into a memoir of Poe, and that it never would have done so had proper inquiries been made. Griswold never cared to make inquiries, and if he had, he was in his normal condition too unclean a man ever to have made *proper* inquiries.

Dr. Griswold's next fabrication is in regard to the details of Poe's appearance as a competitor for the prizes offered by the proprietor of the " Saturday Visitor " at Baltimore. The prizes were one for the best tale and one for the best poem. Dr. Griswold states that, attracted by the beauty of Poe's penmanship, the committee, without opening any of the other manuscripts, voted unanimously that the prizes should be paid to "the first of geniuses who had written legibly." On the contrary, there appeared in the Visitor, after the awards were made, complimentary comments over the committee's own signatures. They said, among other things, that *all* the tales offered by Poe were far *better than the best* offered by others, adding "that they thought it a duty to call public attention to them in these columns in that marked manner, since they possessed a singular force and beauty, and were eminently distinguished by a rare vigorous and poetical imagination, a rich style, a fertile invention, and varied and curious learning." It is not a matter of great importance, but Dr. Griswold's famous pen-photograph of Poe's personal appearance when summoned by Mr. Kennedy to receive his prize-money, is also untrue. I have not the copy of the letter at hand, and therefore cannot recall the precise words of Mr. Kennedy ; but I have in my possession a copy of an original letter which most positively states that Poe's appearance, although somewhat shabby, was not by any means absolutely poverty-stricken, and that the details of the absence of shirt and stockings, mentioned by Dr. Griswold, are false. This statement is interesting as, in a way, confirmatory of my impression that Poe was not so far reduced as he has been represented at this time. And when it is remembered that there is evidence that he had influential friends at that very time working to secure a commission for him, is it probable that they would have permitted him to go about in such a shocking condition as has been represented ? The theory that he was at this time living with friends, is palpably more probable.

That his success in securing the prizes decided him upon enlisting in a literary career, there can be no doubt ; hence it is a matter of no surprise that we hear no more of the army project at this time.

From other dates which have come to me from private sources, I learn that he met Virginia Clemm when she was but six years of age, that he undertook her tuition at ten, and married her when she was but fourteen. From this, it is, again, not only evident, but undoubted, that he was at least a frequent visitor at the Clemms' at the period of his career about which so little is known to the world. An amusing instance of Griswold's pettiness and want of common-sense judgment, even in his endeavor to demean the position and character of his subject as much as possible, is found in the following paragraph in the biography. Speaking of the poet's connection with the *Literary Messenger*, he writes : " In the next number of the *Messenger*, Mr. White announced that Poe was its editor, or, in other words, that he had made arrangements with a gentleman of approved literary taste and attainments, to whose especial management the editorial department would be confided, and it was declared that this gentleman would 'devote his exclusive attention to his work.' " Having put this down in black and white, following his statement that Mr. White was a man of much purity of character, the redoubtable biographer evidently feels that he has set Poe up a peg too high, and immediately planes him down to an endurable level in the next sentence : " Poe continued, however, to reside in Baltimore, and it is probable that he was engaged only as a *general contributor* and *writer of critical notices of books.*" Apropos of these book reviews, Dr. Griswold dismisses them as follows : " He continued in Baltimore till September. In this period he wrote several long reviews, which for the most part were abstracts of works rather than critical discussions." As a matter of fact, the *Messenger* was in its seventh month, with about four hundred subscribers, when Poe assumed the editorship. Poe remained with this journal until the end of its second year, by which time its circulation had been increased fourfold. A contemporary of Poe writes that " the success of the *Messenger* has been justly attributable to Poe's exertions on its behalf, but especially to the skill, honesty, and audacity of the criticism under the editorial head. The review of " Norman Leslie " may be said to have introduced a new era in our critical literature." But Griswold could see nothing in Poe's book reviews of which he cared to speak, for reasons which will be apparent later.

Dr. Griswold's next mendacious allusion to Poe is in connection with his account of his secession from the *Gentleman's Magazine*.

After mentioning a personal correspondence between Burton and Poe, in which the views of the latter, whatever they may have been, are carefully suppressed, Dr. Griswold romances as follows : " He [Burton] was absent nearly a fortnight, and on returning he found that his printers had not received a line of copy, but that Poe had prepared the prospectus of a new monthly, and obtained transcripts of his subscription and account books, to be used in a scheme for supplanting him. He encountered his associate late in the evening at one of his accustomed haunts, and said, 'Mr. Poe, I am astonished. Give me my manuscripts, so that I can attend to the duties which you have so shamefully neglected, and when you are sober we will settle.' Poe interrupted him with, 'Who are you that presume to address me in this manner ? Burton, I am the editor of the *Pennsylvania Magazine*, and you are — hiccup — a *fool!*' Of course, this ended his relations with the *Gentleman's*." That this alleged conversation, so plausibly narrated as to pass current *nem. con.*, were it not for the existence of more reliable documentary evidence, is an audacious invention, has been made apparent to me from the written testimony of gentlemen connected with the *Gentleman's Magazine* at this time.

Dr. Griswold devotes considerable space to his next misstatement, which relates to Mr. Poe's reading of an original poem before the Boston Lyceum. Our lecture managers and lecture public were more exacting twenty-five years ago, on some points, than at the present time. Now, it suffices for a reputable celebrity to *show* himself upon the rostrum. Provided he does not occupy too much time (one hour or an hour and fifteen minutes is about the fashionable limit), he may be sure of copious applause, of fervent congratulations from beaming managers, and a plethoric purse upon retiring. *Then*, O insatiable manager and exacting public! the best literary work expressly performed for the occasion was demanded, or woe betide the celebrities who failed to meet these requirements!

Poe was probably fully conscious of this, and, not unlike other geniuses in the history of the literary world, was driven wellnigh frantic in contemplation of his task of the "written-expressly-for-this-occasion poem." It ended as most of these unequal contests between inspiration and necessity have ended time and time again. The day arrived, and no new creations had been evolved from the goaded and temporarily irresponsive brain. He went to Boston to fill his engagement, nerved to meet the ordeal by a spirit which brought him compensation for his anxiety, — a spirit which Mr. E. P. Whipple, the distinguished essayist, at that time immediately associated with Poe, most admirably describes as intellectual mischief.* He could not do what he had been invited to do; well, he would make them believe that he had filled the demand, if he could, and then honestly own up, and let them laugh at him and with him.

* Poe's connection with the Text-Book of Conchology, of which Dr. Griswold makes such a point, is undoubtedly attributable to this same spirit of intellectual mischief. No other cause can reasonably be assigned for the publication of the book under the circumstances. There was no money in such a venture, and the action partakes so much of the color of Poe's purely mischievous pranks in other fields, that I cannot but assign it to the same species of impulse.

Dr. Griswold makes a labored effort to show that Poe's failure to meet his engagement to the letter was due to cares, anxieties, and "feebleness of will." The charge of feebleness of will, applied to Poe in his strictly literary capacity, is perhaps one of the most sapient bits of analysis of which the reverend and profound doctor has delivered himself. As regards Dr. Griswold's mention of the assistance of Mrs. Osgood, desired by Poe, it is so manifestly absurd, that the biographer's ingenuity and invention fail to enlist any credence in this bit of fiction.

The literary world of Boston twenty-five years ago was marked by characteristics that rendered it anything but liberal and indulgent. Had Poe had the fortunate tact to disarm his audience by "owning up" at the outset, and in advance, deftly knuckling, as he might have done, to its boasted literary acumen and perceptiveness, all might have been well. But he chose rather to indulge his mischievous propensity, to his cost, as it afterwards proved. In his card in the *Broadway Journal*, the poet, in acknowledging his confession to a company of gentlemen at a supper which took place after the reading, truly says, in closing, "We should have waited a couple of days." He should indeed have waited; for among the company was a pitcher that could not contain the water, and the premature leak being made public, naturally aroused a storm of indignant criticism upon the poet's assumption. His long poem had been applauded to the echo, and the reading of "The Raven" afterwards, had sent the audience home in the best of spirits. Poe was too frank and impulsive to keep the joke to himself, and, finding that he had not taken in *all* of the men with brains who received him, he, without a word of suggestion, made a clean breast of it.

How did the truth get to the papers, is the question. We're young indeed, then, it is true. But must not the full-fledged interviewer of the present day have been a grub at some time? and, if so, may not he then have lain snugly ensconced in the comfortable folds of Poe's black frock?

It is difficult to meet with absolute documentary evidence such a statement as Griswold makes in regard to the poet borrowing money of a lady, and then, when asked to return it as promised, threatening to exhibit a correspondence that would make the woman infamous. Griswold manages, however, to admit that whatever his subject might have been with men, he was "*different*" with women; and the numerous letters which I have seen in the poet's hand to the select circle of his near lady friends, mark his relations with them as characterized by uniform delicacy, deference, and chaste feeling. That this glittering generality of Griswold's, in this instance of the borrowing, is another glaring falsehood, every known attribute of the poet tends to show.

As regards Mr. Poe's letters alluding to his dangerous illness, concerning which Mr. Griswold states that Poe was not dangerously ill at all at the time, I have the testimony of a most estimable lady now living, at whose house Mr. Poe was a frequent visitor, that Mr. Poe was almost at death's door at the time from an attack of congestion of the brain, which was in reality the final cause of his death. I have also the testimony before me in Mr. Poe's own hand, spite of Griswold's statement that there was no literary or personal abuse of him in the journals of which Poe complained, that at this very time he (Poe) brought a suit for libel against one of his vilifiers and obtained "exemplary damages."

Speaking of the severing of Poe's connection with *Graham's Magazine,* Dr. Griswold writes : " The infirmities which induced his separation from Mr. White and Mr. Burton at length compelled Mr. Graham to find another editor " ; and also in the same connection, " It is known that the personal ill-will on both sides was such that for some four or five years *not a line by Poe was purchased for Graham's Magazine."* The italics are Dr. Griswold's. He evidently believes with Chrysos, the art patron in W. S. Gilbert's play of " Pygmalion and Galatea," that when a person tells a lie, he "should tell it well."

It is a patent fact, that, among the indignant refutations of Griswold's mendacious memoir of Poe, which was published both in newspaper and magazine form previous to its being included with Poe's works, was a manly and spirited defence of the poet written by Mr. Graham in the *New York Tribune.* Mr. Graham, a few months later, wrote in his own magazine a more extended review of Griswold's memoir, from which we append the following significant extracts : " I knew Mr. Poe well, — far better than Mr. Griswold ; and, by the memory of old times when he was an editor of *Graham's,* I pronounce this exceedingly ill-timed and unappreciative estimate of our lost friend *unfair* and *untrue.* It is Mr. Poe as seen by the writer while laboring under a fit of the nightmare ; but so dark a picture has no resemblance to the living man. It must have been made in a moment of spleen, written out and laid aside, and handed to the printer, when his death was announced, with a sort of a chuckle. He is not Mr. Poe's peer, and I challenge him before the country even as a juror in the case." Of the parallel drawn between Poe and Bulwer's Francis

Vivian in "The Caxtons," in which Dr. Griswold paints in lurid colors the alleged envy and vaulting ambition of the poet, Mr. Graham writes : "Now this is dastardly, and, what is worse, it is false. It is very adroitly done, with phrases very well turned, and with gleams of truth shining out from a setting so dusky as to look devilish. Mr. Griswold does not feel the worth of the man he has undervalued, he has no sympathies in common with him, and has allowed old prejudices and old enmities to steal, insensibly perhaps, into the coloring of his picture. They were for years totally uncongenial, if not enemies ; and during that period Mr. Poe, in a scathing lecture upon ' Poets of America,' gave Griswold some raps over the knuckles of force sufficient to be remembered.

"Nor do I consider Mr. Griswold *competent*, with all the opportunities he may have cultivated or acquired, to act as his judge, — to dissect that subtle and singularly fine intellect, to probe the motives and weigh the actions of that proud heart. His whole nature — that distinctive presence of the departed which now stands impalpable, yet in strong outline before me, as I knew him and *felt* him to be — eludes the rude grasp of a mind so warped and uncongenial as Mr. Griswold's."

This statement of Mr. Graham's was in the form of an open letter to Mr. N. P. Willis, and carefully avoided any specific personal charges, demonstrating more exactly the basis of Dr. Griswold's unscrupulous and malignant animus. As Dr. Griswold never presumed to make any detailed public reply to this or similar articles derogatory to the fairness of his views, it is perhaps as well that the more specific charges that might have been made, have been reserved for the present time.

Mr. Graham is now living, and when I last saw him he was in excellent health. I was then, of course, intent upon securing data in regard to the life of Poe, and in a conversation with Mr. Graham, some peculiarly significant facts touching Griswold's veracity in particular were elicited.

Mr. Graham states that Poe never quarrelled with him, never was *discharged* from *Graham's Magazine;* and that during the "four or five years" italicized by Dr. Griswold as indicating the personal ill-will between Mr. Poe and Mr. Graham, over *fifty* articles by Poe were accepted by Mr. Graham.

The facts of Mr. Poe's secession from *Graham's* were as follows : —

Mr. Poe was, from illness or other causes, absent for a short time from his post on the magazine. Mr. Graham had, meanwhile, made a temporary arrangement with Dr. Griswold to act as Poe's substitute until his return. Poe came back unexpectedly, and, seeing Griswold in his chair, turned on his heel without a word, and left the office, nor could he be persuaded to enter it again, although, as stated, he sent frequent contributions thereafter to the pages of the magazine.

The following anecdote well illustrates the character of Poe's biographer. Dr. Griswold's associate in his editorial duties on *Graham's* was Mr. Charles J. Peterson, a gentleman long and favorably known in connection with prominent American magazines. Jealous of his abilities, and unable to visit his vindictiveness upon him *in propria persona*, Dr. Griswold conceived the noble design of stabbing him in the back, writing under a *non de plume* in another journal, the *New*

*York Review.* In the columns of the *Review* there appeared a most scurrilous attack upon Mr. Peterson, at the very time in the daily interchange of friendly courtesies with his treacherous associate. Unluckily for Dr. Griswold, Mr. Graham saw this article, and, immediately inferring, from its tone, that Griswold was the undoubted author, went to him with the article in his hand, saying, "Dr. Griswold, I am very sorry to say I have detected you in what I call a piece of rascality." Griswold turned all colors upon seeing the article, but stoutly denied the imputation, saying, "I'll go before an alderman and swear that I never wrote it." It was fortunate that he was not compelled to add perjury to his meanness, for Mr. Graham said no more about the matter at that time, waiting his opportunity for authoritative confirmation of the truth of his surmises. He soon found his conjectures confirmed to the letter. Being well acquainted with the editor of the *Review*, he took occasion to call upon him shortly afterwards when in New York. Asking as a special favor to see the manuscript of the article in question, it was handed to him. The writing was in Griswold's hand.

Returning to Philadelphia, he called Griswold to him, told him the facts, paid him a month's salary in advance, and dismissed him from his post on the spot.

So it becomes evident that the memory of Poe's biographer, confused upon the point of his discharge from *Graham's*, has saddled Poe with the humiliation and disgrace that alone belonged to him. The probing of the personal history of Rufus W. Griswold is like stirring up a jar of sulphuretted hydrogen, — it exhales nothing but foul and loathsome odors. Most of the associations of this man in private life are too vile to

place before refined readers.    One anecdote I may be permitted
to give, to illustrate his utter heartlessness and depravity.

At one time in his career he met and became well acquainted with two ladies (sisters) from South Carolina, who
were reputed to be very wealthy.    He paid them every atten-
ion, and finally became engaged to one of them, whom he
shortly afterwards married.    On the very day of the wedding,
and almost immediately after the ceremony, he was informed
that the estimable lady whom he made his wife was a por-
tionless bride.    There had been no attempt made by the lady
to create the impression that she was wealthy, nor did she
dream for a moment that a supposed fortune, and not herself,
had secured the villain's attachment.    Dr. Griswold made
short work of sentiment and conscience.    On the day after
the wedding, he coolly informed his bride at the breakfast-table
that they must part forever, giving for the pretext a reason so foul, so monstrous, that its repetition in these pages
is impossible, from the shocking indecency of the atrocious
subterfuge.    Spite of tears and protestations, he deserted
the bride of a day, never to return to her, nor com-
municate with her again.    It is a matter of surprise that a
man capable of such diabolical mendacity as Dr. Griswold has
shown himself to be, should have found anything favorable to
say in his memoir, nor would he have done so, probably, had
not the poet's pre-eminent genius made the few truths to be
found in the biography as familiar as household words to the
literary world.

The next important statement made by Dr. Griswold, and,
unquestionably, the most heinous falsehood to be found in
the whole tissue of fabrication which has been so extensively

copied as "the life of Edgar A. Poe," is the statement in regard to Poe's alleged breaking of his engagement with Mrs. Sarah Helen Whitman, of Providence, Rhode Island. I may be permitted, in introducing what I have to offer on this subject, to present a letter elicited by Mr. Griswold's original statement, written by Mr. William J. Pabodie an esteemed and influential citizen of Providence : —

To the Editors of the New York Tribune : —

In an article on American Literature in the *Westminster Review* for April, and in one on Edgar A. Poe in *Tait's Magazine* for the same month, we find a repetition of certain incorrect and injurious statements in regard to the deceased author, which should not longer be suffered to pass unnoticed. These statements have circulated through half a dozen foreign and domestic periodicals, and are presented with an ingenious variety of detail. As a specimen, we take a passage from Tait, who quotes as his authority Dr. Griswold's memoir of the poet : —

"Poe's life, in fact, during the three years that yet remained to him, was simply a repetition of his previous existence, notwithstanding which his reputation still increased, and he made many friends. He was, indeed, at one time, engaged to marry a lady who is termed 'one of the most brilliant women in New England.' He, however, suddenly changed his determination ; and, after declaring his intention to break the match, he crossed the same day into the city where the lady dwelt, and, on the evening that should have been the evening before the bridal, 'committed in drunkenness such outrages at her house as made necessary a summons of the police.'"

The subject is one which cannot well be approached without invading the sanctities of private life ; and the *improbabilities* of the story may, to those acquainted with the parties, be deemed an all-sufficient refutation. But, in view of the rapidly increasing circula-

ion which this story has obtained, and the severity of comment
which it has elicited, the friends of the late Edgar A. Poe deem it
an imperative duty to free his memory from this unjust reproach,
and oppose to it their unqualified denial. Such a denial is due,
not only to the memory of the departed, but also to the lady
whose home is supposed to have been desecrated by these dis-
graceful outrages.

Mr. Poe was frequently my guest during his stay in Providence.
In his several visits to the city I was with him daily. I was acquainted with the circumstances of his engagement, and with the
causes which led to its dissolution. I am authorized to say, not
only from my personal knowledge, but also from the statements of
all who were conversant with the affair, that there exists not a
shadow of foundation for the stories above alluded to.

Mr. Poe's friends have no desire to palliate his faults, nor to
conceal the fact of his intemperance, — a vice which, though never
habitual to him, seems, according to Dr. Griswold's published statements, to have repeatedly assailed him at the most momentous
epochs of his life. With the single exception of this fault, which
he so fearfully expiated, his conduct, during the period of my acquaintance with him, was invariably that of a man of honor and a
gentleman ; and I know that, in the hearts of all who knew him
best among us, he is remembered with feelings of melancholy interest and generous sympathy.

We understand that Dr. Griswold has expressed his sincere regret that these unfounded reports should have been sanctioned by
his authority ; and we doubt not, if he possesses that fairness of
character and uprightness of intention which we have ascribed to
him, that he will do what lies in his power to remove an unde-
served stigma from the memory of the departed.

WILLIAM J. PABODIE.

PROVIDENCE, June 2, 1852.

In answer to this, we find Dr. Griswold in the rôle of a bully, impudently attempting to put down Mr. Pabodie's dignified statement, *vi et armis*. He writes to Mr. Pabodie a private letter as follows : —

NEW YORK, June 8, 1852

DEAR SIR, — I think you have done wrong in publishing your communication in yesterday's *Tribune* without ascertaining how it must be met. I have never expressed any such regrets as you write of, and I cannot permit any statement in my memoir of Poe to be contradicted by a reputable person, unless it is shown to be wrong. The statement in question I can easily prove on the most unquestionable authority to be true ; and unless you explain your letter to the *Tribune* in another for publication there, you will compel me to place before the public such documents as will be infinitely painful to Mrs. Whitman and all others concerned. The person to whom he disclosed his intention to break off the match was Mrs. H——t. He was already engaged to another party. I am sorry for the publication of your letter. Why you did not permit me to see it before it appeared, and disclose in advance these consequences, I cannot conceive. I would willingly drop the subject, but for the controversies hitherto in regard to it, with which you are acquainted. Before writing to the *Tribune*, I will await your opportunity to acknowledge this note, and to give such explanations of your letter as will render any public statement on my part unnecessary.

In haste, yours respectfully,

R. W. GRISWOLD.

W. J. PABODIE, ESQ.

To this insolent and impotent letter, which was tesselated with scandalous and irrelevant stories respecting Mr. Poe's relations with some of his most esteemed and valued friends,

Mr. Pabodie replied by calmly reiterating his published statement in the *New York Tribune*, and by adducing further proof of Griswold's audacious fabrications. The tone of this letter is in striking contrast to that of Griswold's virulent and threatening note. Its forbearing mildness indeed renders it open to criticism on this ground.

June 11, 1852.

MR. RUFUS W. GRISWOLD.

DEAR SIR, — In reply to your note, I would say that I have simply testified to what *I know to be true*, namely, that no such incident as that so extensively circulated in regard to certain alleged outrages at the house of Mrs. Whitman, and the calling of the police, ever took place. The assertion that Mr. Poe came to Providence the last time with the intention of breaking off the engagement you will find equally unfounded when I have stated to you the facts as I know them. In remarking that you had expressed regret at the fact of their admission into your memoir, I had reference to a passage in a letter written by Mrs. H. to Mrs. W., which was read to me by the latter some time since. I stated in all truthfulness the impression which that letter had left upon my mind. I enclose an extract from the letter, that you may judge for yourself : —

"Having heard that Mr. Poe was engaged to a lady of Providence, I said to him, on hearing that he was going to that city, 'Mr. Poe, are you going to Providence to be married?' 'I am going to deliver a lecture on Poetry,' he replied. Then, after a pause, and with a look of great reserve, he added, 'That marriage may never take place.'"*

I know that from the commencement of Poe's acquaintance with

* In another letter Mrs. H. writes, referring to this conversation, indignant at the use which Dr. Griswold had made of these innocent words more than a year after she had reported them, "These were Mr. Poe's words, and these were all."

Mrs. W., he *repeatedly urged her to an immediate marriage.* At the time of his interview with Mrs. H., circumstances existed which threatened to postpone the marriage indefinitely, if not altogether to prevent it. It was, undoubtedly, with reference to these circumstances that his remark to Mrs. H. was made, certainly not to breaking off the engagement, as his subsequent conduct will prove. He left New York for Providence on the afternoon of his interview with Mrs. H., not with any view to the proposed union, but at the solicitation of the Providence Lyceum ; and on the evening of his arrival delivered his lecture on American Poetry, before an audience of some two thousand persons. During his stay he again succeeded in renewing his engagement, and in obtaining Mrs. W.'s consent to an immediate marriage.

He stopped at the Earl House, where he became acquainted with a set of somewhat dissolute young men, who often invited him to drink with them. We all know that he sometimes yielded to such temptations, ar.d on the third or fourth evening after his lecture, he came up to Mrs. Whitman's in a state of partial intoxication. I was myself present nearly the whole evening, and do most solemnly affirm that there was no noise, no disturbance, no " outrage," neither was there any "call for the police." Mr. Poe said but little. This was undoubtedly the evening referred to in your memoir, for it was the *only* evening in which he was intoxicated during his last visit to this city ; but it was not " the evening that should have been before the bridal," for they were not then published, and the law in our State required that they should be published at least three times, on as many different occasions, before they could be legally married.

The next morning, Mr. Poe manifested and expressed the most profound contrition and regret, and was profuse in his promises of amendment. He was still urgently anxious that the marriage should take place before he left the city.

That very morning he wrote a note to Dr. Crocker, requesting him to publish the intended marriage at the earliest opportunity, and intrusted this note to me, with the request that I should deliver it in person. You will perceive, therefore, that I did not write unadvisedly in the statement published in the *Tribune.*

For yourself, Mr. Griswold, I entertain none other than the kindest feelings. I was not surprised that you should have believed those rumors in regard to Poe and his engagement ; and although, from a regard for the feelings of the lady, I do not think that a belief in their truth could possibly justify their publication, yet I was not disposed to impute to you any wrong motive in presenting them to the public. I supposed rather that, in the hurry of publication and in the multiplicity of your avocations, you had not given each statement that precise consideration which less haste and more leisure would have permitted. I was thus easily led to believe, from Mrs. H.'s letter, that upon being assured of their incorrectness, and upon learning how exceedingly painful they were to the feelings of the surviving party, you sincerely regretted their publication. I would fain hope so still.

In my article in the *Tribune,* I endeavored to palliate their publication on your part, and to say everything in your extenuation that was consistent with the demands of truth and justice to the parties concerned. I would add, in regard to Poe's intoxication on the evening above alluded to, that to all appearances it was as purely accidental and unpremeditated as any similar act of his life. By what species of logic any one should infer that in this particular instance it was the result of a malicious purpose and deliberate design, I have never been able to conceive. The facts of the case and his subsequent conduct prove beyond a doubt that he had no such design.

With great respect,

Your obedient servant,

REV. RUFUS W. GRISWOLD.                    WILLIAM J. PABODIE.

It will be seen by this correspondence that the attempt of Dr. Griswold to browbeat Mr. Pabodie was courteously but firmly and unanswerably met. Dr. Griswold never paid the slightest attention to this letter, contenting himself with leaving on record the outrageous scandal that has since obtained an almost unprecedented circulation in the numerous memoirs of Poe, based upon Dr. Griswold's malicious invention, that have been published. The introduction of the story of the banns would seem to come under the head of what lawyers call "an accessory after the fact." Dr. Griswold had probably heard that the banns were *written*, if not *published*, and took advantage of this information to adroitly garnish his story with them. To set this question at rest forever, I have obtained permission to quote the following passages of a letter received from Mrs. Whitman in August, 1873 : —

"No such scene as that described by Dr. Griswold ever transpired in my presence. No one, certainly no woman, who had the slightest acquaintance with Edgar Poe, could have credited the story for an instant. He was *essentially* and *instinctively* a gentleman, utterly incapable, even in moments of excitement and delirium, of such an outrage as Dr. Griswold has ascribed to him. No authentic anecdote of coarse indulgence in vulgar orgies or bestial riot has ever been recorded of him. During the last years of his unhappy life, whenever he yielded to the temptation that was drawing him into its fathomless abyss, as with the resistless swirl of the maelstrom, he always lost himself in sublime rhapsodies on the evolution of the universe, speaking as from some imaginary platform to vast audiences of rapt and attentive listeners. During one of his visits to this city, in the autumn of 1848, I once saw him, after one of those nights of wild excitement, before reason had fully recovered its throne. Yet even *then*, in those frenzied moments when the doors of the mind's 'Haunted Palace' were left all unguarded, his words were the words of a princely intellect, overwrought, and of a heart only too sensitive and too finely strung. I repeat that no one acquainted with Edgar Poe could have given Dr. Griswold's scandalous anecdote a moment's credence.

" Yours, etc.,

"S. II. WHITMAN "

In regard to Mr. Griswold's professed friendship for Poe, which he endeavors to demonstrate in copies of a correspondence which I cannot refrain from thinking was extensively "doctored" by the doctor, to suit his purpose, I am able to present an extract from an autograph letter of Dr. Griswold written to Mrs. Whitman in 1849.

The object of this was evidently to cool Mrs. Whitman's friendship for Mrs. Clemm, thus preventing their further intimacy. This was desirable to Dr. Griswold for evident reasons.

NEW YORK, December 17, 1849.

MY DEAR MRS. WHITMAN, — I have been two or three weeks in Philadelphia attending to the remains which a recent fire left of my library and furniture, and so did not receive your interesting letter in regard to our departed acquaintance until to-day ; I wrote, as you suppose, the notice of Poe in the *Tribune*, but very hastily.

I was not his friend, nor was he mine, as I remember to have told you. I undertook to edit his writings, to oblige Mrs. Clemm, and they will soon be published in two thick volumes, of which a copy shall be sent to you. I saw very little of Poe in his last years. . . . . I cannot refrain from begging you to be *very* careful what you say or write to Mrs. Clemm, who is not your friend, nor anybody's friend, and who has no element of goodness or kindness in her nature, but whose whole heart and understanding are full of malice and wickedness. *I confide in you* these sentences for your own sake only, for Mrs. C. appears to be *a very warm friend to me.* Pray destroy this note, and, at least, act cautiously, till I may justify it in a conversation with you.

I am, yours very sincerely,

RUFUS W. GRISWOLD.

This brief note affords a tolerably good specimen of the utter duplicity of the man. In his printed memoir of Poe, he quotes a correspondence indicating professed friendship ; in private, he squarely owns that no friendship ever existed between Poe and himself.

He writes that Mrs. Clemm is a friend to no one, and stigmatizes her character, and in the same breath speaks of her warm friendship for him.

Had Griswold lived in Othello's time, no one could have disputed with him the position of "mine ancient," honest Iago.

From a correspondence from Mrs. Clemm, who, there can be no reasonable doubt, is correctly described by Willis as "one of those angels upon earth that women in adversity can be," we find the most positive testimony that Dr. Griswold's association with collecting the works of Poe, and of writing a memoir of the author, was purely voluntary and speculative.

It presents simply the fact of a designing and unscrupulous man, prompted by hatred and greed of gain, taking advantage of a helpless woman, unaccustomed to business, to defraud her of her rights, and gratify his malice and his avarice at her expense.

A miserable pittance having been given to Mrs. Clemm in exchange for Poe's private papers, Dr. Griswold draws up a paper for Mrs. Clemm to sign, announcing his appointment as Poe's literary executor, not omitting of course a touching allusion to himself. This is duly signed by Mrs. Clemm, and printed over her signature in the published editions of Poe's works. But if the wording of this curious paper be carefully observed, it will be noted that nothing whatever is said in it of any request by Poe that Dr. Griswold should write a memoir of his life. This duty was properly assigned to Mr. Willis, — of all men, familiar with the subject, the most competent to fulfil such a task, — and his tender and manly tribute to the stricken genius was all that could have been wished, all that the world called for.

Mrs. Clemm had no idea, at the time she signed the paper which she scarcely understood, that Dr. Griswold had any intention of supplementing Mr. Willis's obituary with any memoir by his own pen: It was a piece of gratuitous malice, — the act of a fiend exulting over a dead and helpless victim.

The tone of Poe's critique of Griswold, in his review of the "Poets and Poetry of America," which unquestionably inspired the reverend doctor's malignant hatred, scathing as it is, will impress the reader with its outspoken manliness and integrity of purpose. What a contrast to the biography that, while undermining the very foundations of Poe's moral and social character, yet hypocritically professes to be dictated by friendship, and written in a *generous* spirit! I fear that Dr. Griswold's precious specimen of his generosity will go on record in the history of literature as an everlasting monument of his despicable meanness!

Dr. Griswold was, take him all in all, about as well fitted to be Poe's biographer, as Mr. Preston Brooks would have been to have written an impartial life of Charles Sumner. And, indeed, whenever it becomes possible for a Rufus W. Griswold to write a true transcript of the life of an Edgar A. Poe, then will perpetual motion have become possible, the world will find it easy and comfortable to arrest its revolutions at pleasure, and balloon voyages to the planets will become as popular and as practicable, as is a trip to Saratoga at the present day.

# LETHE.

# LETHE.

By C. McK. LEOSER.

'ERBORNE with carking grief and weary weight
   of sin,
   Yearneth the patient Christian for the time
   When, to the ringing seraph-song sublime,
   Falleth the load, and proud he entereth in,
   Escaped the world's annoy and Satan's gin ;
  And, fain to leave the worn and tasteless joys,
  And all the bitter glare and hollow noise,
Seeth his everlasting life begin.
So toward thee, Lotos, home to sweet souls given,
  The outworn toiler in the muck of trade,
  Or where the opinion of the public 's made,
Turns at the hour to which his thought has striven ;
  Then, the dull burden from his shoulders laid,
Forgets his care in thee, thou gentler earthly Heaven.

# THE MIRACLE OF THE FISHES.

# THE MIRACLE OF THE FISHES.

## By ROBERT R. ROOSEVELT.

N these modern days the public affects a taste for sporting. Whether in imitation of the recreations of the aristocratic and leisure-loving nations of the Old World, or impelled by an increase of sedentary occupations among ourselves, Americans are given more and more to spending their holidays in the chase of beast, bird, or fish. In the spring, as soon as the frost lets go its grip of the waters, the young New-Yorker's fancy lightly turns to thoughts of visiting the trout-ponds of Long Island, — the Mattowacs of the jovial J. Cypress, Jr., of glorious memory ; the sportsman's Paradise of the more sententious and didactic Frank Forester, — where trout are "frighted from their natural propriety" by many strange devices in the way of fishing-tackle. During the summer the effectual fires of that hottest of resorts, Saratoga, pale before the attractions of the Adirondacks, and our deluded men about town exchange the miseries of stifling nights and villanous aperients for the tortures of merciless black gnats and tunefully triumphant mosquitoes. And in the fall the knights of the quill and yard-stick drag their unaccustomed limbs over "stony limits" and through meadowy morasses in an imaginary devotion to sportsmanship, and a praiseworthy, if unrewarded, pursuit of quail. Diana is worshipped even more assiduously than Venus, whose longest trains and biggest chignons are not as alluring as a lively trout-brook, a lovely snipe-bog, or a stand on the bass rocks by the "sounding sea." All this is healthful, and promises well for the "millions yet to be" on this continent, of whom it will be said, —

"They can jump, and they can run,
  Catch the wild goat by the hair, and hurl their lances in the sun."

Metaphorically, of course, as the only goats worth catching — reference clearly not being intended by the poet to the docile creatures that roam about the shanties of Goat Town, and alternate their diet between old hats and bits of paper — are those of the Rocky Mountains, who are not given to letting themselves be caught in their inaccessible fastnesses even by the most agile hunter of the liveliest poetical imagination; while the discovery of gunpowder has converted the romantic lance into the prosaic, but game-compelling, breech-loading rifle or shot-gun.

Fortunate as is this change, and promising, as it does, an immense increase of muscular Christianity, it has its defects, and of course it inflicts much suffering by compelling the experienced sportsman to listen to the puerilities of the beginner, — the skilful angler to have his soul harrowed up by being asked about the virtues of a fishing *pole*, or graciously informed of the special attractions of some favorite *tail* fly, till he feels his "torture should be roared in dismal hell," — or the accomplished shot to be assured by some bungler that a muzzle-loader "shoots stronger than a breech-loader"; but, trying as these are, they are not the only points to be condemned. The system itself is wrong. At present there are

ut two classes in the community who consider game at all ;
ne of these regards it simply as something to be eaten, the
ther looks upon it solely as something to be killed. The
irst may be dismissed with scarce a word, as utterly beneath
he contempt of well-regulated minds : for it has been the
roper thing to condemn indulgences of the stomach from
he days of the dishes of peacock's tongues to the times of
*pâtes de foie gras ;* and the latter class alone is worthy of our
tender care and wise advice. These individuals, these sportsmen, as they call themselves, vainly consider they have attained their ends when they have had a good day's sport,
when they have filled their bags or their creels, when they have
drunk deep draughts of the breath of the morning and feasted
their eyes on the pictures drawn by Nature's golden pencil,
when they have cast the fly delicately and accurately, when
they have tossed the bass-bait into the combing crest of the
outermost breaker, or when they have shot straight and " held
true." Poor fools, they have put their happiness into a con-
densed pill, and swallowed it up at a gulp ; they have had
but a moment's pleasure in what should have been "linked
sweetness long drawn out." In their "dull, untutored minds"
they never dreamed of what a " thing of beauty and a joy
forever" a fish could be made, and only used him in the last
stage of his existence, and, by opposing, ended him. They
thought only of the trout that were in the brook or the bass
that were in the sea, wished that there were more, but never
speculated how they came there. At this point science and
morality alike come in and say, "What thou sowest, that shalt
thou also reap ; if thou wouldst have fish, fish must thou
even plant, precisely as thou plantest corn ; if thou wantest

whiskey and beans, if thou desirest soup, how canst thou
expect a crop when thou art always harvesting and never
planting ?

It may not seem romantic to grow game for pursuit, as a
market-man raises beef for the table ; and the fisherman might
imagine he was being degraded into a fishman ; but the
sporting pleasures of modern times must be tempered by the
influences of scientific discoveries, or our utilitarian age, with
its proud nets and its improved weapons, will sweep them out
of existence.  It is true that a "glorious nibble" may reward
the sublimated angler, living in the highest heaven of his
art, for a day of patience, but the rest of mankind would like
a rise or a bite now and then, just for variety.

The delights of a day on Long Island are not to be denied, but they are different from what they once were.  In
former days, when the genial and brilliant J. Cypress, Jr., visited Raccoon Beach — now misnamed Fire Island — to kill
ducks, and his friend, Ned Loftus, cast a fly so "far and delicately and suspendedly" that it took wings and flew away, ducks
and snipe were so abundant that you did not have to whistle,
and they came to you, my lad, and you could cast your lines
into any brook with a full and abiding faith that trout were
there to see.  Now, the Madeira is good, — yea, verily, we
know whereof we speak, — and the sherry came over before
any other emigrant, and the champagne flows in a never-
ending stream ; but the preserves are bare of fish, and the
gentle angler has to trust to a French cook to fill his stomach, that should be cloyed with trout.

Nor is this the fault of the fish ; the finny tribe are not
to blame ; they are willing to do their part.  A trout lays

en thousand eggs ; imagine such a reckless amount of ma-
ernity ! Ten thousand eggs, ten thousand fry, ten thousand
ngerlings, ten thousand "speckled beauties," in their well-
ounded proportions ; ten thousand atoms of fishing happiness.
Nurse the little ones, teach them to play at hide-and-seek
when their natural enemies are about, protect them from evil
ssociates, warn them against wicked ways, and keep their
ins from the paths that lead down to death, and they will
rowd the waters, stock all the preserves, and, lifting up their
voices, beg to be caught. An Englishman was once invited
o visit a friend, who allured him to the country under the
pretence of having a fine carp pond, whereas he had only
brought fifty fish, thinking that enough for a week's sport,
and turned them loose a few days previously. Conceive the
host's horror when his sporting friend caught forty-seven the
irst morning, before breakfast. In American preserves, etiquette requires the fisherman to return to the water the trout
that he catches, that he may catch them over again, or leave
hem to the next guest. But if the sportsman insists that there
s no great enjoyment in raising fish, and that he would rather
hoe corn and dig potatoes for amusement, not to speak of
profit, he should console himself with the recollection of the
benefit he confers on society, of the addition he makes to
he supply of fish food, that monument of the brain, that
estorative of the machine-shop of ideas, that fertilizer of in-
elligence, which the students of man's body affirm it to be.
He should contemplate the advance to be effected in the
human race when the intellect is developed by unlimited
condiment. Though the fisherman be a member of the Lotos,
and may think, from his surroundings, that a development of

brain is not necessary, he should still have pity and consideration for the benighted world outside the gifted few, and help the common mind into a higher sphere of development. Therefore, whether the fisherman be a philanthropist, a sportsman, or even a member of the Lotos, he should allow no blind ideas of present recreation to keep him from a duty he owes mankind, and should not presume to wield the rod till he has worked the breeding-trough.

Suppose there are ten thousand sportsmen, and each should supervise the incubation of but one pair of fish, raising ten thousand young, and every pair of those young should subsequently raise their ten thousand, it would require a syndicate or statistician to compute the result. The lakes and rivers and the ocean itself would become crammed with fish, till the traveller could make the voyage to Europe dry-shod on their backs; ships would get fish-bound, and have to be cut out: mankind would have to go without washing, and drink whiskey. to allow the fish sufficient water; and such a millennium of sportsmanship would have arrived as was never dreamed of in the wildest reaches of sporting philosophy. Then there would be no empty creels, no blank days, none of those perverse hours when trout will not rise, and none of those painfully insinuating questions, when the sportsman at last returns with a goodly mess, as to where he bought them and how much he paid for them. The jeers of the unbelieving would then be in vain, and the hearts of the best of the human species would be made happy by the miraculous reproductiveness of fishes.

# THE LOTOS-EATERS.

# THE LOTOS-EATERS. *

By ALFRED TENNYSON.

"COURAGE!" he said, and pointed toward the land,
"This mounting wave will roll us shoreward soon."
In the afternoon they came unto a land,
In which it seemed always afternoon.
All round the coast the languid air did swoon,
Breathing like one that hath a weary dream.
Full-faced above the valley stood the moon ;
And like a downward smoke, the slender stream
Along the cliff to fall and pause and fall did seem.

A land of streams ! some, like a downward smoke,
Slow-dropping veils of thinnest lawn, did go ;
And some thro' wavering lights and shadows broke,
Rolling a slumbrous sheet of foam below.
They saw the gleaming river seaward flow
From the inner land: far off, three mountain-tops,
Three silent pinnacles of aged snow,
Stood sunset-flush'd : and, dew'd with showery drops,
Up-clomb the shadowy pine above the woven copse.

* This poem is the only article in the volume not written by a member of the
Lotos Club.   It is inserted for the reason that it suggested the name of the Club,
and in acknowledgment of Mr. Tennyson's acceptance of the dedication. — Eds.

## LOTOS LEAVES.

The charmed sunset linger'd low adown
In the red West : thro' mountain clefts the dale
Was seen far inland, and the yellow down
Border'd with palm, and many a winding vale
And meadow, set with slender galingale ;
A land where all things always seem'd the same!
And round about the keel with faces pale,
Dark faces pale against that rosy flame,
The mild-eyed melancholy Lotos-eaters came.

Branches they bore of that enchanted stem,
Laden with flower and fruit, whereof they gave
To each, but whoso did receive of them,
And taste, to him the gushing of the wave
Far, far away did seem to mourn and rave
On alien shores ; and if his fellow spake,
His voice was thin, as voices from the grave ;
And deep-asleep he seem'd, yet all awake,
And music in his ears his beating heart did make.

They sat them down upon the yellow sand,
Between the sun and moon upon the shore ;
And sweet it was to dream of Fatherland,
Of child, and wife, and slave ; but evermore
Most weary seem'd the sea, weary the oar,
Weary the wandering fields of barren foam.
Then some one said, "We will return no more ";
And all at once they sang, "Our island home
Is far beyond the wave ; we will no longer roam."

## CHORIC SONG.

### I.

HERE is sweet music here that softer falls
Than petals from blown roses on the grass,
Or night-dews on still waters between walls
Of shadowy granite, in a gleaming pass ;
Music that gentlier on the spirit lies,
Than tir'd eyelids upon tir'd eyes ;
Music that brings sweet sleep down from the blissful skies.
Here are cool mosses deep,
And thro' the moss the ivies creep,
And in the stream the long-leaved flowers weep,
And from the craggy ledge the poppy hangs in sleep.

### 2.

Why are we weigh'd upon with heaviness,
And utterly consumed with sharp distress,
While all things else have rest from weariness ?
All things have rest : why should we toil alone ?
We only toil, who are the first of things,
And make perpetual moan,
Still from one sorrow to another thrown :
Nor ever fold our wings,
And cease from wanderings,
Nor steep our brows in slumber's holy balm ;
Nor hearken what the inner spirit sings,
"There is no joy but calm !"
Why should we only toil, the roof and crown of things ?

### 3.

Lo! in the middle of the wood,
The folded leaf is woo'd from out the bud
With winds upon the branch, and there
Grows green and broad, and takes no care,
Sun-steep'd at noon, and in the moon
Nightly dew-fed ; and turning yellow
Falls, and floats adown the air.
Lo! sweeten'd with the summer light,
The full-juiced apple, waxing over-mellow,
Drops in a silent autumn night.
All its allotted length of days,
The flower ripens in its place,
Ripens and fades, and falls, and hath no toil,
Fast-rooted in the fruitful soil.

### 4.

Hateful is the dark-blue sky,
Vaulted o'er the dark-blue sea.
Death is the end of life ; ah, why
Should life all labor be ?
Let us alone. Time driveth onward fast,
And in a little while our lips are dumb.
Let us alone. What is it that will last ?
All things are taken from us, and become
Portions and parcels of the dreadful Past.
Let us alone. What pleasure can we have
To war with evil ? Is there any peace

In ever climbing up the climbing wave ?
All things have rest, and ripen toward the grave
In silence ; ripen, fall and cease :
Give us long rest or death, dark death, or dreamful ease.


5.

How sweet it were, hearing the downward stream,
With half-shut eyes ever to seem
Falling asleep in a half-dream !
To dream and dream, like yonder amber light,
Which will not leave the myrrh-bush on the height ;
To hear each other's whisper'd speech ;
Eating the Lotos day by day,
To watch the crisping ripples on the beach,
And tender curving lines of creamy spray ;
To lend our hearts and spirits wholly
To the influence of mild-minded melancholy ;
To muse and brood and live again in memory,
With those old faces of our infancy
Heap'd over with a mound of grass,
Two handfuls of white dust, shut in an urn of brass !


6.

Dear is the memory of our wedded lives,
And dear the last embraces of our wives
And their warm tears ; but all hath suffer'd change ;
For surely now our household hearths are cold :
Our sons inherit us : our looks are strange :

And we should come like ghosts to trouble joy.
Or else the island princes over-bold
Have eat our substance, and the minstrel sings
Before them of the ten years' war in Troy,
And our great deeds, as half-forgotten things.
Is there confusion in the little isle?
Let what is broken so remain.
The Gods are hard to reconcile:
'T is hard to settle order once again.
There *is* confusion worse than death,
Trouble on trouble, pain on pain,
Long labor unto aged breath,
Sore task to hearts worn out by many wars
And eyes grown dim with gazing on the pilot-stars.

### 7.

But, propt on beds of amaranth and moly,
How sweet (while warm airs lull us, blowing lowly)
With half-dropt eyelids still,
Beneath a heaven dark and holy,
To watch the long bright river drawing slowly
His waters from the purple hill, —
To hear the dewy echoes calling
From cave to cave thro' the thick-twined vine, —
To watch the emerald-color'd water falling
Thro' many a wov'n acanthus-wreath divine!
Only to hear and see the far-off sparkling brine,
Only to hear were sweet, stretch'd out beneath the pine.

8

The Lotos blooms below the barren peak :
The Lotos blows by every winding creek :
All day the wind breathes low with mellower tone :
Thro' every hollow cave and alley lone
Round and round the spicy downs the yellow Lotos-dust is
    blown.
We have had enough of action, and of motion we,
Roll'd to starboard, roll'd to larboard, when the surge was
    seething free,
Where the wallowing monster spouted his foam-fountains in
    the sea..
Let us swear an oath, and keep it with an equal mind,
In the hollow Lotos-land to live and lie reclined
On the hills like Gods together, careless of mankind.
For they lie beside their nectar, and the bolts are hurl'd
Far below them in the valleys, and the clouds are lightly
    curl'd
Round their golden houses, girdled with the gleaming world :
Where they smile in secret, looking over wasted lands,
Blight and famine, plague and earthquake, roaring deeps and
    fiery sands,
Clanging fights, and flaming towns, and sinking ships, and
    praying hands.
But they smile, they find a music centred in a doleful song
Steaming up, a lamentation and an ancient tale of wrong,
Like a tale of little meaning tho' the words are strong ;
Chanted from an ill-used race of men that cleave the soil,
Sow the seed, and reap the harvest with enduring toil,

Storing yearly little dues of wheat, and wine and oil ;
Till they perish and they suffer — some, 't is whisper'd —
      down in hell
Suffer endless anguish, others in Elysian valleys dwell,
Resting weary limbs at last on beds of asphodel.
Surely, surely, slumber is more sweet than toil, the shore
Than labor in the deep mid-ocean, wind and wave and car ;
O rest ye, brother mariners, we will not wander more.

PLAYERS IN A LARGE DRAMA.

# PLAYERS IN A LARGE DRAMA.

By I. H. BROMLEY.

OUBTLESS there are people in the world who coddle themselves with the idea that they are utterly and absolutely sincere ; that though in a general sense it may be true that "all the world 's a stage and all the men and women merely players," there is at least no ringing up of curtains or strutting before the footlights in their own profoundly earnest lives.  Is it cynicism to dispute them in their fond delusion ; to say that no such thing is possible ; that with all their efforts to be simple, direct, natural, they are forever artificial, — artful in manner, address, features, step, and even in the very attitude of worship and the diction of prayer ?  Art wedded Nature on that bridal morn in Paradise when our Mother saw she was unclad, and plucked her wardrobe from the fig-tree ; and there has been neither divorce nor separation since.  Then began costumes, and from the fig-leaf flowed the infinite pageantry of soft and silken stuffs, of lace and muslin, satins and embroideries, with which brides, wives, and mothers have come rustling down to us from Paradise, bringing with them, with all their art and artifice, the garden's fragrance and the garden's light and life and joy.

Since the exodus from Eden, Nature has been kept in flower-pots and set in windows, framed behind foot-lights, with curtain at the front and wings at the sides, pieced out with stove-pipe hat and fringed with claw-hammer coat, surmounted and crowned with the chignon, built upon with the pannier, and draped with the polonaise. Art and artifice and artfulness and all things artificial came in with the curse, and will go out only with the millennium. This. is the trail of the serpent over us all, that we are always acting, that we can never be utterly sincere. Is it a hard statement? Do you believe that, in your serious, solemn work in the world, there is no little bell to ring up your curtain, no audience to act before, no mimicries nor tricks nor deceptions, nor strutting back and forth, nor rolling up of eyes, nor phrasing of sentences, nor any of the thousand things that make a play a play? Have you ever sat before a camera and listened to the stereotyped address of the photographer, " Sit easy now, and look natural"? Do you think you did it? There are easy-sitting, natural-looking Matilda Janes and Charles Augustuses enough hanging on walls and shut up in albums to girdle this round globe with such a belt of ghastly caricature as would haunt the day with fearful visions, and distort our dreams with nightmares; and every mother's Matilda Jane and Charles Augustus of them all, though they sat cramped and gasping before the portrait-painting sun, thought it was nature, and that they were altogether sincere; and even when they rose from their constrained ease and unnatural naturalness, and stretched themselves with weariness, never dreamed they had been fooling themselves while they tried to fool the sun. Let us be frank about it, for we are all together in it;

who is there that has not some time sat with folded hands
and vacant stare before the dreadful camera?

Some one not long ago defined a "bore" to be "a person
who persists in talking about *him*self when you want to be
talking about *your*self." The readiness with which the newspapers — most of which, I may be permitted to say, know a
good thing when they see it — snapped up the definition, and
the general acceptance of it as a crisp, bright truth, were
proof enough that to the average man it came as a sort of
revelation. Men who had encountered bores, and been annoyed by them, did not know that the difference between
themselves and the bore was only in opportunity, — did not
know, indeed, that they were bored by egotism only in the
degree in which it hindered them from being egotistical themselves. But this touchstone of some quaint philosopher revealed themselves to themselves in such manner as to raise
a smile at their own absurdity. We do not know how absolutely selfish we are till some such thing uncovers us and
shows us as we are, — acting small deceptions to ourselves
with no audience but the looking-glass. We are hide-bound
— pachydermatous — with egotism. Largely as we may talk
of patriotism and its sacrifices, of religion and its tender
offices, of humanity and universal brotherhood, we are all so
self-centered that we never, for country, church, or fellow-man,
rise above ourselves entirely ; our wings forever touch the
ground, and the highest attainment of our very best endeavor
is in reaching a line of conduct whose motives are freest
from what is sordid, mean, and base.

There are several thousand men who, in their daily walk
down Broadway, for at least half a block before they reach

the full-length mirrors which stand for a sign on the side-walk before a picture-dealer's shop, are oppressed with anxiety lest some conceited coxcomb shall get between them and the glass. Not one of them believes he is conceited or vain, and not one of them but thinks the man in front who obstructs the glass is a disgusting puppy who has not the sense or the modesty to keep his vanity and foppishness from public sight. It's a long procession that goes daily down Broadway, but to these reflections concerning the brutal stupidity and vanity of the person in front, each one succeeds as naturally and regularly as to his order in the line and his place before the glass. What a world of mincing and smirking and strutting the Broadway mirrors witness every day, and how many thousand times a day is the question, " How do I look ? " put to them by men who would actually be surprised should they catch themselves at it ! Of all forms of selfish-ness, the one reckoned most contemptible, fit to be treated only with derision and jeers, is the vanity of personal beauty or good looks. It is that sort of self-engrossment that has hardly body enough to be called a vice, a harmless hollowness that can only be despised or pitied. No one likes to confess to this weakness. And yet everybody knows that the softest and easiest approach to everybody else can always be reached by judicious and not overdone allusions to personal attractions.

The truth is, that we not only never open our hearts to each other, but we do not open them to ourselves. Shall I say, then, that in our moments of serenest joy or or our crises of supremest need, when, helpless and hopeless, we lift our weak hands upwards, we do never consciously strip our-selves bare of all concealments ? Shall I say that before God

ve are in some sense playing parts, and that if he reads us,
t is through his own omniscience, and not because in our
most secret devotions we open the book and turn its pages
before him ?   Abel's altar of sacrifice, Abraham's memorial of
he covenant, Moses receiving the law behind the curtain
of cloud in the wondrous drama of Sinai, the ark of the cov-
nant, the hangings of the tabernacle, the paraphernalia of the
emple, the priestly garments with their tinkling bells, the cere-
nonial observances and the grand ritual of worship, the teach-
ngs of allegory and parable, the stoled and surpliced priests,
he chant of solemn organ, the summons of church bells, the
pulpit vestments, the groined arches and dimly lighted aisles,
he well-dressed worshippers, the attitude of devotion, the rhyth-
nic flow of praise, and the choice rhetoric of prayer, attest
hrough all the ages the symbolism by which alone we may
approach the Uncreated.   In our worship we are but actors.

As individuals we act to ourselves and others ; as nations
and aggregate humanity we play our parts.   History is but an
acted play, and human progress an unwritten drama.    It is
but a difference in degree between the strutting royalty of the
boards and the kingly carriage of the real ruler.   Each to his
audience.   Congresses and parliaments are but the "people"
of the stage, sometimes unravelling and sometimes tangling
the plot, burdened always with a sense of importance, as though
they were making the play, when in fact they are only swept
along by it.   The great events of history have always been
dramatic, always set on in tableaux, and all the great characters of the world, robber-kings, regicides, crusaders, command-
ers, heroes, saints, and martyrs, have posed themselves in
dreary and pitiful self-consciousness for the pen of the his-
torian or pencil of the artist.

No one of the thousands who were present can ever forget the dramatic features of the great Chicago Convention of 1860. A vast auditorium was crowded almost to suffocation ; upon the great stage in front sat delegates from all the Northern States, while in the center the representatives of the press were plying busy pencils. A party that had never been in power, and had no strength in any Southern State, was in convention to nominate a President. The scene, the occasion, the surroundings, the vast multitudes of men, and the distinguished actors engaged, were all combined in one intensely dramatic effect. Some of the most earnest and thoughtful statesmen in the country were there, called by what they deemed a momentous crisis to act together for the country and for humanity. There was an indescribable something in the air which presaged disturbance. It was a close, oppressive atmosphere, like that which goes before the wild simoom. The feeling was general that the country was on the eve of some great sweeping change, but how grand were the possibilities, how woful the sacrifices, and how complete the regeneration that lay in the near future, the wisest had not dared to dream. The curtain was ringing up on the first act of a tremendous drama, and these were the players ; earnest and serious, yet players. Preliminaries were settled and organization effected, and the Convention came to its work. The audience adjusted itself, the army of reporters sat with pencils poised, the telegraph-operators handled their keys nervously, — the roll-call of the States began. Maine, New Hampshire, Vermont, were called, and as if they were nothing more than the dead numerals of a process, the chairman of each delegation announced the scattered votes. The

Secretary called "Massachusetts." Over at the right of the chair a man not much known then outside his State, short in stature, with a full round face that had in it the rare combination of womanly tenderness with heroic firmness, stood up in his seat and said, "Mr. President." The President said, "The gentleman from Massachusetts!" There was an instant's pause. Hardly had the hush fallen when, in a voice that itself was music, John A. Andrew said, "Mr. President, the Commonwealth of Massachusetts casts twenty-one votes for William H. Seward, four votes for Abraham Lincoln." No more than that. Only the announcement of a vote. But here was more in it than figures. In all that multitude there was no one so obtuse as not to know that here came on the stage a royal knight among the heralds. "The Commonwealth of Massachusetts" was his announcement, and with that there came not merely the sapless factors in a process of mathematics, but a grand and stately Commonwealth, crowned with the memories of all her lofty sacrifices and glorious achievements, proud of her line and lineage, of her storied places and her battle-fields, her statesmen, heroes, scholars, martyrs, and, above all, of her front rank in devotion to freedom and human rights, swept into the line with a kingly consciousness of right of precedence. Dramatic, but wonderfully well acted, on no small stage and in no small way.

Then Rhode Island and Connecticut were called, and gave their answers as merest matter of statistics. The Secretary called "New York." At the head of the New York delegation a tall man, thin and spare, rose slowly to his full height and then stepped upon his chair. Then, in a metallic ringing voice, with distinct articulation, as though about beginning an ora-

tion, Mr. William M. Evarts said, "Mr. President," and the
President replied, "The gentleman from New York." There
was just the suggestion of noise, a low whispering buzz in the
great wigwam that hindered the silence from being complete.
But here was an actor who did not underestimate effect. "Mr.
President," said he, "I wait till the Convention is in order."
It was hardly necessary for the President to use his gavel or
to say, "The Convention will be in order." The hush that
followed his last word was absolute. Every head leaned forward, every eye was bent upon the gentleman from New York.
Then, when he knew he had them all, bristling forward, eager,
intent, — although his announcement had been discounted, and
they knew precisely what was coming, — he said, " Mr. President, the State of New York casts seventy votes for William
Henry Seward." And the Convention broke into the wild and
vociferous cheering which the practised orator and actor had
planned for with such careful arrangement of details. The
dramatic effect which, by skilful pauses, deliberate utterance,
and the magnetism of voice and eye, conveyed to the Convention a sense of the personal affection and tender regard,
combined with loyal devotion and unbounded admiration, with
which Mr. Seward was regarded by the citizens of the great
State of New York, was carefully studied and wonderfully
well done. These were but touches of by-play, however, in
the larger drama.

There were two ballots. — Seward leading, Lincoln following
and gaining. There was a feeling, as the third call began,
that this was not only to end the balloting, but to name the
President. The excitement was intense. Nimble pencils followed down the list of States, catching up the changes that,

according to their significance, were received with a ripple of
sensation or a burst of cheers. Before the last State was
called the event had been discounted ; and though there were
then four votes lacking to a choice, the result was deemed to
have been reached. Instant on the response of the last State,
Ohio, by her chairman, transferred four votes from Mr. Chase
to Mr. Lincoln. The full-voiced Secretary turned his face
upward to the skylight in the roof above him, and called out
the vote to men who, without stopping to record it, ran to the
sides of the wigwam and shouted the news to the surging multitudes outside. Within the building grave and serious men
embraced and kissed each other, old men danced and young
ones cheered and shouted and flung aloft their hats, the rafters
rang with multitudinous roar ; and as the wave of sound rolled
through the doors and windows, the streets took up and echoed
it and rolled it back, cheer answering cheer in one great
jubilee of joy. With the first burst of it a gunner standing
by his loaded piece with lighted match reached forth his
hand ; there was a little flash, — a puff of cloud, — and into
the midst of that wild tumult of applause there leaped from
the brazen belly of the gun a roar that crowned and drowned
all. The curtain fell on the first act, of a new historic period.
The roar of artillery that was to be the music of the drama
in its stately progress, with a sublime fitness which there was
no prophet to recognize, had greeted the occasion and saluted
its hero. That moment a great, grand man, whom the world
then scarcely knew, stepped out with modest self-distrust upon
a career such as the world had never seen, laid his hand
with solemn sense of responsibility upon the great task before him, and never ceased to bear its burdens grandly, while

he wore its honors meekly, till from under the assassin's hand, his labor done and his fame complete, God called and crowned him.

Magnificent acting there was in all this, and magnificent beyond description or power of expression was the acting which came after it. How, at the drawing of the crimson curtain of the war, the world beheld a million men in arms, and saw their camp-fires stretched across a continent, — how the stage was crowded with heroes great and petty, — how the guns were shotted, and the blood was real, and the madness and the fury of the charge were hot and earnest, — how utterly genuine were the agony of parting and the anguish of bereavement, — and how real and remorseless the Death that brooded over loved ones, — we may all freshly and tearfully remember. Grand and tremendous tragedy, and for the most part grandly acted! Possibly we are not yet far enough away from the smoke and the roar of the conflict and the glamour of the fields to adjust this political revolution fairly to the motives out of which it proceeded and upon which it was carried along. We are apt to idealize epochs and peoples as we invariably do individuals. It seems very plain that men were only puppets in the play. While men were spinning threads to patch a sail, God took their puny policies for the strands of his eternal purpose, and twisted them together in a cable that should hold a ship at anchor, while it offered rescue to a race. Let us not deceive ourselves as to man's work or man's purpose in the war. It was not nearly so large, so pure, or so noble as we try to think. Into it entered all manner of motives, — ambition, hatred, envy, jealousy, love of strife, and the passion for notoriety, as well as

igh and holy love of country, solemn sense of duty, sympa-
hy with the oppressed, love of humanity, and the knightly
entiment of chivalry. Out of the fiery furnace into which
ll these diverging purposes were turned, there came, through
he chemistries of God's grace, pure gold. Here let us walk
with unshod feet and reverent head, as one who treads on
holy ground and witnesses the mystery of miracle.

It is no detraction from the dignity and importance of
man's work in the world to judge of it as done altogether
and always with foot-lights at the front. To our eyes, level
with the stage, the acting all seems very grand ; the sweep
of royal robes and the glitter of coronets and crowns, the
retinues that wait on kings, the assemblies where laws are
made and the courts where they are administered, the officers
of justice, marching armies, noise of tumult, din of strife, shift-
ng and mingling tableaux of nations, states, and peoples, are
all as real to us as emotion or pulsation. Go up a hundred
feet or more, and from some tower window look down upon
it all. How much less it seems! Go still higher, till your
men become insects and your horses creeping things, and all
the glitter and spangle of trappings and dress are the merest
flash of phosphorescent foam ; and higher still, till you lose
all perception or discrimination of writhing, gliding, twisting,
individual men, and see below you only Man. Ah ! from even
here, a short rifle-range above the world, what petty things
men are, and how petty their pursuits ! But look ! how large
the world itself ; how broad and beautiful, as from this height
we gather in the view ! Men are little, but the world is
large, and Humanity is great. Let us be frank with and to
ourselves, acquaint ourselves with our own limitations, not

overestimate our capacities or our importance. Our parts are assigned, — we have them to act. That our mission in the world is no more nor less than this, should not deter us from the loftiest ideals and a supreme endeavor. For you who stand at the wings waiting to go on, there need be no discouragement in this discovery. Make up your mind that you take with you in this great venture all the infirmities that came down from Eden, with all the possibilities of being great and true that stretch out from Calvary. You are no Atlas bearing up the world. Your responsibility ends with your own acting, and does not reach to God's disposing. Because you may not attain perfection, is no excuse for not struggling in a great and hearty way toward it. Truth is as absolute as perfection. Go toward it, not as a child toward a bawble, hoping to grasp and hold it fast, but follow it reverently as the chosen people followed the fiery pillar to the shores of Jordan and the Land of Promise. Strip yourself first of the deceit that you are not acting, and then act well your part. They are the greatest actors who enter into the character they play, and utterly forget themselves. And they who act grand characters themselves become grand. Make your ideal grand, lofty, pure; saturate yourself with its spirit, walk in your conception of it, act it, be it. The world's applause is not all that's worth living for, but it is not to be despised. Accept it modestly, deserve it faithfully, but never bow the knee to reach it, or be distracted by it from your purpose and your work. You all things invite; for your fresh face and springing step and all your youthful possibilities, a hearty welcome and sincere applause await. The curtain rises, the play is called: go on, and God go with you!

# BERTHA KLEIN.

# BERTHA KLEIN.

*A STORY OF THE LAHN.*

By W. J. FLORENCE.

DOCTOR, will you hear my story?
Thank you.

I was a student at the University of Bonn, and during my vacations often went fishing up the Lahn. The Lahn, you know, is a charming river that empties into the Rhine opposite Capellen and the beautiful castle of Slolzenfels. During these excursions I made my headquarters at the " Drei Kronen," a delightful little German inn, situate on the right bank of the river, a few miles above Lahnstein, and kept by one Caspar Lauber. From Caspar I learned where were to be found the best fishing-spots, and after our day's sport we would sit under the vines and tell stories of the past. He related anecdotes of the Austrian campaign, — he had been a soldier ; I would speak of my American home, far away on the Ohio : and as we watched the smoke curling from our meerschaums of canaster, we would intermingle the legends with staves of " Die Wacht am Rhein " and " Tramp ! tramp ! the boys are marching." I had been two summers thus passing my holidays between Nassau and Lahnstein, doing duty with rod and reel, when one day, while at my favorite pastime, I became aware I had a companion; for above me on the bank stood a pretty girl intently watching my endeavors to hook a Barbillion that had evaded my attempts to land him.

"O, so near! 't is too bad!" said she with a pretty Nassaun accent. "If the Herr try his luck over there, above the ferry-boat, he will have fine sport." And then, as if she felt ashamed at having spoken to a stranger, she dropped her eyes, while a blush at once overspread her face.

"Thank you, pretty one," said I. "I supposed I had known all the favorite fishing-spots on the river; but if the Fraulein will conduct me, I will go and try above the ferry-boat."

"Philip Becker always fishes there when he visits Fachbach, and never without bringing in a well-filled pannier"; this in a half-timid, half-sad voice.

"Well, show the way, Fraulein." She led the way to the place indicated, when I ventured to ask her name.

"Bertha Klein," she said.

"And do you live near, Fraulein?"

"Yes, over there near the Lahneck. Father works at the Eisensmeltz. I am returning from there now. I bring him his dinner at this hour."

"Every day at this hour you cross the ferry with papa's dinner, do you?"

"Yes, Herr."

"And who is Philip Becker, of whom you spoke a moment since?"

"Philip, he lives at Nassau with Keppler the chemist." And at pronouncing Philip's name I thought I saw a dark shadow pass over Bertha's pretty face. "Philip is coming to Fachbach next week, so papa tells me." And Bertha's pretty face again grew darkly sad.

She was of the blond type of German girl, blue-veined, with large bright eyes, fringed with silken lashes, long and regular, while her golden hair hung down in twin braids at her back.

"Good day, sir."

"Good day, Bertha." And she tripped quickly up the bank and disappeared.

The evening found me at the Drei Kronen, with a well-filled basket of carp and barbel.

" There, landlord," said I, " you may thank the pretty Bertha Klein for my luck to-day. She it was who told me where to throw my line."

" Oh! oh! Have you seen Bertha? She is one of the prettiest girls in the Duchy, and good as she is beautiful." And then Caspar gave me a history of her family. Her father was foreman at the Eisensmeltz, or furnace. Bertha was an only child. Philip Becker, a chemist's clerk at Nassau, was a suitor for her hand ; and although Philip was an ill-favored, heavy lout, Bertha's mother thought him every way worthy of her child. "I do not think the girl likes him," said the landlord, "nor should daughter of mine wed him." And we drank a glass of Ashmanshauser to the health of the pretty Bertha Klein.

Day after day Bertha would stop a moment to speak a few words to me as she journeyed to and from the furnace. Our acquaintance ripened into friendship, friendship into — Well, you will see, doctor. One day, while climbing the hillside together, picking wild flowers, stopping ever and anon to listen to the rushing of the river at our feet or the loud roaring of the iron furnace across the stream, Bertha, suddenly stooping, cried, " O Albert, see here! Look! oh, look! Here is the *Todesblume*." *

" The Todesblume! Where, Bertha ? "

" Here at my feet ; and, see, the mountain-side is full of them. Do you know the legend of this flower ? "

" No, darling, tell it me."

We seated ourselves on a large mass of stone, portions of the fallen ruin of the old castle Lahneck, that towered for a hundred feet above our heads ; and while Bertha's clear blue eyes sparkled with a strange mixture of mystery and earnestness, and betimes referring to the bunch of small white flowers in her hand, she related to me the LEGEND OF THE TODESBLUME.

" This old castle up there behind us was once the stronghold of the famous old freebooter, Baron Rittenhall, who, although considered a wicked, reckless, wild man by the world in general, yet loved his young and beautiful wife with the greatest possible affection. And, indeed, 't was said the immense treasures he had levied from vessels passing up and down the Lahn were spent in jewels, trinkets, and precious stones to decorate the person of his lovely wife, the Lady Rittenhall.

" One day a pilgrim passing the castle begged for alms. The pious Baroness gave him succor, while he in return gave her a single sprig of green. 'This,' said the holy man, 'if planted in early spring, will bear a small white flower, which is of rare virtue, for on St. Anne's day the possessor of this little flower may summon from the dead the spirit of his departed love.'

* Death-flower.

"'The spirit of one's departed love'? echoed the Baroness.

"'Yes, daughter,' rejoined the friar, 'at midnight on St. Anne's day, whoever will dissolve this flower in a goblet of Emser red wine, while repeating these words, —

> "From earth, from sea,
> From brook, from fen,
> From haunt of beast,
> From homes of men,
> Form of one I loved most dear,
> By Todesblume, appear! appear!"

shall bring to earth the loved departed one. Remember, daughter,' continued the pilgrim, ''t will require a brave heart to summon from the grave.' And, blessing her, he took his leave.

"On the following day the Lady Rittenhall, with her own white hands, planted the sprig in a pretty, bright spot, near where we are now sitting," said Bertha; and her pretty voice grew sweetly tremulous as though it had tears in it.

"Day after day would the beautiful Lady of Lahneck watch the little flowers budding from the stems, until they seemed to grow under the sunlight of her eyes, so that when the Baron returned from an incursion among the neighboring mountains, he found the hillside whitened with them.

"'This is thy work, dear one,' said the Baron, as, descending from his saddle at the drawbridge, he pointed proudly to the carpet of white flowers at his feet.

"'I knew 't would please thee,' smilingly replied she; and, leading to the dining-hall, while the Baron and his retainers washed 'their draughts of Rhenish down,' she related the story, as told her by the pilgrim.

"'By my falchion,' said the Baron, ''t is a well-told tale; and here I pledge me, should fate or fortune take thee from me, bride of mine, I swear by my sword to summon thee to earth again. In token of the promise, I drink this goblet to the table round.'

"That night, while the Baron held high revel with his brother troopers in the dining-hall, the Lady Rittenhall sat trembling in her chamber; a strange dread seemed to possess her, a belief that she should be doomed by fate to test the powers of the Todesblume. A cold hand seemed to clasp her heart, and scarcely had her maids been summoned to her apartment, before the good lady was a corpse.

"The Baron, once so wild and reckless, now became sad and morose. He was inconsolable. Now clasping in his arms the form of his once beautiful wife, now pacing the long corridors of the castle that echoed gloomily his stifled sighs, he was indeed broken in heart and spirit.

"Scarce had they laid the body in the grave before the Baron again remembered his pledge to test the death-flower. St. Anne's day was now fast approaching, and his oath must be fulfilled." Here Bertha stopped, and, looking quietly about her, asked me if I did not hear a footstep.

"No, darling," said I; "go on with your story; there is no one near us."

"I am sure, Albert, I heard a footfall in the bushes behind us," continued she; and her voice again grew tremulous and tearful.

"You are mistaken, Bertha," said I, reassuring her. "Let me hear your story out."

"Well, the Baron shut himself up in the very chamber where

is lady had breathed her last, and on the morning of St. Anne's day was found lying dead, while on the table stood a goblet of Emser red wine, in which floated the broken petals of the Todesblume ; and they do say," whispered Bertha, "that a small white dove was seen flying from the upper window of the castle at midnight of St. Anne's day."

"Very well told, Bertha," said I. And my boyish heart was filled with a wild desire to test the maiden's love. " I would do as much for you, my Bertha, should you be taken from me. I would call you back to earth if it were possible, and here I swear it," said I, rising to my feet.

" O Albert, do not, I implore you!" cried Bertha, wildly throwing her arms about my neck.

" Very pretty ! very pretty !" growled a rough voice behind us, —"very pretty ; I am sorry to disturb your love-song, Fraulein." And a heavy, thick-set young man, with stooping shoulders, and straight long hair, put back behind his ears, came out of the bushes at our back. His eyes, heavy and leaden-colored, seemed half closed, while he hissed his words between two rows of singularly white and even teeth.

" Pardon, Herr American. Bertha's mother sent me in quest of her. 'T is near sunset, and the gossips at Fachbach might say evil things of the Fraulein if they knew — "

" Philip Becker, stop! I know what you would say," cried she. " Do not insult me. Tell my mother I will come."

" She bade me fetch you," hissed Philip Becker, while his eyes slowly closed their lids as if they were too heavy to keep open, — " to fetch you, Fraulein ! — fetch you."

" Hark you, friend," said I. " You have delivered your message. Your presence is no longer needed. I will accompany Miss Bertha home."

"I spoke not to *you*," said Philip, fairly yellow with rage.

"But I spoke to you, sir! You see, you frighten the girl. Take your dark shadow hence, or I will hurl you into the river at my feet."

With a wild yell the chemist's clerk sprang at my throat, and would have strangled me, but with a sudden jerk I struck him full in the face with my head, and, throwing him off his feet at the same moment, I sent him spinning down the hillside ; nor did he stop till he reached the river, from whence I saw him crawl, dripping wet.

"Very pretty, Fraulein! Very pretty, Herr American!" shouted Philip, as he shook his clinched fist at me, and disappeared at the foot of the hill. Bertha, who had screamed and hid her face, now became alarmed for my safety. "He will do you some fearful harm, I know he will ; he is vindictive and relentless. O Albert! it is all my fault," sobbed the pale girl ; and, picking up her flowers, we journeyed toward the village. "I did not know he had arrived from Nassau," said she, "though mother told me he was coming soon. I hate him, and I shall tell him so, though I am sure he knows it already."

We had reached the garden of the Drei Kronen, when Bertha said, "Come no farther with me. Leave me here, Albert. I must go on alone, now ; 't is best." And giving me the sprig of the Todesblume, she tripped away towards her home.

Placing the flowers in my letter-book, I strolled into the tavern, where I found the landlord endeavoring to dry the dripping Philip Becker with a flask of Ashmanshauser. The moment Philip saw me enter, he dropped his glass, and with a curse on his heavy lip darted out of the door.

"He has told me all about it," said the landlord, roaring

with laughter ; "and it served him right. Egad, I wish I had been there to see it." So we took our pipes, and after had related the story of my struggle with Philip on the hillside, took my candle from the stand and went to bed, of course to dream of Bertha Klein.

Day after day during the long summer would we meet at the foot of the Lahneck, there to renew our vows of eternal constancy. Philip Becker had gone back to Nassau, vowing vengeance on the entire American nation, and myself in particular. Bertha and I would often laugh at the remembrance of poor Philip's appearance dripping on the river-bank, and with a prayer for his continued absence, we would again pick Todesblumes at the old trysting-place.

Thus matters went till near the month of September, when I was summoned home to America. My mother was dying with a sorrowing heart, and, torn between love and duty, I broke the news to Bertha.

"And must you go ?" cried Bertha. "O darling, I shall die ! "

" I shall return in the spring, my beloved, if God will spare me. The time will pass quickly ; you will hear from me by every mail, I promise you ; and here, where I first listened to your words of love, I again pledge my faith." So, kissing Bertha, I tore myself away.

"I will never see you again, my own, my only love." were the last words that caught my ear ; and, looking back, I saw poor Bertha, with her face buried in her hands, at the foot of the tower, where she first told the story of the death-flower.

With all speed I returned to Bonn, where I found letters awaiting me. I must at once return to the States. So, bidding my fellow-students adieu, I took my departure for Liverpool, and, securing passage by a Cunarder, in ten days reached New York ; four more days brought me to my mother's bedside. She had been very ill, but now gave promise of a slow recovery. Days, weeks, months, passed away, and I was constantly in receipt of letters from Bertha. The same old trusting love, the same pure, innocent sentiments, filled her pages, while an occasional small white flower would recall our meetings on the hillside at the Lahneck. " Here," Bertha would write, " is the Todesblume, to remind you of the little girl who awaits your return on the banks of the flowing Lahn."

It had been arranged that I should return to Germany in the spring ; and as my mother's health was fast returning. I looked forward to the date of my departure with great joy, when suddenly Bertha ceased to write to me. Several weeks elapsed, the holidays passed, and still no letter from my heart's idol. Can Bertha's mother have insisted upon her marrying Philip Becker ? Perhaps she is ill. Can she have forgotten me ? These and a thousand other surmises filled my brain, and I was in despair, when one day the postman brought me a letter with a German post-mark, but the address was not in Bertha's handwriting. I hastily tore it open ; it was from Caspar Lauber, landlord of the Drei Kronen.

Great God ! Bertha had been murdered ! found dead with three cruel stabs in her neck and breast ; and there at the very spot where I had left her on the hillside was the deed committed. Suspicion had fallen on Philip Becker, who had fled the country, while a reward was offered for his apprehension. I could read no further, but with a groan fell fainting o the floor. A long and serious illness followed, and for months I lay just flickering between life and death. In my moments of delirium I would often call for Bertha Klein, and with a maddened scream vow vengeance on the chemist's clerk. My dreams were of the river Lahn and its vine-covered hills. Then my fancy would picture Bertha struggling with Philip, and while he plunged the knife into her pure heart, I was held by a stalwart demon, who spat upon me and mocked my frantic efforts to free her from the murderer's grasp. Then the old castle of the Lahneck would fill my disordered vision, and at its foot, among the vines, I saw two youthful forms, — the one a tall, dark-haired youth, the other a blue-eyed German girl. In her hand she held a small white flower, and as she looked through tears of joy into the young man's face, the figure of a low-browed, wild, misshapen man arose behind them. Noiselessly he crept to the maiden's side, and with a hissing, devilish laugh, dashed headlong down the mountain-side into the river below, leaving the loving pair transfixed with fear and wonder.

When the bright spring days came, I grew somewhat better, but the physicians said my recovery would be a slow one.

My attendants would tell me of my ravings, of my constantly calling Bertha ; and, to humor my caprices, had brought, at my request, a small box containing Bertha's letters and the various love-tokens she had given me. In my porte-monnaie I found the little flower, — Bertha's gift, when she related the story of the Todesblume. It was pressed between two small cards, and indeed seemed almost as fresh as when the Fraulein gave it me. " This flower," said I, " will bring her back to me for a moment at least ; and when I am grown strong and well, I 'll try the spell."

The last day of June found me sufficiently recovered to journey to Saratoga, at the recommendation of my physician. I reached New York City, when I determined to go no farther until I tested the power of the death-flower.

To this end I put an advertisement in the paper: "A gentleman desirous of making some experiments in chemistry would like an unfurnished apartment in the upper portion of the city. The advertiser would prefer such apartment in a house not occupied as a residence. Apply," etc., etc., etc.

The third day after my advertisement appeared, an elderly German gentleman waited on me at my lodgings. He had just the apartment I desired, over a druggist's shop; in fact, the upper floor of a three-story house, unoccupied save by the old gentleman, who kept the drug-store beneath, and situated in a quiet up-town street, near one of the avenues.

I at once engaged the rooms, and on the following day made an inspection of the premises. I found the upper story to consist of two rooms of equal size. One room was entirely empty, and the other contained a long table, three wooden-bottomed chairs, while a large glass mirror over the mantel completed the furniture of the apartment.

"I have occupied this house but a few weeks," said the old German; "and as I am alone here, I shall be glad to have your company; so, if the Herr will take the apartments, he shall have them at his own price." And the old druggist bowed to the very ground in Teutonic politeness.

"What door is this?" said I, pointing to a small trap in the wall, about two feet wide, and just large enough to admit a man, stooping. This door had been concealed by the back of one of the chairs, and I thought the old gentleman seemed startled at my discovering it.

"I do not know for what purpose that door could have been constructed," said the old man; "but you see it leads to the other room." And, passing through, we found ourselves in the empty apartment.

After a word or two of necessary agreement, I hired the apartments for one month from date, and on the following Friday, St. Anne's day, I determined to try the potency of my magic flower.

At midnight, on the 26th of July, 1869, I sat alone in that chamber. Upon the table stood a silver goblet filled with Emser red wine. At the head of the table I had placed a chair, while I occupied another at the foot. The clock of St. Michael's Church commenced to strike the hour of midnight; at the first stroke I extinguished the light, and, dropping the flower into the goblet, slowly spoke the words, —

"From earth, from sea,
From brook, from fen,
From haunt of beast,
From homes of men,
Form of her I love most dear,
By Todesblume, appear! appear!"

As the echoes of the last stroke of twelve died upon my ear, a thin cloud of vapor rose from the goblet; at first it was of a violet hue, when suddenly it changed into bright crimson color, and, growing gradually dense and heavy, soon filled the room, while through the misty veil I saw globes of golden pearl dancing before my astonished vision, strange soft music played in sweetest strains about my ears, and, growing giddy at the sound, I felt I was falling from the chair. With a determination to resist the power that was pressing on my brain I held fast to the table, and cried again, "Appear! appear!"

The mist was now fast disappearing, and while the room grew bright, as though lighted by a thousand candles, I saw seated in the chair at the head of the table, dressed in the cerements of the grave, the ghost of Bertha Klein; her golden hair no longer braided down her back, but hanging loosely about her face; her eyes pure and blue as of old, but sad and weeping. A clot of blood upon her neck marked the spot where the murderer's knife had entered. Frozen with horror at the sight, I sat motionless for an instant; but her pitiful face and sorrowful look seemed to ask for words of compassion.

"Speak to me, Bertha; let me hear your voice," cried I.

Quick as a flash she rose, and with a cry of horror that chilled me to the heart's core, she screamed, "Look behind you quick, Albert! quick!"

I turned just in time to save my life; for the old druggist had stealthily entered through the trap-door in the wall, and was about to plunge a large dirk-knife in my back, when I caught his arm; in the struggle that ensued, I tore the wig from his head, and, making one desperate blow, I sent the knife intended for me into the heart of *Philip Becker*.

Now, doctor, I thank you for your attention. I have but one more favor to ask. Won't you speak to the chief physician? Appeal to my friends to have me released from this asylum, for I assure you I am no more a lunatic than you are.

# Nine Tales of a Cat.

# NINE TALES OF A CAT.

*A LEGEND OF MURRAY HILL.*

RESPECTFULLY DEDICATED TO THE PRESIDENT OF THE A. S. P. C. A.

By J. BRANDER MATTHEWS.

YOUNG De Jones was one of those nice young
  men,
    Supposed to belong to the upperest ten ;
    His manners were soft and aristocratic ;
He waltzed in a way that the girls called ecstatic,
While he flavored his talk with a wit that was Attic.
They said that his form was patrician in mould ;
        He had wealth untold,
        He had stores of gold ;
He had ancestors too, in the days of old ;
Yet his enemies called him a Fifth-Avenoodle,
Cause he parted his hair in front, like a poodle.

Returning one night from the joys of the dance,
To the house where he dwelt with his two maiden aunts,
He entered his chamber and cast off his clothes,
Then he sprang into bed, softly seeking repose.
He dreams, while he sleeps, of the blond Miss Tressyllian;
The fair dam-sell with whom he had danced the cotillon,
Whose father, 't was said, was worth more than a million.

In the midst of his dreams,
It suddenly seems
That he hears a shrill sound that no mortal could utter ;
Right through him it went, — like a hot knife through butter.
So he jumped to the window, threw open the shutter ;
On the fence in the yard he beheld a huge Cat !
Which was singing a song in the key of Z flat.
He shouted out " Scat ! " but the beast would not scatter.
Then he swore ; he said, Darn her ! and Dang her ! and Drat her !
And affirmed with an oath, could he only get at her,
He would beat her and bat her,
And reduce her indeed to inanimate matter !
He, in short, was as mad as a hare or a hatter.
But the Cat kept on yelling, to pause still refusing.
Right or wrong,
She continued her song,
In a way that, perhaps, she considered a-mew-sing.
De Jones thought for a second ;
He rapidly reckoned
All the ways that existed of trying to still her,
And at length he resolved upon murder ! he 'd kill her !
In the East, every city is ruled by a Mayor ;
In the West they are ruled by the Colt, au contraire.
So De Jones takes his pistol from out of his bureau,
With a fierceness suggesting the banks of the Douro,
With an ardor recalling the hot sun of Cadiz,
He takes aim, and he fires, and the Cat goes to Hades !
And De Jones goes to bed,
And to sleep, it is said,
With the hope in his heart that the Cat is now dead.

On the evening succeeding
This murderous proceeding,
n his room he was sitting, some poetry reading,
When he suddenly heard,
As he after averred,
\ most horrible noise : what could have occurred ?
t was dreadful, and dire, and supremely absurd !
t was ghostly and ghastly and ghoulish !
Ie threw open the shutter, and he felt rather foolish,
'et he stood firm and fast, though the night air was coolish.
One firmness, infirmity,
Or whate'er you may term it, he
'ossessed in abundance ; his temper was mulish.
\nd besides he felt sure that a sound like that
Could be naught but a Cat !
t might be a Tom or it might be a Tabby ;
It sounded indeed like a muscular babby !
Then he heard it again, — in the key of Z flat ;
T was the beast he had killed, — he was certain of that !
The ghost of the Cat
Had returned ! that was pat !
So he snatched up his pistol, and said, " The joke played is ! "
He took aim, and he fired, and the Cat went to Hades.

On the evening after
He was shaking with laughter ;
In the midst of his fun there arose a shrill sound ;
It came up from the ground.
It was not a shriek, it was not a moan,
It was not a growl, it was not a groan,

But its hollow tone
Chilled De Jones to the bone;
'T was the ghost of that Cat!
He was certain of that!
He began to be frightened, in spite of his boasts:
If a Cat have nine lives, can a Cat have nine ghosts?
He threw down the book he was reading ("Lord Bantam"),
For he feared that the phantom
Was going to haunt him,
To fret him and fright him; — it never shall daunt him!
So he snatched up his pistol, — 't would frighten the ladies, —
He took aim, and he fired, and the Cat went to Hades.

He lies tossing and turning throughout the long night;
Not a wink can he sleep, on account of his fright.
At the earliest light
He arises and walks to his office, — poor wight!
He 's a real-estate broker, but — strange metamorphosis —
Although customers come, he can scarce let 'em offices;
At his window, I 'm told,
He had caught a bad cold,
And his partners affirmed, they ne'er heard such a cough as his.
Young De Jones often wished, when he thought of the Cat,
To be deaf as a post, or as blind as a bat:
He would hear not and see not the terrible ghost,
Which returned night by night to his favorite post.
That evening again on the fence there sat
The ghastly old Cat,
With her horrible song in the key of Z flat!
Now no saint could endure an infliction like that,

So he snatched up his pistol, — his soul more afraid is, —
He took aim, and he fired, and the Cat went to Hades.

When the beast had been killed some six times or seven,
The cold he had sent De Jones straight to heaven.
     With two lives left,
     Of but seven bereft,
She may dance where his corpse 'neath the turf gently laid is.
The old Cat may rejoice without fear of hot Hades,
She may warble her song in the key of Z flat,
     She may scoff, she may laugh
     At his epitaph,
"Here lies young De Jones who was killed by a Cat!"

- - -

P. S. — MORAL.

When this tale was begun, with its horrible fun,
     I had morals in plenty,
     Some fifteen or twenty.
This tale now is done, and I cannot find one!
Just to keep you from thought and from wearisome dizziness,
I suggest as a moral, "Mind your own business!"

# JOHN AND SUSIE.

# JOHN AND SUSIE.

*A STORY OF THE STAGE.*

By CHANDOS FULTON.

## I.

Y friend Colton was one of those quiet, retiring, unostentatious men, whose many noble qualities of head and heart are not discovered except in the intimacy of friendship. Wordsworth must have had such a man in his thoughts when he wrote : —

> " He is as retired as noontide dew,
>   Or fountain in a shady grove ;
> And you must love him, ere to you
>   He will seem worthy of your love."

Not that, like the snail, my friend Colton kept within his shell, and had to be sought (though in his slow, methodic manner there was some analogy between him and that testacean) ; for he was not, by any means, a man to be 'drawn out," as the phrase is, by any species of social inquisition, and had to be known to be appreciated. His almost childish simplicity and candor of manner, and correct, straightforward conduct, left a favorable impression on all with whom he had business intercourse ; but few gave

him credit for the high-mindedness, the delicacy of sentiment, warmth of heart, and cultured refinement which constituted the sterling worth of the man. He cultivated few
friendships; not that he did not value the love of his fel-
low-beings, or was slow to discover good in others, or was
distrustful of humanity, or was reserved and retiring from
any motives of pride, but because his affection was too sincere and cogent to be diffusive.

Such men as John Colton are common, although, keeping
within the intimacies of friendship, they are little known ;
and it is seldom that such beautiful, though passive characters are employed by the dramatist or novelist in the elab-
oration of their wonder-exciting plots. In the whirlpool of
society they are sometimes caught, but speedily dashed out,
and float quickly back into the calmer waters of domestic
quiet. Such men are the true disciples of Him who died
to save us ; without any ostentation they are continually
doing good, and showing by their own happiness that it is
easy to make life enjoyable.

Colton did not marry till late in life, because, for many
years, his early widowed mother, and his two sisters, both
younger than himself, were dependent on him for support ;
for his father had always lived up to every cent that he
made, and, dying shortly after his son had gone into business, had left his family entirely destitute. Besides, he did
not believe that a man ought to marry until he could see
his way to comfortably provide for a wife ; and it was not
until he had seen his sisters married and settled, and purchased a home for himself, and installed his mother there-
in, that he was in this position ; and then he was a staid

middle-aged man, with plenty of ideas (or ideals?) on the
subject of marriage, but no definite purpose.

A great war now agitated the country, and his thoughts
were of Mars rather than of Venus.

A man of his nature naturally shrinks from the semi-barbaric
life of the soldier; but he would have enlisted and "gone
to the war," had not his friends convinced him he would
be of more service at home, — in many ways, such a careful, thoughtful, reliable man would be useful in such a time
of trust, judgment, and energy. He raised and subscribed
funds to recruit regiments; he prepared banquets for soldiers passing through the city *en route* to the seat of war;
he got up "war-meetings" to inspire the people and encourage the men in the field. In the great Sanitary Fair
he was a leading spirit; indeed, if it had not been for his
exertions, the great Christian enterprise would never have
been initiated in his city. He was chairman of various
committees, and devoted his whole time to the work. He
was in the building from morning until night, superintending
and assisting the arrangements. He was thus brought into
acquaintanceship with many ladies and gentlemen whom he
otherwise would probably never have met, for all gathered
together and united in the Samaritan's work; but, unmind-
ful of them, he attended to his business in his usual quiet
way, accomplishing a great deal and saying nothing about it..

It was at this time and in this way that he met
Miss Susie Jones, a petite, pretty, elfish brunette, whose
sharp black eyes flashed mischievously as she said something sarcastic and smart. And Susie, who was very vivacious and affable, was always saying something sarcastic and

smart, now bringing the laugh on herself as well as her neighbor, and some might have thought, indeed some openly declared, that she was malicious and cruel-hearted, and delighted to tantalize and provoke people by her remarks: these did her great injustice; they misjudged her entirely. She was kind-hearted and sympathetic, and in every respect a lovable character; but she had been endowed with the talent of sarcasm and repartee, which she frequently indulged, often inconsiderately, it must be admitted, but from an innocent, fun-loving spirit, and not from any cruel feeling. To many this characteristic was a sort of spice or seasoning of the dainty little dish, and rendered her society charming. It gave her individuality. If it had not been for this gift of epigram and repartee, which many dreaded, she would frequently, in the goodness of her heart, have been imposed on.

Once Susie said something that was quite cutting to Colton, which hurt his feelings very much, although no one would have thought so, for he was not a man to show his trouble any more than his many good qualities, except when occasion developed them. Susie soon perceived the effect of her words, and in her regret at having so thoughtlessly uttered them, she suffered greater heart-pangs than those she had inflicted, although John was extremely sensitive. She felt very sorry, yet could not well make an apology, as there was no excuse for one; but she resolved to make all reparation in her power in the future by kindness and deference to him, as she recognized in him a superior man. When she wanted some one to aid her in tying the evergreen festoon over the table, she asked John's assistance, instead of calling rich young Mr. Thomas, whom all the girls were

ifter, but who had sooner come to her than to any one
ilse ; and so she favored or honored him on every occa-
ion, much to the concealed merriment of many who thought
he was doing this merely to trouble him. The difference
n their ages, his being over double hers, prevented any
matrimonial surmises.

A pleasant acquaintance sprang up between John and Susie,
which, as the fair drew to a close, ripened into friendship, and they began to discover each other's many good
characteristics. John recognized the fact that there was none
of the sharpness in her heart that there was on her tongue ;
that she liked to plague him purely from innocent fun and
not maliciousness ; and she was equally quick to learn that
his plain appearance and quiet manner were accompanied
by the noblest characteristics of man.

If it had not been for that Sanitary Fair, I do not believe John ever would have married, — and, of course, he and
Susie were married.

They were married in the springtime, and their bridal tour
was extended throughout the summer to the fall, in travelling over the New England and Western States. John had
long thought, and Susie coincided with him, that one should
see the beauties of his own land before viewing those of the
Old World ; and this is why they travelled over this country,
instead of joining in the fashionable hegira across the ocean.
Susie had previously, with her parents, travelled over a portion of the tour ; but John had always, from necessity, been
kept closely to business, and could not until now take the
time, or much less afford the trip.

## II.

WHEN they returned in the fall, Mrs. Colton had the house ready for their occupancy, and immediately abdicated in favor· of the younger Mrs. C., having promised to visit in turn her two daughters.

John and Susie had gotten along together admirably, and he did not believe anything ever could occur which would mar their happiness ; such an idea never entered her head, for from temperament she was always accu tomed to look on the bright side of the picture.

It is true, John, quite sensitive now about his age, was nettled somewhat when quizzed about his marrying a girl young enough to be his daughter, and testily changed the conversation ; but when the remark was made to Susie, she would ask, —

" Now, would you like to know why I married John ? "

" Yes," of course all those questioned answered.

" Why, because I loved him ! Was n't that reason enough ? "

" Ho ! ho ! " John would exclaim, if within hearing. " But that is not the reason she gives me ! Why do you think she tells me she married me ? "

" For your money ? " some one would venture to re-mark.

" Pshaw ! "

" O, I was merely joking, of course ! What then ? "

" Let her explain herself. What was it, or rather why was it, Susie, dear ? "

" Why, because he asked me ! " Susie would laughingly

:ply ; and in time these unpleasant remarks no longer an-
oyed John.

He learned to bear the quizzing of Susie, and when in the
100d she was unmerciful.

John and Susie went much to the theatre, their cultivated
1stes enabling them to appreciate good performances ; and at
certain establishment a higher order of entertainment was
iven, and this they frequently attended.

One of the leading actors in the company, whom they both
dmired, was about the same age as John, as Susie learned
rom a reply in the " Answers to Correspondents " in a
veekly paper ; but he looked young enough almost to be
iis son, on the stage ; and as he always wore the same
:urly wig in public, few outside of the theatre knew it was
ine ; and beside him, off the stage, John, with his clear, full,
uddy cheeks, and slightly gray, though luxuriant hair, was
lecidedly the youngest looking, for the other, prematurely
roken by the arduous labors of his profession, showed his
/ears in his bearing and face as well as in his scant capil-
ary covering.

Susie could not refrain from quizzing John about the better
iooks of the actor ; and as often as they went to the theatre,
:he as frequently alluded to the subject, never supposing that
he took the matter to heart.

John, however, was annoyed, and evinced the fact, and his
mischievous, though devoted little wife did not spare him.

He availed himself of the excuse of a shower or any trivi-
ality not to take her to the theatre ; and she, surmising
the reason, provokingly declared he was jealous of the actor.

It soon became evident to his friends that there was something on John's mind that was worrying him, in his set, sorrowful features, intent though unattentive manner, and occasional half-suppressed sigh.

He managed, however, to assume his wonted smile and cheery manner in the presence of his wife, and so she did not notice the change in him which was perceptible to others.

A few days of mental worry will wear a man more than weeks of physical pain. In a few weeks John really did begin to look aged.

"O, I might have known it was no match for me!" he exclaimed one day, evidently unconscious or obvious of my presence at the adjoining desk.

I instantly decided to avail myself of the exclamation to ask an explanation, at the risk of being considered impertinent, in the hope that I might be able to cheer him up.

"Why, what is the matter?" I inquired.

"O, nothing!" he answered hastily, recalled to himself. He arose, took his hat, and was about leaving, when I detained him, alluded to ·the changes perceptible in him, and advised him to confide in me, assuring him that a confession of one's sorrows or crimes alike relieves the mind.

At first he insisted I was entirely mistaken, but after a while confided to me his trouble.

I — I knew the actor off the stage, minus his youthful wig and mustache : I shocked him by laughing outright in his face ; I could not help it.

"I don't blame her!" he observed with desperation. "Of course *he* would be better preserved than *I* am ; *he* has had nothing to do all his life but to play-act!"

"Nothing to do but to 'play-act'! That is enough to do! His life has been more arduous than yours, my dear friend!"

But "outsiders" have the idea that "play-acting" is so easy and simple that there is no work or wear in it; that, in fact, an actor's life is one long-drawn-out pleasure; and it was in vain that I endeavored to argue the point with John.

"Look at that man!" he would exclaim; and, supposing that he was more familiar with the actor's career than I was, though acquainted with him, I dropped the subject.

I went home to dine with him, and found that Susie had added to her collection of photographs of celebrities one of the venerable actor in a popular modern character, in which he appeared in all the glory of his curly wig, luxuriant mustache, etc., etc.

Of course, while showing this she did not miss the opportunity to give a sly thrust at John, and I spoke to her about the actor's art of "making up," and how deceptive in such cases appearances were, mentioning an actor whose mustache in the daytime is decidedly sandy, but which is jet-black on the stage. John being in another room, I asked if she did not think she worried him in thus quizzing him about his age, and she said no; for, it must be remembered, he carefully concealed his vexation of spirit from her.

"Don't blame her!" he said afterwards, — "don't blame her! O no, she does not think of me; this comes from the heart, and she is enamored of him; if it was merely a thought, a matter of the head, she would think of me as well!"

"Nonsense, man!"

He would not, however, listen to reason; he was satisfied

his wife no longer loved him, — at least as she had; she was enamored of the actor.

An idea occurred to me. I proposed to John, supposing he was acquainted with the actor, to have him to dine with him at his house.

"I don't know him!" he replied angrily.

"I will introduce you!"

"I don't want to know him!"

"Be advised, my friend."

"You are mad to propose this!" he responded indignantly.

We were walking down town; whom should I see coming up but the actor?

As he approached, I perceived that John did not recognize him off the stage; and I boldly introduced them, regardless of the probable consequences.

John was completely taken aback, and looked at me twice before accepting the actor's proffered hand, as if to assure himself he had not misunderstood me.

After a few pleasant words (on my part), we separated and passed on.

John burst out laughing as soon as out of hearing of the receding actor. I then explained to him how completely, by the aid of art, the theatrical artists could, and are often compelled by the exigencies of their profession to, metamorphose themselves, great actors making the matter a study.

"O, what a joke on me!" he exclaimed.

"You can make it a joke on Susie," I ventured to suggest.

"How?"

"By presenting him to her," I replied. "He is not all

hat fancy painted or the sun photographed, and you 'll have
he laugh on her!"

He acquiesced, and a day was appointed for the dinner. I
arried the invitation to the actor, who was an educated,
vell-bred gentleman, and prevailed on him to accept.

Susie was not altogether pleased at the idea of meeting
he actor, but appeared in her newest and finest dress at the
inner.

I arrived early, in order to witness the introduction. If
er husband was taken aback by the difference in the ap-
earance of the actor off and on the stage, she was dumb-
ounded ; for it was several minutes before she could speak.

After a very pleasant dinner I told "the story," having pre-
iously obtained John's permission to do so ; and it was as
nuch enjoyed by Susie as by the actor, who recalled the
anecdote of Garrick, on which Robertson's charming adapta-
ion is founded. Now the actor is a welcome visitor to the
Coltons, and has told them enough of his professional career
to convince even Mr. C. that "play-acting" is arduous and
vexatious.

# THE THREE GREAT SYMPHONISTS.

# THREE GREAT SYMPHONISTS.

*HAYDN, MOZART, AND BEETHOVEN.*

By JAMES PECH.

O art has perhaps undergone more various changes, or has continued, from its revival, in the Middle Ages up to the present time, in such a constant state of progression, as music. The later improvements in the instrumental kind, both with respect to performance and composition, are alone sufficient to demonstrate the fact. The strongest proof of the gradual perfection of this branch is discoverable in the increasing estimation in which the *symphony* is held ; and the cause of this very general tendency towards instrumental music is to be traced to the splendid productions of genius, that are now sent almost daily into the musical world. Indeed, knowledge and taste are even more universally diffused by the reproduction of the greatest masterpieces in every variety of shape ; and when we have had such men as Clementi, Hummel, and Liszt, lending their superior talents to the arrangement of symphonies for the piano-forte, by which one of the highest forms in musical art is widely distributed amongst every portion of the community, we compare them to philosophers who, by microscopic observations, bring to common view natural beauties known previously but to the few.

The *symphony* is, perhaps, as strong an instance as can be cited of the rapidity and extent of the improvement of music within the last one hundred and fifty years. In the beginning of the eighteenth century, this species of composition was unknown; and now, towards the close of the nineteenth, to what a pitch of excellence has it arrived! This has all been effected by the talents of a Haydn, Mozart, and Beethoven; and subsequently by Mendelssohn, Sphor, and Schumann.

To some it may be instructive, and it may not be uninteresting to others, if we attempt an analysis of the different means by which Haydn, Mozart, and Beethoven, in their time, produced such wonderful effects, compare their styles, and endeavor to describe the particular beauties of each. We are apt to consider and to believe that music is a language in which the mind and character of the composer are as clearly portrayed as is the genius of the poet in his works. The one speaks as forcibly by means of notes as the other by words, to those who love and understand them. A person enthusiastically fond of the philosophic Mendelssohn was asked, "How can you admire a man so much with whom you never had an hour's conversation?" The reply was, "I have conversed with him for months past through his 'Elijah.'" May we not, then, by studying the symphonies of Haydn, Mozart, and Beethoven, discover the powers which wrought such wonderful effects, and learn to revere the superiority of the minds that produced them? If we draw a comparison between these minds, we shall not find much difficulty in tracing, nor perhaps in accounting for, the distinguishing features of the style adopted by each.

The regularity of Haydn's middle and later life, his habits of neatness and precision, the polished and cheerful tone of his music, denote a mind regulated by certain fixed principles of action, and warmed by a naturally fertile and elegant fancy. As circumstances of early youth tend principally to the formation of character, so the privation and restraint to which he was subjected at this period probably prevented his imagination from bursting forth, and delayed its luxuriance ; but at the same time they confirmed him in habits of industry, strengthened his powers of independent reason and judgment, and thus prepared him for an after period, when, aided by concurring circumstances, he became the inventor of that melodious conversation, that fine combination of various and beautiful effects, — the *symphony*. Mozart, on the contrary, nurtured in the sunshine of affluence, enjoying the warmest encouragement, and surrounded by every possible stimulant to genius from his earliest years, was of a totally different mould. His ardent mind modelled itself by the luxury to which he was a constant witness, and by the life of ease and pleasure which his circumstances allowed him to lead. His music is accordingly distinguished by its richness and voluptuousness. He was naturally indolent, — he wrote only "when the fit was on him," — and it is probable that had he lived before Haydn, we might never have possessed his splendid symphonies composed after the model of the latter. By these remarks we do not mean to detract from the merit of Mozart ; his genius was of a kind not to be daunted by obstacles ; but it is probable that from the peculiarly opposite situations of the composers, perfectly opposite effects were produced. There was, moreover, a melancholy in Mozart's temperament,

— prompted perhaps by an overwrought imagination, — and he possessed a more ardent, though not such constant and unbending, enthusiasm as Haydn in the cultivation of his art.

There cannot well be a greater contrast than between these two masters and the highest follower of their steps, Beethoven, both as regards character and style; yet he was the scholar of Haydn. Beethoven, however, appears to have imbibed from his master little more than the technical means which enabled him to follow his own path to fame, and which he opened through obstacles that would have dismayed any but so strong a character as his was. He neither possessed the luxury of Mozart nor the elegance of Haydn, but from his subjects, which are by far more simple though scarcely so beautiful as theirs, he has worked out quite as striking and more novel effects than either. His music is marked by originality, strength of design, and romantic grandeur. His great predecessors arrived nearer perfection in the polish of their productions, but in conception we apprehend (in the symphony) he has aspired to heights more sublime than either of them. The source of this is his extreme originality, or rather *eccentricity*, which at the same time excites astonishment and lays him open to the severity of criticism. At that time Haydn, we are told, censured this quality, and was of opinion that if not curbed by a nice discrimination, and guided by a just idea of effects, it would be likely to lead the way to a wrong estimate of the beautiful. The defects of a great artist in any line are always the soonest imitated and disseminated, and thus it has been with the eccentricity of Beethoven. They whom his original vein and his astonishing force delight are little aware of the power required to pursue is course. The mere effort exhausts the strength allotted to common natures, and many who have tried his arms have proved only their own "ineffectual fires." At the same time, the disposition to extravagance seems to have grown by what fed on in the mighty master himself, for all propensities are increased by indulgence, as some of his later works afford evident proofs of the dangerous tendency of the habit of exaggeration.

In the regular process of our essay, however, we shall proceed to examine the foundation on which Haydn raised his splendid superstructure, and for this purpose we must refer to the early periods of the cultivation of instrumental music. The overture, which is the earliest indication of anything like the symphony, and almost of any species of instrumental music, owes its origin to Lully. About the middle of the seventeenth century he composed it for the *Bande des petits Violons* of Louis XIV. Before his time, in the few trios and quartettes, which were composed simply for the violin and violoncello, the other parts were generally subordinate to the first violin. But Lully, in his compositions, allotted to each instrument an almost equally prominent part to sustain ; he added to the number by drums, etc. ; and lastly, by the introduction of discords, he varied the monotony of the former system of composition, as well as by the genius and originality of his passages themselves. Until the appearance of Lully's overtures, such a prelude was never thought of, and, what is even more singular, by their novelty and excellence, they continued for a long time to hold their place and pre-eminence, and were played before operas composed by Vinci, Leo, and Pergolesi, nearly a century after the date of their original production.

Scarlatti was the next composer of overtures. Then followed the *Concerti grossi* of Corelli and Vivaldi, and lastly the concertos and overtures of Handel, Bach, Jomelli, Porpora, and Bononcini, with others of less note. In all these, however, the fugue was the principal object, and one prominent part was given to the violin or some single instrument. Of all the old masters we should say the Padre Martini is one to whom Haydn may be the best compared, if he can be justly likened to any. But truly sublime and unequalled as they were in certain branches of their art, at what a distance were they left by Haydn in the composition of instrumental music! By him were the peculiar properties and characteristics of every instrument developed; by him each was made to speak in its own melodious language to the heart and the imagination. It was given to him to reply to the query, "Que veux tu sonate?" for he made the symphony descriptive. He it was who first avowed that he formed a little story as a guide to the workings of his spirit. In truth, the design of Haydn's symphonies is more clearly developed, and his ideas can be better understood than either Mozart's or Beethoven's. This it is, perhaps, that renders them more generally pleasing, assisted by the lively tone of feeling that to a certain degree pervades them throughout. Thus their characteristics are clearness of design, purity and elegance of taste, yet not without depth of conception, and they are always tempered by a nice and judicious perception of effects, which never allowed him to wander beyond the sight or transgress the bounds of sympathy in his audience. The hearer is not, perhaps, so raised as by Beethoven, or so deeply touched as by Mozart, but the feelings never sink below a certain equable and just level;

he attention is never strained to understand him, and the
ar is always interested, always satisfied. He is original, but
ever eccentric ; and though never dazzling, refined and deli-
ate to the highest degree. The general analysis of one of
is symphonies will, perhaps, illustrate our ideas on the sub-
ect more clearly, and we select the Seventh, because it is
most generally known, and, as it appears to us, comprises all the
distinguishing traits of his style.

The short opening *adagio* is in D minor. In the *Encyclo-
pédie de Musique* there is an article on the symphony by
Monmigny, who decides that the character of this movement
s of a religious cast, and he interprets it to be a prayer.
n this view, however, we cannot agree ; for if the composer
had commenced his work in such a frame of mind, it is
scarcely possible that in one single page he should have so
completely divested himself of the emotions which must have
been awakened, as to take up his *allegro* in a manner wholly
unmarked by elevated feeling. It is difficult but not impossible to trace the succession of ideas in the mind of another,
and as contrast, though not unconnected, is generally aimed at
n the *adagio* and *allegro* of a symphony, we should rather
imagine the opening of the present to have been constructed
upon a less exalted foundation. The subject is contained in
three measures, the last of which

consists in responses between the higher and lower instruments; the whole of it has the character of expostulation,
which is beautifully expressed by the ascent of semitones,
commencing after it has modulated into F major.   That this
expostulation succeeds in its object is evident, from the *piano*
repetition of the opening burst, and from its subsequent
transition from D minor to the softened key of E flat.   This
is a beautiful idea.   To the ordinary observer the movement
may seem to present nothing particularly worth notice in its
construction.   What then does it contain that finds its way to
every heart?   Simplicity, superior taste, and variety;   for it
will be seen that, although short and constantly repeated, the
subject is so exquisitely diversified as never to appear monot-
onous.   This is another capital distinction of Haydn's style,
though he can scarcely be said to possess it to the same degree as Mozart.

The *allegro* opens with a graceful and winning subject in

D major, developed by the stringed instruments, and followed

y a spirited *tutti*. It is then reproduced in A major, and
with his usual care to prevent sameness, the accompaniments
re varied. But how manifold are the resources of art, and
et what slender means does it require to produce the finest
ffect!

The next subject which the composer selects is merely the
econd and third measures of his first. This displays his
unity and clearness of design. Although this movement is of
light and exhilarating character, the connection is still to be
ept up between it and the *adagio*, and the new subject par-
akes of its character just so much as to awaken the same
rain of ideas, though less vividly. The response is made by
he basses, and this serves as another link in the chain, whilst
he variations of the passage by the wind instruments, the
eautiful conversation maintained between them, and the bril-
iant keys through which it modulates, continue the elevated
tate of the mind, and keep both the intellect and the ear in
onstant expectation and interest.

At length the commencement is resumed, and with what
ase and brilliancy are the two themes (from their intimate
onnection) worked up together? During the first pages
he former becomes the groundwork for the same *tutti* which
opens the movement; a few measures before its conclusion,
the latter is heard from the wind instruments; it then forms
a few measures of beautiful contrast, leads off to the concluding *tutti*, and during this is incorporated with the first,
and closes the movement with proportionate vigor and effect.
It is perhaps in the *andante* that Haydn's power lies; for in
such movements there is more room for the display of his
delicacy and taste. His theme in the present instance is

soothing, but not mournful, and is made so prominen
throughout as to be the principal object in the picture.

Indeed, although there are in some places several subjects
moving at once, yet they all spring, as it were, from one root,
and are, like the same flower in its various stages of growth,
all different modifications of the same beautiful creation,
whilst it continues, like its prototype, in a constant state of
progression, acquiring at every fresh period of its existence
some addition in richness and beauty.

It is evidently the design of the composer to draw the
principal attractions of this movement from simplicity, delicacy of expression, and fine harmony. Aware, however, of the
effect and almost necessity of contrast, he has ingeniously
availed himself of this resource without departing from his
original plan. Thus he has reproduced his subject in a minor
key, in a trio between the flute, oboe, and fagotto, which is
followed by a *tutti;* not a mere union to produce change by

he contrast of tone, but the addition of instruments, each
aving a part to perform that is necessary to the general design.
hat good taste, however, may not be offended by an instant
eturn to the theme, after this burst, the composer wins his way
ack to it by a passage "fine by degrees and delicately less,"
hus displaying exquisite judgment and taste. Being fully
ware that his subject was of too nice a texture to bear immediate or violent contrasts, he has made them steal gradually
upon the ear, and in the same manner the movement fades
away at the conclusion. The genuine master has adhered to
his plan and to the character of his air; there is nothing
abrupt, nothing incongruous, — all is smoothness and purity.

Haydn was particularly happy in the composition of his
minuets and trios. As these movements are too short to be
susceptible of any powerful effects, that is to say, in connection with the body of the symphony, they should consist of
fanciful and brilliant traits of melody, pleasing for their *naïveté*.
They may be compared to the *divertisemens* in an opera; they
produce variety and captivate the ear, whilst they afford a
point of repose to the attention, and thus the hearer is prepared to follow the composer with fresh energy through his
rondo. Hadyn's are models in this style.

One of the finest proofs of genius is the power of producing
great effects by simple means. The subject of the rondo is

introduced on a *pedale* bass ; and is taken in trio by the first and second violin and tenor. A *forte* of two notes follows, sufficient to rouse the attention of the audience and produce contrast ; but Haydn, aware of the quaintness of his subject, has treated it with a corresponding singularity. This *forte*, which has but one note for the trumpets and drums, has for answer three notes from the first violins ; and here we must observe that, short as the subject is, consisting only of thirteen notes, the characters of the two phrases into which it is divided are distinguished through the whole movement. But that which is susceptible of the most contrast, and is of the gravest and deepest cast, is put under the care of the corresponding part of the orchestra, whilst the other, which is of an opposite expression, is consigned to the lighter instruments. In fact, the orchestra may almost be compared to opposing casuists, engaged in illustrating their several opinions of the same question in different ways, — the serious and the gay. The entire movement is by this means rendered a complete conversation. The *tuttis* are rare, the burden of the dialogue being alternately borne by prominent instruments, always changing, always quaint, always interesting and original. Towards the end the combat deepens, and in the winding up the composer has infused into his treatment of the subject all the force and fire of which it is capable. He had previously invested it with enough only of these qualities to prevent monotony, and has reserved this masterstroke till he has presented it in every possible guise. The manner is by turns quaint, lively, persuasive, decided ; and at last, when we have followed these transitions with increasing interest through all their diversity, the theme bursts upon is full of vigor, energy, and brilliancy, at a time when we think every protean change has been exhausted. Through all this variety, however, the design is clearly and substantially maintained. We enter into the composer's ideas as we do into those of an enlightened person in conversation, without effort and without weariness. His melodies dwell in the memory ; the effects produced in treating them are impressed on our minds ; and this, after all, is the true test of an author's perfect success.

This general analysis will give some idea of the mode of construction adopted by Haydn in all his symphonies. By a similar examination of one of Mozart's and one of Beethoven's, it is our object to ascertain how far we have been accurate in our description of the principal differences in the three styles, and to discover if any improvements have been made by the two latter in the models left them by the illustrious inventor of the symphony.

If the orchestra in the hands of Haydn be considered as carrying on an eloquent and enlightened conversation, under the direction of Mozart each instrument appears to speak in the language of a beautifully descriptive poem. We have already referred to the opposite circumstances in the life of the two composers, which we conceive tended to the formation of two totally different styles ; and if they are recalled, these exemplifications of their manner will, we think, be found clear and expressive. We may then proceed to an analysis of Mozart's Symphony in E Flat.

In the opening *adagio* the principal feature is contrast, and the design appears to be to elevate the mind. It commences with a full and powerful *tutti*, succeeded by a descending scale, *piano*, for the first violin, and this is repeated three times, modulating into F minor, when the violin has a syncopated trait of melody of tender expression. The running passages are then resumed, the flute varying effect by a few broken notes, and the drums, trumpets, and horns being heard in an undertone. Having modulated to the subdominant, which is sustained by the violins and wind instruments, the running passages are taken up by the tenors and basses. But here Mozart consults equally both the character of his instruments and the variety which he is ever anxious to preserve, and thus the scale is reproduced, *ascending*, and with the difference of a flat seventh, which on the second and third repetition is augmented by that of a flat ninth, while the instruments are increased and break off as abruptly on the chord of F with a seventh and flat ninth, leaving the violins and fagotti to close the movement by a *legato* passage of semitones of a wailing expression. In this movement emotions of a totally opposite nature and yet equally strong are awakened. We are elevated, we are awed, we are softened, and these effects are wrought nearly by the same passages judiciously varied and employed. What Mozart may be said to have chiefly aimed at in his music * was to excite the different passions in their most extreme degrees, and this is the principal distinction between him and Haydn. The latter always preserves a certain medium, above and below which we are seldom either elevated or depressed. But Mozart revelled with more freedom in the realms of fancy, and consequently the

---

* It must be remembered that our remarks are entirely confined to the instrumental music of these composers. The same reflections will not so strictly apply to their compositions for the voice.

:elings are more alive to his touches than the judgment.
'o support this position, we only ask the reader to note and
ecall the emotions which are aroused by hearing the *adagio*
) Haydn's Seventh Symphony and those which arise on lis-
ening to that we have just analyzed, and to compare his
:ensations. The *allegro*, introduced by a melancholy passage,
; *legato* and *cantabile*, and a soothing effect is imparted to it
·y the mellow and rich tone of the horns, which take up
he first strain of the subject in answer to the first violin,
he second being answered in a similar manner by the fagotti,
vith the same effect.

Here there is a link in the chain of connection between
his movement and the *adagio*. The descending scales which
here form the principal feature are again introduced, com-
)ined, however, by passages of a bold and decided character.
)ne of Mozart's greatest beauties is the power which he pos-
:esses of reproducing one idea in so many and yet such
:qually beautiful forms, and the present is a striking example.
Ne have already shown that these simple passages, by a slight
:hange, were made to answer two purposes in the first part,
·oftening and *exalting* the mind, and now again they serve
o exhilarate merely by the alteration of the time and man-
1er of their accompaniment, or rather connection. We now
urrive at some exquisitely expressive solos for the clarionet
ind fagotto, which are succeeded by a strongly contrasted
·utti, and then follows the first *reprise*. Here a new subject
s worked from the accompaniment to the ᴦlarionet solo,
und is held in play principally between the stringed instru-
nents. It commences in G minor, passes through the domi-
1ant to A flat, where the violins take up the clarionet solo

considerably varied, and modulate to C minor. Then the
basses are heard, and a *tutti* succeeds, leading to the repetition of the commencement. It will be remembered that the
descending passages which formed the *tutti* were in the first
part introduced in the original key of E ; but in the present
instance, by an alteration of the harmonies, the same idea is
reproduced in A, and consequently a pleasing variety is the
result, as, although there is no material change or new subject
to the end of the movement, yet the former subjects acquire
fresh novelty and attraction from this surprise to the ear, as
they pass through different modulations and are heightened in
effect by the almost imperceptible graces which Mozart never
fails to append every time he retouches a trait of melody.
The *andante* which follows

is in character exquisitely tender and perfectly describes to
our minds "the luxury of grief." It is in A flat, and is commenced by the stringed instruments, flute, and fagotto. After

he subject has been simply developed, the horns and clari-
net are added, and the second part is led by an exquisite
olo for the flute into F minor, the violin remaining prin-
ipal for some time. The first phrase is then resumed in a
onversation between the instruments, till we arrive at a deli-
ious solo for the clarionet, answered by the flute and fagotto.
But now comes the master-stroke. Whilst the subject is car-
ying on in dialogue between the stringed instruments, the
larionets, flutes, and fagotti are recalling old associations by
he repetition of three *descending scales*, and thus is the sim-
le idea produced for the *fourth* time. in a totally different and
till more delightful shape. We recognize it again some way
urther on, transferred to the second violin and tenor, whilst
he subject is taken by the wind-instruments. The beautiful
conversation of the fagotto and clarionet, with the other
nstruments, is one of the principal distinctions of this movement, as is likewise its *cantabile* style. The parts literally
sing, so exquisitely are they blended together. There is about
he whole a languor, from its perfectly legato style, and yet a
richness and warmth that give rise to emotions the most
absolutely luxurious. A great love of contrast is, however (as
we have remarked), to be found in Mozart's music, and thus
the minuet which follows is exceedingly animating. The trio
consists of beautiful solos for the clarionet and violin, supported by the horns and stringed instruments.

The subject of the *finale* is lively and graceful, and is led
off by the violins.

After the first *tutti*, which is of a kind to raise the spirits
from languor, to which they would have sunk during the *andante*, the modulation becomes somber, when, having returned

to the dominant, the air, so to speak, is " trifled with " by
the clarionet, fagotto, and violins.   Throughout the *finale*, in-

deed, all the instruments may be said to trifle.   Nor is this
disposition of the parts without design ; but to trace this
design we must follow the flights of the gayest fancy, — we
must pursue a butterfly flitting from flower to flower, whilst
every new reflection of the sunbeams on its painted wings
brightens its tints and exalts their beauty.   Thus we catch
perpetual glimpses of the subject, which, as it recurs, we hear
everywhere perpetually varying ; it keeps the mind in the
never-ceasing anticipation of new pleasure, and the expectation is never disappointed.   Its characteristics are delicacy,
grace, and *naïveté ;* and these traits are sustained throughout.

It should appear then, from this general inquiry, that the
chief differences in the styles of Haydn and Mozart may be
comprised in a few words.   The genius or imagination of
Mozart was richer and more varied, that of Haydn more regular and more concentrated.   The former opened to his talents a wider field of action, and his forte lay certainly in
vocal music ; whilst the number and beauty of the instrumental
compositions of the latter, taken as a whole, may be said to

urpass his productions for the voice.* Mozart has, to a cer-
ain degree, infused into his symphonies many of the proper-
ies which belong to vocal music. Hence the languor, the
enderness and intensity of feeling, which characterize most
f them, and the correct and beautiful manner in which he
uits the genius of each particular wind-instrument ; these being
nore analogous to the different species of tone to be found in
voices, and being better adapted to the tenderness, volup-
uousness, and warmth of his ideas. Nevertheless, Mozart is
sometimes so completely guided by his enthusiasm and his
ancy, that he appears to forget those rules to which others
send, and sometimes his ideas appear to press upon him in
such rich and varied profusion as to take from the clearness
and unity of his design. This, although a splendid fault, is
one which Haydn would not have committed. His plan
was laid at first, and it guided him steadily to the last. Nor
was he ever drawn aside by the desire of producing an *effect*,
however striking, if it were not in perfect consonance with
his design.

We must now turn to the last great model of the school of
these composers. Beethoven may indeed be considered as
having followed them, and at the same time as having enlarged so considerably the extent of the way they struck out,
as to have left only slight traces of their steps. After what
we have already said on the subject of the eccentricity of
Beethoven, it will, perhaps, be thought singular that we should

---

* We are aware that many will be disposed to differ from us in this opinion,
but the test of the merit of music is the general estimation in which it is held.
Haydn's instrumental compositions are more frequently performed than his vocal,
whilst some of Mozart's operas still stand proudly pre-eminent.

assert that the germs of this characteristic are to be found in Mozart. They who have studied his works will, however, we doubt not, agree with us. For a striking instance, we refer the reader to the passage immediately after the double bar in the *finale* to his symphony in G minor. We have selected Beethoven's First Symphony in C for our analysis, because, being one of his earlier productions, it possesses only enough of this quality to render it original, and because it is one of the most esteemed, though by no means the best.

The first two chords of the *adagio* display the desire of novelty, as, instead of beginning on the reputed key of C, a flat seventh is inserted in its place, which resolves into the chord of the subdominant. Then we have the dominant also with a seventh, which, by raising the bass one tone, passes into A minor, and again we have D with a seventh, which resolves into the chord of the dominant, in which key the *plan* of the movement may be said to begin. It consists only of twelve measures, and leads by a running passage for the stringed instruments to the *allegro con brio*. There is no single word in the English language which describes the character of this movement, and the *finale* to the same symphony, so well as the Italian one of *Brioso*, especially the latter; in the present, perhaps, there is a little too much intensity, — not however, the intensity of Mozart, for Beethoven is seldom or ever tender, his melancholy is of a higher cast, —

> " A solemn, strange, and mingled air,
> 'T was sad by fits, by starts 't was wild," —

and in his movements of a higher character the same wildness is to be found in a less degree.

There is nothing striking or even pleasing in the subject of he present : —

Indeed, in the allegros of Beethoven this is frequently the case. It appears as if he wished to display his power of producing great effects by slender means ; consequently they gain upon us as they proceed, instead of at once riveting the fancy, as happens when we listen to the beautiful *morceaux* on which similar movements of Haydn and Mozart are built. After the development of his theme, and the first *tutti*, which may be considered in all symphonies as the mere prelude to what follows, a simple but beautiful trait of melody is made *the subject of conversation* between the flute and oboe, subsequently the clarionet and fagotto are introduced, as it were, by gradations, and lastly the violins. The accompaniment to his passage, which in the present instance is formed from the last bar of the subject, is of a kind peculiar to this composer,. and is introduced in the same manner in his overture to *Prometheus.* The modulation being carried into G minor, the same solo somewhat varied is taken up by the basses, and leads to a return of the subject in F sharp. We may here remark that one of the leading characteristics of Beethoven's style consists in the power and character which he gives to his basses. In this respect he might almost be termed the *Handel* of symphonists. If they be ever so simple, they are distinguished by a solidity and originality that always invests the whole composition with grandeur. At the second *reprise* the subject passes through A, D, and G to C minor, and the movement here takes a mysterious form ; a tremando is kept up by the second violin and tenor, whilst the short strain before alluded to as peculiar to Beethoven is distributed in alternate solos between the first violin, fagotto, flute, and oboe ; after this, the dialogue becomes very singular. A passage, evidently formed on the third and fourth measures of the subject, is led off by the stringed instruments, whilst the first and second measures are kept in constant response by the wind-instruments through several keys, till a rolling bass concludes it in unison on E, and the flutes, clarionets, oboes, and fagotti lead back to the opening by a *sostenuto* passage also in unison. After a *tutti* which differs considerably from the first, the solo before taken in G by the flute and oboe is here transferred to the flute and clarionet in C, and it is ultimately conducted again to C minor, while it is taken by the basses, thus producing a fine contrast. In the concluding *tutti* we have another alteration. The first measures of the subject are taken by the basses, whilst the last is taken by other instruments. This had never before this time been the case ; but the composer was aware of the strength of this passage, when referred to a situation to bring it out, and he judiciously reserves it for the winding up, where it produces a magnificent effect.

The characteristics of this *allegro* are unity of design, simplicity in melody, and strong contrast. In the first there are evident traces of the master *Haydn*, as may be noticed from the fact that, with one exception, every passage is formed on

he original subject. In clearness, however, he falls very short
f his model ; he has not the same pertinacity in adhering to
is plan, that is to say, he is contented with keeping up a
hain of connection formed of the more prominent parts of his
lea, without attending to those finer links which assist so
aaterially, though almost imperceptibly, in awakening previous
ssociations. In the same manner he has not the same well-
onstructed plan in the use of his instruments as Mozart, who
rill make one or two very prominent, and assign to them a
ertain passage which they alone shall work upon, and which
rill form a _landmark_, as it were, in his ocean of melody,
rhilst Beethoven will, for the sake of contrast, transfer an
lea from one instrument to another, so that, if we would re-
all it, it comes to the mind in twenty different forms. At
he same time, Beethoven produces greater and more striking
:ffects from simpler means than either of his predecessors ;
iis combinations are more novel, and there is an innate
trength and vigor in his music which can hardly be found
:lsewhere.

The _andante_ is upon an extremely simple subject, of a
cheerful, though smooth character, and it is so contrived that
the instruments take it up one after another in the style of
the fugue, which has a rich and novel effect. It becomes
gradually more playful as it proceeds, and the first part concludes with a staccato passage of triplets for the violins and
clarionet. In the second part we have a good contrast ; the
key is changed from F to C minor, and again the instru-

ments drop singly on a succession of minor thirds and fifths, till, leading to a staccato accompaniment for the fagotto and stringed instruments, the thirds and fifths are brought in spasmodically and give a wild and complaining effect. Gradually the subject is resumed in the major key, and is most beautifully varied, in a manner approaching to a fugue, though it does not conform to the laws of that species of writing. The principal ideas guide the composer the whole way though.

The minuet and trio are, the one spirited, the other graceful and fantastic, to a very high degree. Beethoven makes more of this part of the symphony, we are inclined to think, than either of his predecessors. He infuses into it a larger portion of spirit and contrast, and renders it more important to the body of the work. The trio is between the horn, clarionet, and violin, and is a most exquisite bit of dialogue.

In the subject of the *finale* there is more to please the fancy than we have yet met with. It catches at once by its airiness and simplicity ; how beautifully is this effect heightened by the passage given to the violoncellos in the second strain ! and again, what an animating contrast is found in the passage for the basses, beginning at the twenty-fourth measure ! In this movement there is nothing but what is lively and easy, but there is not the same mastery of construction that is to be found in the *allegro*. The composer appears to write more for the pleasure than the instruction of his hearers ; there it was agreeable reflection, here it is pure recreation and enjoyment. This, we are aware, is the general character of the finales to both Haydn and Mozart, but scarcely to the same degree. Those of the former are more refined and chastened, those of the latter richer and more luxurious ; and in both they are more elaborate than Beethoven. They appear to us to possess a freedom from all restraint, an exuberance of spirit that carries everything along ; yet the hand of the master is to be observed in the formation of the design and its preservation to the conclusion ; and here, where he is not so constantly aiming at effect, the style is more perspicuous.

We have now completed a sufficiently minute analysis of three of the best works of these great masters, to enable us to compare their different styles, and to determine whether any decided improvements had been made in the symphony as it was left to Mozart and Beethoven by its immortal inventor. We have already shown on what slender foundations Haydn raised this lasting fabric. The materials for its formation he drew from the fertile resources of his own mind. He gave character and importance to every instrument,* assigning to each a part adapted to its powers ; he classified them, and taught them the language that is not only intelligible, but delightful to the ear of the musician, and he established certain rules by which he formed a new species of descriptive music, and gave to the mere "concord of sweet sounds" a definite character which it never before possessed, except when in conjunction with, or rather subordinate to, the human voice. Besides the simple invention of the symphony, it cannot be determined how far this very circumstance might tend to the improvement of the *overture*, which was then, comparatively speaking, at a low ebb, and which has since improved so materially. Be this as it may, the invention itself was sufficient to immortalize the composer, and as a proof of the sta-

* Beethoven's Ninth Symphony, and the Symphony-Cantata, by Mendelssohn.

bility of the principles on which it is founded, its form has been but slightly altered, except in one or two cases ; it still consists of the *adagio, allegro, andante, minuetto*, or *scherzo, trio,* and *finale,* and these are still distinguished by the same characteristics that were first assigned to them.

It could not, however, be supposed, particularly when such a composer as Mozart followed in the path of Haydn, ·that the symphony would not, like everything else, continue in a state of progression, even although its external form remained unaltered.   The genius of Mozart was cast in ˙too superb a mould to imitate in any closer manner than that of working on the same principles and aiming at the same end as his predecessor.*   Consequently, the styles of Haydn and Mozart in instrumental music differ nearly as widely as in vocal.   We have already pointed out in what these differences consist ; it remains to show in what particulars or in what degree the latter added to the beauty of the symphony.   The distinguishing trait in Mozart's style is warmth and richness of imagination, inasmuch as he possessed this quality in a greater degree than Haydn, so he was able to shadow out his musical pictures with more glowing colors and to invest them with a greater degree of interest.   Thus, in his use of the wind-instruments, he has shown a more vivid perception of the beautiful than Haydn, and in this it is that his grand improvement lies.   He has made nicer distinctions between their several qualities, has allotted to each a more decided character ; he has, in fact, treated them more as the *singers*

---

* Mozart dedicated a set of his light quartettes to Haydn, saying, " This dedication is only due to him, for it was from Haydn that I learned to compose quartettes," and he might have added also symphonies.

f the orchestra, from their analogy to the human voice. In
ther respects, what he has done for the symphony has been
ɔ enrich it by a more vivid, and to elevate it by a loftier, vein
f fancy. At the same time the very ardor which has guided
im so rightly in one sense has misled him in another, by
ometimes carrying him beyond the limits of that pure and
elicate taste which Haydn never overstepped, and by causing
im to lose sight of the clearness and unity of design which
onstituted one of the greatest perfections of his illustrious
redecessor.

When Beethoven entered upon his musical career, it is to
e supposed naturally that, from being the scholar of Haydn,
nstrumental music would first absorb his attention. The
ymphony, at once the newest and highest species of composi-
ion, opened a wide and splendid field to the exertions of the
spiring composer ; but, if we consider the state of perfection
n which it was left by Haydn and Mozart, it is evident that
Beethoven would be constrained either to become a copyist
or to strike out a new path for himself, and how dangerous
would this attempt be to any one of the most powerful talents ? Such, however, did Beethoven possess. In his earliest
productions, which consisted of sonatas, trios, quartettes, and
quintettes for the piano-forte and other instruments, he was
accused of crude modulation, and an attempt rather to be singular than pleasing. It appears, then, that originality was his
earliest distinction, and this it is that has placed him by the
side of Haydn and Mozart in the symphony, without his being
the imitator of either. It cannot be denied that in his first
productions of this kind — for instance, in the one we have
analyzed — traces may be found in the general construction

of the style of his masters, yet as a whole no style can be more decidedly opposed to those of his two predecessors than that of Beethoven.

The mind of this master was, as is generally known, of a very peculiar formation, and, if we read his works aright, we should say that he possessed a lofty, though not rich imagination, and that this, combined with great simplicity and strength of conception, raised him nearer the sublime than either of those who preceded him. At the same time he appears to have possessed an inexhaustible fund of originality, from which he drew so constantly as to render it sometimes a failing rather than an excellence. This is, we regret to say, too much the case in the Ninth Symphony. We mention this work more particularly, because in it was introduced the first innovation upon Haydn's original plan, before alluded to, in the shape of a chorus, which formed a part of the fourth and last movement, as also in the symphony opening with an *allegro*, and having no minuet or trio. Beethoven is not generally considered to have succeeded in the attempt to unite the two opposite styles of vocal and instrumental music. Even in the present day, its effect, when it is occasionally performed, is such as to leave upon the public mind a feeling of disappointment and fatigue. Its length alone will be a never-failing cause of complaint to those who reject monopoly in sounds.

The fact is clear to the philosophic observer, that there must be a natural tendency in the mind to vocal music, as presenting definite ideas to the mind ; consequently, when instrumental is combined with vocal, the latter takes the lead, as it were, in the train of association, the former falls from a principal to a subordinate, and the combination thus belongs to no class, and possesses no distinct character, or, if any, becomes a chorus. It appears, therefore, that the symphony retains its original form unchanged, and that Beethoven has aided its advance towards perfection by strength and sublimity; whilst at the same time his own particular style is distinguished, besides these attributes, by originality, simplicity, beauty of melody, and great power of description, which is alone displayed in that really stupendous work, his Pastoral Symphony.

The result of this investigation, to our conception, is that, by a happy concurrence, three minds more perfectly formed for the establishment of this magnificent invention could not have succeeded each other than those of Haydn, Mozart, and Beethoven. The first gave it form and substance, and ordained the laws by which it should move, adorning it at the same time with superior taste, perspicuity of design, and beautiful melody; the second added to the fine creation of his fancy by richness, warmth, and variety; and the last endowed it with sublimity of description and power. When will the *artist* appear who shall combine all these attributes? — for what others can be *added?*

THE END

Check Out More Titles From HardPress Classics Series In this collection we are offering thousands of classic and hard to find books. This series spans a vast array of subjects – so you are bound to find something of interest to enjoy reading and learning about.

Subjects:
Architecture
Art
Biography & Autobiography
Body, Mind &Spirit
Children & Young Adult
Dramas
Education
Fiction
History
Language Arts & Disciplines
Law
Literary Collections
Music
Poetry
Psychology
Science
…and many more.

Visit us at www.hardpress.net

CPSIA information can be obtained
at www.ICGtesting.com
Printed in the USA
BVHW081349230819

556642BV00020B/1856/P